Understanding criminology

CRIME AND JUSTICE
Series editor: Mike Maguire
Cardiff University

Crime and Justice is a series of short introductory texts on central topics in criminology. The books in this series are written for students by internationally renowned authors. Each book tackles a key area within criminology, providing a concise and up-to-date overview of the principal concepts, theories, methods and findings relating to the area. Taken as a whole, the *Crime and Justice* series will cover all the core components of an undergraduate criminology course.

Published titles

Understanding drugs, alcohol and crime
Trevor Bennett and Katy Holloway

Understanding youth and crime 2nd edition
Sheila Brown

Understanding crime data
Clive Coleman and Jenny Moynihan

Understanding white collar crime
Hazel Croall

Understanding victims and restorative justice
James Dignan

Understanding justice 2nd edition
Barbara A. Hudson

Understanding crime prevention
Gordon Hughes

Understanding social control
Martin Innes

Understanding violent crime
Stephen Jones

Understanding risk in criminal justice
Hazel Kemshall

Understanding psychology and crime
James McGuire

Understanding community penalties
Peter Raynor and Maurice Vanstone

Understanding public attitudes to criminal justice
Julian V. Roberts and Mike Hough

Understanding criminology

Current theoretical debates

Sandra Walklate

3rd edition

Open University Press

Open University Press
McGraw-Hill Education
McGraw-Hill House
Shoppenhangers Road
Maidenhead
Berkshire
England
SL6 2QL

email: enquiries@openup.co.uk
world wide web: www.openup.co.uk

and Two Penn Plaza, New York, NY 10121-2289, USA

First published 2007
Reprinted 2009

A catalogue record of this book is available from the British Library

ISBN 13: 978 0 335 22123 3
ISBN 10: 0 335 22123 8

Library of Congress Cataloging-in-Publication Data
CIP data has been applied for

Typeset by RefineCatch Ltd, Bungay, Suffolk
Printed in UK by Bell & Bain Ltd., Glasgow
www.bell-bain.com

The McGraw·Hill Companies

Contents

Series editor's foreword viii
Preface and acknowledgments to the 3rd edition x

1 Introduction: understanding some key features of criminology 1
Some domain assumptions within criminology as a discipline 2
Criminology and modernity 2
How to define the criminal 5
What influences talk about crime? 6
What do we know about crime? 7
What is known about criminal victimization? 10
Criminology, politics and criminal justice policy 11
Conclusion: what are the key features of criminology? 14
Further reading 16

2 Perspectives in criminological theory 17
The behaviour of criminals 17
The criminality of behaviour 22
The criminality of the state 28
Conclusion 36
Further reading 36

3 Understanding 'right realism' 38
Socio-biological explanations: the work of Wilson and Herrnstein 39
Rational choice theory 42
The routine activity approach 44
Administrative criminology 45
Right realism: a critique 47

Ways of thinking about the family and crime 49
Conclusion 56
Further reading 58

4 **Understanding 'left realism'** 59
What is 'left realism'? 60
Left realism UK style: a critique 66
Left realism US style 74
The modernist dilemma 77
Left realism and New Labour: politics, policy and process 78
Conclusion 81
Further reading 82

5 **Gendering the criminal** 83
The gender blindness of criminology 83
Feminism and criminology 84
Feminisms and criminology: contradictions in terms? 89
Ways of thinking about men within criminology 90
Sex role theory and criminology 91
Categorical theory and criminology 95
Doing gender as criminology 96
Biography and the psychoanalytical turn 99
Reflections on masculinity and criminology 100
Summary: gendering the criminal or gendering criminology? 101
Conclusion 103
Further reading 104

6 **Crime, politics and welfare** 105
Understanding the welfare state 106
Why it is important to understand the relationship between the citizen and the state 111
New Labour, new policies? Young people and crime 113
Young people, crime and antisocial behaviour 115
Conclusion: questions for criminology 117
Further reading 118

7 **Criminal victimization, politics and welfare** 119
What is victimology? 119
A challenging victimology? 128
Rebalancing the criminal justice system 129
Feminism, policy and violence 136
Ethnicity and hate crimes 140
Conclusion: criminal victimization and social responsibility 142
Further reading 144

8 **Conclusions: new directions for criminology?** 145
Positivism, modernism and gender 145
A word on cultural criminology 148
Gender, race and class 150
Criminology and risk 151
Criminology and trust 154
Criminology, the citizen and the state 157
Criminology, political economy and social capital 159
Conclusion 160

Glossary 161
References 164

Index 177

Series editor's foreword

This is the third edition of Sandra Walklate's *Understanding Criminology*, which first appeared in 1998 as the third book in Open University Press' *Crime and Justice* series, and went to a second edition in 2003. The success of her book helped to establish the series as a key resource in universities teaching criminology or criminal justice, especially in the UK but increasingly also overseas. The aim of the series has been to produce short but intellectually challenging introductory texts in key areas of criminological debate, which will give undergraduates and graduates both a solid grounding in the relevant area and a taste to explore it further. Although aimed primarily at students new to the field, and written as far as possible in plain language, the books are not oversimplified. On the contrary, the authors set out to 'stretch' readers and to encourage them to approach criminological knowledge and theory in a critical and questioning frame of mind.

Professor Walklate's book, now substantially revised and updated, tackles the challenging subject of criminological theory, which is of course fundamental to any university course in criminology or criminal justice. No short text can hope to do justice to the huge body of theoretical writing which has influenced criminology over more than a century and, like all other authors who taken on this task, she has had to be highly selective in her coverage. Her approach, however, differs markedly from the standard approach of simply giving a chronological account of the history of the main landmarks in criminological thought. Rather, she takes as her central focus some of the key concerns which have driven both theory and research over the last 30 years. While giving due deference to the past, she shows that criminology has now become a very different (and far more complex) discipline, in which theorists have to take account of many new kinds of data and knowledge, fundamental changes in social structures and institutions, and major developments in other academic fields. The core questions she grapples with include the nature of the relationships between crime and gender, crime and social exclusion, crime and the (fast changing) household and – fundamental to understanding current theoretical debates – changing relationships between the citizen and the state. She also examines key concepts which have begun to transform criminological thinking over the past ten years, including globalization, risk, trust, social capital, masculinities and restorative justice. In exploring these issues, she provides clear expositions of the contributions, strengths and weaknesses of, *inter alia*, feminist theory, left realism and right realism, post-modernist theory, the emerging 'cultural criminology', and theories built around the controversial concept of the 'underclass'. She also devotes particular attention to core debates in 'victimology', a field in which she has herself made a significant and original contribution, and argues ultimately for a self-reflexive criminology in which a concern with *social justice* is placed at the heart of theoretical debate. Throughout, she manages to communicate sophisticated and complex ideas in a succinct and accessible manner, without either grossly over-simplifying arguments or assuming too much initial knowledge on the part of readers.

Other books previously published in the *Crime and Justice* series – all of whose titles begin with the word 'Understanding' – have covered justice and penal theory (Barbara Hudson), crime data and statistics (Clive Coleman and Jenny Moynihan), youth and crime (Sheila Brown), crime prevention (Gordon Hughes), violent crime (Stephen Jones), community penalties (Peter Raynor and Maurice Vanstone), white collar crime (Hazel Croall), risk in criminal justice (Hazel Kemshall), social control (Martin Innes), psychology and crime (James McGuire), victims and restorative justice (James Dignan), drugs, alcohol and crime (Trevor Bennett and Katy Holloway), public attitudes to criminal justice (Julian Roberts and Mike Hough), desistance from crime (Stephen Farrell and Adam Calverley) prisons (Andrew Coyle) and political violence (Vincenzo Ruggiero). Four are already in second editions and other second editions are in preparation. Other new books in the pipeline include texts on race and crime, modernization and criminal justice, criminological research methods, 'cybercrime', and policing. All are topics which are either already widely taught or are growing in prominence in university degree courses on crime and criminal justice, and each book should make an ideal foundation text for a relevant module. As an aid to understanding, clear summaries are provided at regular intervals, and a glossary of key terms and concepts is a feature of every book. In addition, to help students expand their knowledge, recommendations for further reading are given at the end of each chapter.

Mike Maguire
February 2007

Preface and acknowledgments to the 3rd edition

It is now 10 years since I first wrote *Understanding Criminology*. During that time the discipline of criminology has grown apace as an area of study at both undergraduate and postgraduate level. When the idea for this book was first mooted, referees for the proposal expressed some concern that a book of this kind would result in the 'dumbing down' of the discipline. It was, therefore, with some interest that I read some of the reviews for the proposal for a third edition of this book. Several of those reviews expressed a concern that it was too advanced for use at first-year level. I leave the reader to conclude what might be taken from this shift in opinion, but I hope that, at whatever level this is read, it will constitute an interesting and valuable challenge for the reader. Moreover, I would like to thank the anonymous reviewers whose opinions were sought on the possibilities of a third edition. Their considered views have not always been followed but they were very much appreciated. In addition I would like to thank Laura Dent and Catriona Watson at McGraw-Hill/Open University Press for their help and support and, finally, Mike Maguire whose role and input as series editor over the last 10 years has been invaluable.

Sandra Walklate
Eleanor Rathbone Chair of Sociology
School of Sociology and Social Policy
University of Liverpool

chapter one

Introduction: understanding some key features of criminology

Some domain assumptions within criminology as a discipline
Criminology and modernity
How to define the criminal
What influences talk about crime?
What do we know about crime?
What is known about criminal victimization?
Criminology, politics and criminal justice policy
Conclusion: what are the key features of criminology?
Further reading

A book like this one, entitled *Understanding Criminology*, begs a number of important questions about its subject matter in its very title. Such a title makes a number of claims: that there is an area of study clearly identifiable as criminology; that that area of study has a clearly definable subject matter; that there is some agreement as to what that subject matter comprises; and that there is a range of concepts that are commonly used and commonly understood with which to talk about that subject matter. Each of these claims is contentious. In this Introduction we shall endeavour to examine the nature of these claims in an effort to appreciate the problems inherent in talking about crime. First of all, it will be useful to develop some appreciation of what characterizes criminology as a discipline and how its subject matter might be defined.

Some domain assumptions within criminology as a discipline

Criminology as a discipline has been described as a rather tenuous area of study (Rock 1986). It is defined not by a particular unit of social reality (as psychology is definitively concerned with the individual or sociology with social relationships) but by a substantive concern: crime. Consequently, it is a 'discipline' inhabited by practitioners, policymakers and academics, all of whom share a common interest in that substantive issue but all of whom may be committed to quite different disciplinary ways of thinking about it. Those disciplinary concerns can range from psychiatry to sociology. This, then, gives criminology a multidisciplinary rather than a unidisciplinary character.

As Garland (2002) has pointed out, it is possible to identify a variety of ways, historically, in which talk about crime entered public discourse, through the work of essayists and clergymen, for example. However, to argue that there was some continuous thread of common concern between these different ways of talking about crime glosses over not only the differences between them but also the historically contingent and specific nature of some of those concerns. This does not mean that views about crime (roguery, sinfulness, or other ways of depicting offensive behaviour) were not being articulated or did not represent authentic concerns. It does mean, however, that it may be mistaken to talk of those concerns as if they represented some coherent body of evolving knowledge called criminology. Indeed, Garland (1988: 1) states that: ' "Criminology" as a professional academic discipline did not exist in Britain before 1935, and was established only gradually and precariously thereafter.'

The question remains, however, as to what characterized this emergent discipline and influenced its later development. Despite the presence of different ways of talking about crime or criminal behaviour, there is a common thread to the construction of 'criminological' knowledge about such behaviour. That common thread can be traced historically through the influence of the Enlightenment and the common adherence to one way of thinking about knowledge and the knowledge construction process: positivism. It will be of some value to consider the influence of the ideas associated with positivism in a little more detail.

Criminology and modernity

Criminology, like other social science disciplines, is often characterized as being rooted in 'modern' ideas. What is meant by the term 'modern' is, however, open to interpretation. In this context it refers to the features of social and cultural life that, arguably, became embedded in social structural processes consequent to the impact of the Enlightenment, a period of time that is associated with the move from a pre-modern social world to a modern one. Cooke suggests that the Enlightenment had the effect of producing the belief that:

> Reason could be used to make the future a malleable one, and could interrupt the flow of history, overturn traditional hegemonies. Modernity was now to be understood as the very expression of individual and collective reason to bring about the achievement of some great social project.
>
> (Cooke 1990: 5)

This belief in the power of reason, and of the reasoning capacities of men in particular (Seidler 1994), had a powerful effect on the role that other beliefs had previously played in society, especially religious beliefs. Indeed, the belief in the power of reason, in some respects, not only took the place of religion but also put in its place a belief in the reasonable power of science and the scientific enterprise. These ideas, associated with the Enlightenment emerged during the eighteenth century. As we shall see, they set the agenda for the later emergence of positivism that has had a powerful influence on criminology. But why did this belief in reason take such a hold? This requires further explanation.

In our current everyday lives we are surrounded by technology and technological developments that reflect features of a modern society that we have come to take for granted – computers, cars, televisions, mobile phones, iPods, etc. Science and technology have been remarkably successful in changing the nature of people's everyday lives in quite fundamental ways in the production of such artefacts. However, the belief in the role and importance of science in modern societies is arguably more fundamental than even the production of such artefacts suggests.

Underpinning this kind of productive process is a presumption that it is through the knowledge produced by science that man could control the environment (nature). This presumption became rooted not only in the natural sciences and the technological developments that have been made as a consequence as the examples just referred to illustrate, but also in the emergent social sciences. In other words, the social sciences, modelled on the natural sciences, could provide the data on which social life, including social problems, could be not only managed but also controlled. These beliefs, embedded in the notion of a modern society, have underpinned criminological work since its inception and have tied criminology implicitly to the policymaking process: that is, to the belief that policies could be formulated that would better control and/or manage criminal behaviour. The basis on which those policies were (are) to be formulated is connected to the influence of positivism, mentioned earlier, and how the knowledge production process is to be understood.

Many reviews of the origins of criminology refer to the influence of positivism. Positivism is a term used to describe one way of thinking about the basis on which knowledge can claim to be scientific. The claim to produce scientific knowledge has been made by criminology through its historical commitment to objectivity; to understanding the determined nature of criminal behaviour; and by its ability to measure criminal behaviour (Taylor et al. 1973). These ideas, that criminal behaviour can be objectively measured through understanding the social, psychological or biological factors that produce it, reflect a commitment to the scientific endeavour as being fundamentally concerned to produce universal explanations one of the key features of positivism.

This desire to construct an explanation of crime that would apply to all situations has constituted a key characteristic of criminology and is connected to the implicit desire to formulate policy. Of course, the kinds of explanation that have been produced have varied according to the disciplinary concerns of the producers. This, in part, accounts for the confusion which academic criminology both reflects and thrives on. It also, in part, contributes to the tensions between academic talk about crime and common sense talk about crime.

As an area of study, then, peopled in this way and informed by a fundamental concern to produce universal explanations of crime, are the factors that contribute to the confusion as to whether or not there is anything clearly definable as *criminological* knowledge. Moreover, recognition of factors such as these makes it especially important to understand what is being said, by whom, and how that knowledge has been generated. In other words, there are not only competing theoretical perspectives on crime (as there are competing perspectives in other social science areas of study) but also quite distinct competing presumptions about the unit of analysis with which to even begin to think about the crime problem – from individual biology through to the role of the state.

To summarize, in the preface to his book *Talking about Crime and Criminals*, Gibbons (1994) has this to say:

> The title of this book speaks of 'talking about crime' and is intended to draw attention to the fact that much of the time criminologists literally don't know quite what they are talking about. Much of what passes for theorising in criminology involves fuzzy or undefined concepts, propositions that are implicit rather than explicit and/or that are internally inconsistent, and kindred other problems of exposition or logical structure.
>
> (Gibbons 1994: ix)

Of course, criminologists are not the only ones to suffer from problems such as these. Lack of clarity and fuzziness are problems inherent in both professional and 'common sense' discourses on crime. Some of these difficulties lie in understanding the nature of criminology as a discipline as well as understanding what influences how definitions of criminal behaviour are constructed and how talk about crime is constructed. These are separate, though interconnected, issues worthy of further exploration.

How to define the criminal

Defining that behaviour which counts as criminal and that behaviour which does not is neither an easy nor a straightforward process. It is clear, of course, that what is or is not permitted by the criminal law can be taken as the point of reference that defines the kind of behaviour with which criminologists are concerned. In this sense it is possible to say that the substantial concern of criminology is lawbreaking behaviour rather than criminal behaviour. This clearly differentiates the kind of behaviour with which criminology might be concerned from the more emotive use of the term 'criminal' itself, the use of which potentially can prejudge the guilt of the offender or can draw on more deeply embedded notions of 'wickedness'. Both of these tendencies not only fuel debates on crime but also can serve to contribute to the fuzziness associated with those debates. Taking the law as the point at which behaviour comes under the scrutiny of criminology certainly offers up a very broad range of concerns for analysis. However, the implications of defining criminological concerns in this way need to be spelled out a little more clearly.

First, such a definition places the law at the centre of defining behaviour as criminal or otherwise rather than placing the behaviour itself at the centre of criminological concerns. In so doing, however, it must be remembered that such a reference point can only define behaviour in this way at any one particular historical moment. Laws change. Some behaviours are newly defined as criminal (lawbreaking), others are decriminalized (defined as non-lawbreaking). The age of homosexual consent constitutes a good example of an area of the law in which changes have taken place over a relatively short historical period of time. The presumption of this book will be, however, that the central concern of criminology is lawbreaking behaviour.

Second, defining criminological concerns in this way inevitably directs any talk of understanding criminal behaviour towards, in part, understanding the processes whereby that behaviour has come to be defined as criminal – that is, understanding how and why laws change. An emphasis of this kind is somewhat different from an emphasis that focuses on the inherent characteristics of individuals as predefining their criminality – characteristics which, it has been argued, predispose some individuals to engage in criminal activities, such as having a particular kind of personality or possessing a certain chromosomal pattern (see Chapter 2 for a thematic development of this kind of approach). So, defining the central concern of criminology as being lawbreaking behaviour implies that those concerns are much more centrally focused on the *social processes* that lead to some behaviours but not others being defined as criminal and therefore being subjected to 'crime talk'.

Indeed, there exists a good deal of common sense knowledge about crime and criminal victimization. This knowledge, for some of the reasons already suggested, often sits uncomfortably with the rather more tenuous and circumscribed knowledge produced within a discipline called criminology; a discipline that frequently does not agree with itself. These issues notwithstanding, there is some agreement on some fairly general criminological 'truths', which frequently challenge the rather more dramatic media images of crime with which we may be more familiar.

Having, it is hoped, clarified one way of defining the kind of behaviour with which criminology might be concerned, it will be useful to explore some common perceptions about what criminal behaviour is like, who is likely to engage in it and what influences those perceptions.

What influences talk about crime?

Felson (2002) points to a number of fallacies that people often share about crime. One of these fallacies he refers to as the 'dramatic fallacy'. By this he means the extent to which media portrayals of crime, both factual and fictional, serve to equip individuals with particular images of the nature of crime, criminals and criminal victimization. These images tend to overplay the extraordinary crime and underplay the ordinary, routine, mundane nature of most criminal offences that take place.

The dramatization of crime in this way, however, informs 'common sense' talk about crime. Moreover, such dramatization not only informs 'common sense' talk but also frequently informs political talk. Such talk, given its dramatic influences, is often emotive in form and content and constitutes the backcloth against which criminological talk can look very vague and fuzzy indeed. However, by their power and influence, such images make the case for clarity from criminology and criminologists all the stronger. That such clarity appears to be absent is in part attributable to the nature of the discipline as well as to the nature of its chosen subject matter as discussed earlier.

However, Felson (2002) goes on to argue that media images of crime often serve to fuel a number of other fallacies about criminal behaviour. In particular, they fuel what he calls the 'age fallacy' and the 'ingenuity fallacy'. In other words, media images leave us with the impression that both victims and offenders are rather more middle aged than they actually are and that in order to commit crime it is necessary to be daring and ingenious. Media portrayals also frequently distort the nature of the role of the criminal justice professionals in the crime business and what they are more or less capable of. None of these images is borne out by the empirical data on crime, but they nevertheless infuse commonly held images of crime.

It is important to note that there is evidence to suggest that the media play an important role in influencing and shaping public perceptions of crime risks if not crime itself (Banks 2005; Chadee and Ditton 2005) and this seems to be the case across different countries and cultures (see for example, De Maillard and Roche 2005; Oberwittler and Hofer 2005; Smolej and Kivuori 2005). The promotion and/or amplification of issues in the media can contribute towards setting the agenda on an issue or enhancing a sense of threat or danger (Kasperon and Kasperon 1996; Philo 1999; Schlesinger et al. 1991). Cavender (2004: 346) in the context of assessing the media contribution to the increasing disparity between officially recorded crime rates and public perceptions of the nature and extent of the crime problem over the last 25 years states:

> The public had genuine concerns that reflected a changing social reality. But, the media reinforced and reproduced the public's attitudes. The media provided the organising frame, the narrative structure, the story line, and they kept it up for 25 years. Perhaps this is why the public's fear of crime has declined so little despite a decline in the crime rate. Crime has become an ever-present part of our symbolic reality.

Moreover that ever present part is also importantly visual and this visual culture plays on people's feelings and common sense understandings about crime. As Valier (2004) points out, visual culture travels rapidly and can be viewed in locations and circumstances a long way from their point of production. For example, the events that followed the publication of contentious cartoons of the prophet Mohammed in Denmark in early 2006 resulted in widespread demonstrations across the Muslim world and stands as testimony to the power of such visual technology. Indeed, media images of hostages, videotapes of beheadings, at the scene broadcasts of terrorist acts (qua 11 September 2001) are all intended to move us, to encourage us to place ourselves next to the victim. Such representations have a multilayered effect in appealing to moral notions of what a decent society should look like (Cottle 2005; Peelo and Soothill 2000; see also Peelo (2006) on the reporting of murders in such a way as to encourage us all to be witnesses). Such appeals potentially misrepresent the nature and extent of crime along with the chances of criminal victimization. This debate however, while particularly pertinent to the fear of crime, begs the question of what is known about crime (lawbreaking behaviour) by whom and how is that knowledge constructed. As a result this also begs the question of what, then, might a criminological 'truth' comprise?

What do we know about crime?

In answering a question such as this it is usual to refer to the various sources of statistical information on crime. These sources of information include official statistics, survey statistics (especially criminal victimization survey data), and self-report studies. Each of these sources of information offers different kinds of information about crime (and criminal victimization). Coleman and Moynihan (1996) and Maguire (2002) discuss the strengths and weaknesses of these different sources of data about crime (and criminal victimization). Suffice it to say in this context that on the basis of information of this kind, and a whole range of different academic studies of crime, Braithwaite (1989) has identified a number of criminological 'truths'.

Braithwaite (1989: 44–9) states that there are 13 'facts' about crime that criminology needs to explain, which more 'common sense' knowledge can sometimes fail to appreciate:

1 Crime is committed disproportionately by males.
2 Crime is perpetrated disproportionately by 15–25 year olds.
3 Crime is committed disproportionately by unmarried people.
4 Crime is committed disproportionately by people living in large cities.
5 Crime is committed disproportionately by people who have experienced high residential mobility and who live in areas characterized by high residential mobility.
6 Young people who are strongly attached to their school are less likely to engage in crime.
7 Young people who have high educational and occupational aspirations are less likely to engage in crime.
8 Young people who do poorly at school are more likely to engage in crime.
9 Young people who are strongly attached to their parents are less likely to engage in crime.
10 Young people who have friendships with criminals are more likely to engage in crime themselves.
11 People who believe strongly in complying with the law are less likely to violate the law.
12 For both men and women, being at the bottom of the class structure – whether measured by personal socioeconomic status, socioeconomic status of the area of residence, being unemployed or belonging to an oppressed racial minority – increases rates of offending for all types of crime apart from those for which opportunities are systematically less available to the poor.
13 Crime rates have been increasing since the Second World War in most countries, developed and developing. The only case of a country which has been clearly shown to have had a falling crime rate in this period is Japan.

These facts which a theory of crime 'ought to fit' can be tempered in a number of ways. In some respects, for example, they do not quite resonate with the phenomenon of 'white-collar crime'. That kind of lawbreaking behaviour appears to be committed by older, married males. Moreover, caution does need to be asserted more generally about these 'facts' given that they are (and can only be) derived from the variety of sources of information available about lawbreaking behaviour – sources that will always be incomplete in some way or other. Such caveats notwithstanding, these 'facts' certainly challenge some aspects of common sense knowledge about crime and criminal behaviour.

For example, common sense knowledge about crime, for the most part, renders implicit that most crime is committed by men. Indeed, this criminological 'fact' has until recently also remained implicit in much criminological talk about crime (see Chapter 5). Common sense knowledge about crime (and again, until recently, much criminological knowledge) also renders invisible the hidden nature of much criminal activity – for example, 'domestic' violence, rape in marriage, buying stolen goods, failure to enforce health and safety regulations in the workplace, fraudulent activities by business corporations. Indeed, in many respects much criminological work has focused on that kind of lawbreaking behaviour that common sense understandings of crime would most readily identify – juvenile delinquency, burglary and street crime.

However, identifying such 'facts', as Braithwaite does, contentious though some aspects of them might be, does not necessarily provide us with an explanation of them. So, while much criminological work has been concerned to measure the nature and extent of crime – that is, there has been a keen empirical focus central to the discipline – in order to make sense of those 'facts' it is necessary to try to explain them. What might such an explanation consist of? Braithwaite's list of 'facts' foregrounds social characteristics: general patterns of variables characteristic of social groups or social processes which have been identified by more than one empirical study as contributing to the propensity to engage in lawbreaking behaviour. Such social factors may not, of course, explain every individual case of crime committed or every individual criminal, but these factors locate criminology squarely in the domain of the social rather than in the domain of individual psychology. It is important to note that this text will also presume that it is social rather than psychological or biological explanations of lawbreaking behaviour that constitute the prime concern of criminology. The implications of this position are twofold and are interconnected.

First, it implies that we shall not be concerned in the following chapters with recent developments of criminological interest that have put to the fore genetic, hormonal, dietary or more general biological factors as the cause of lawbreaking behaviour. This book will presume that such factors are largely irrelevant in explaining the *patterning* of crime. In other words, if we take lawbreaking behaviour as the starting point of criminological concerns it is difficult to see how hormones or genetics can carry information about (changing, social) laws and thus constitute a meaningful level at which to explain crime.

A further reason for the irrelevance of biological factors is connected with the second implication of foregrounding the social as the arena in which criminological debate is most meaningfully constituted. That lies in understanding the relationship between criminology and criminal justice policy. Before this is discussed in more detail, however, it will be of value to appreciate some additional criminological 'facts'. One of the more recent features of criminology has been its increasing focus on criminal victimization. So having said something about what is known about crime, it will be useful to say something about what is known about criminal victimization.

What is known about criminal victimization?

The concern with and for the victim of crime has been given greater political and academic prominence since the mid–1970s. Miers (1978) argues that this 'politicization of the victim' was inherent in the formation of the Criminal Injuries Compensation Board in 1964 (now the Criminal Injuries Compensation Authority), although it has become many times stronger since then. Such a concern with the victim of crime can be explained in a number of different ways. It is certainly the case that the emergence of support services for crime victims in the form of Victim Support (which received its first Home Office funding in the mid-1980s and has been arguably the most rapidly expanding area of the voluntary sector since the late 1970s) provided a voice for the victim of crime where none existed before. In a different way the first and subsequent use of the criminal victimization survey by the Home Office in 1982 also exposed a fuller picture of the nature and extent of criminal victimization than was previously available and contributed in different ways to the growing concern about crime.

Factors such as these, alongside what appeared to be ever failing policies directed towards crime, fuelled the political debate on law and order that consequently increasingly turned its attention to the victim of crime. That attention was concerned not only to highlight the impact of crime on the victim but also to utilize the victim as a resource in combating crime itself. As Karmen (1990) has observed, as a consequence, policy both in the United States and in the United Kingdom, became increasingly informed not by crime prevention but by victimization prevention. Informing this general shift in policy has been a growing amount of data on criminal victimization.

The criminal victimization survey has been an important resource in identifying key 'facts' about the victim of crime. If that data source were used as the sole source of information about criminal victimization, then it would be possible to assert that young males are not only most often the offenders (the lawbreakers) but also most often the victims of crime. However, such an assertion would be misleading since it reflects a concern with only one form of lawbreaking behaviour taking place in only one set of circumstances.

If we extend our victimological gaze from the street to the bedroom, to the kitchen and to the workplace, then the picture of who the victims of crime are changes. Women feature much more significantly as victims of crime than do young males, although the extent to which young people as a whole (rather than just young males) are subjected to the processes of criminal victimization, from child abuse to mobile phone theft, should not be underestimated. Taking the victimological perspective seriously is also a 'truth' that any criminological explanation should endeavour to address.

To summarize: criminology as a discipline has been characterized historically by the desire to search for a universal explanation of crime. That search has produced knowledge from a range of disparate starting points all of which make competing claims in understanding crime. Those competing claims have frequently contributed to the confusion and fuzziness that surrounds the discipline itself. Nevertheless there are some central tenets of criminology on which there is some consensus among academics, even if those tenets conflict with more common sense understandings and more emotive political assertions. That consensus is a rather tenuous empirical one more than it is a theoretical one, however. In other words, criminologists *might* agree that the lawbreaking behaviour of young males constitutes one of the key issues of concern, but they will not necessarily agree on what underlying factors result in that concern or what can be done about it. It is at this point that the relationship between criminology, criminal justice policy and politics referred to earlier re-emerges.

Criminology, politics and criminal justice policy

As Garland (1985) has lucidly argued, criminology as an area of study has always been closely connected to the formation of criminal justice policy. As has been argued elsewhere, this connection can be attributed for the most part to the dominance within criminology (and other social science disciplines) of one particular version of the knowledge gathering and construction process: positivism. The influence of positivism on criminology has been well documented (see, for example, Roshier 1989; Taylor et al. 1973). One aspect of that influence was felt in the drive to assert a 'positive' influence over the processes of social change that were taking place especially during the nineteenth century. That drive tied criminology to the policymaking process as government extended its sphere of influence over social life and took an increasingly directive role in endeavouring to control the impact of social change. Social policies, including criminal justice policies, were formulated against this backcloth, resulting in an intimate relationship between the contemporary state of criminological knowledge and the formation of criminal justice policy.

Obviously, the kind of criminological knowledge that has influenced policy formation has varied historically. Some of that knowledge has led to policies that have focused on individual differences and deficiencies, whether biological or psychological. More recently, however, policy has been informed by an orientation that has been more generally social in character. Those orientations may, of course, vary in the assumptions they make about human beings and their potential. Our focus here will be to try to unpick some of the general features of criminal justice policy since the late 1970s and to map some of the connections to be made between these features and criminology that will be developed in subsequent chapters. The question might be raised, of course, why since the late 1970s? Part of the answer to this question lies within an understanding of processes that began much earlier.

As has been stated already, criminology is a modern discipline and as such shares in the characteristics of what we call modern society. Within sociology modern societies are commonly characterized as risk societies – in other words, as societies that are not riskier but in which cultural demands are primarily focused on the concern to be free from risk. Put another way, modern societies are societies preoccupied with the future – that is, with safety. Such cultural expectations are deeply rooted and are manifested in all aspects of social life – from issues to do with health to what we expect from the criminal justice system. Since 1945 these processes and expectations have taken a particular toll on the nature of our understanding of the crime problem and our response to it. Indeed some commentators have gone so far as to suggest that in this search for zero risk we now live in a 'culture of fear' (Furedi 1997, 2002). It will be useful to explore this impact in a little more detail.

Young (1999) argues that over the last 30 to 50 years, as our society has moved from a modern society to a late modern society, it has also moved from being an inclusive to an exclusive society. In some respects this analysis invokes an image of the 'Golden Age' of the 1950s with an interventionist state, a consensual social order, and people being unafraid to leave their front doors open. However, the cultural crisis of the 1960s, followed by the economic crisis of the 1970s, resulted in increasing social and economic insecurity. The effect of these processes is that the well off now live side by side with the not so well off in our cities. From this emanates not only an increased sense of relative deprivation (see Chapter 4 for a fuller discussion of this concept) but also an increased desire to draw boundaries around 'us' and 'them'. Put fairly simply, in an inclusive society there is security and tolerance, while in an exclusive society (a term used to describe contemporary social processes) there is insecurity and intolerance. So, not only do people become preoccupied with security (freedom from risk) but also with demonizing what they consider to be the source of their insecurity: the criminal. In this sense, Garland (2001) is correct to assert that we now live in a society preoccupied with control.

As a consequence, in contemporary political debate on crime and criminal justice policy there is little to choose between the main political parties. This is manifested by the various campaigning slogans over the past 10 years or so, from the Conservatives' 'Prison works!' to Labour's 'Tough on crime, tough on the causes of crime'. It is also evident in what might be considered to be more thoughtful contributions on the crime question by the various parties – for example, the adoption of Etzioni's (1996) communitarianism by the Labour Party prior to the 1997 general election or the more recent suggestion of the need to reintroduce neighbourly communities by the Conservative Party Shadow Home Secretary (January 2002). Underpinning all of this is an acceptance that crime is a normal fact of everyday life the risk from which we all need to manage better. Thus, arguably, much mainstream criminological research has become preoccupied with victimization prevention, with much of the work of the criminal justice agencies being similarly focused on responding to the victim of crime and managing risk.

At the same time as many of these processes have become increasingly complex (see Garland 2001 for a fuller exposition of the nature of this complexity), criminology as a discipline has changed beyond recognition. At the beginning of the 1980s the largest employer of criminologists was the Home Office and the academic departments that existed were small and focused primarily on research and postgraduate studies. Since then criminology has grown enormously both in terms of student numbers and in relation to academics claiming the label 'criminologist'. What is interesting about this exponential growth and development is that it has not resulted in a loud or effective academic criminological voice being heard. Thus, over a relatively short period of time we have become a society in which people are preoccupied with managing their security and our criminal justice system, peopled by professionals, has become much more complex and is now charged with delivering that security. At the same time while criminal justice policy has become an increasingly complex arena some social issues have remained the same. For example, the gap between rich and poor has changed little; we have become increasingly aware of and sensitive to the problems faced by people from ethnic minorities in our society, and while some progress in respect of gender inequalities has been made in public life, for many women little has changed in their private life. These features of our society raise questions of social justice: what do we think is a fair and just way of distributing the rewards (and punishments) in our society? Who has access to these rewards and punishments, where, when and how? (One way of thinking about the notion of social capital that we will discuss in the Conclusion to this book.) What do we think is socially just? Expressed in this way the connections between criminal justice policy and processes and social justice become clearer. The way in which criminal justice policy is formulated, who is subjected to that policy and how they are dealt with speaks volumes about the contemporary nature of social justice: the relationship between the citizen and the state; who is responsible for what and when. As a result of the interconnections between criminal justice and social justice, and the relationship between criminology and criminal justice policy, the discipline itself is also implicated in these interconnections. All these issues coexist in a highly politicized context with relatively little attention paid to any in-depth commentary on them.

So a focus on contemporary criminological theorizing and its impact (or lack of it) is of interest, given the wider context in which that theorizing has taken place. Some of that, especially in the early 1980s, was conducted with considerable fervour and that is interesting in its own right. It is also valuable to map the way in which the discipline endeavoured to intervene in political debate and the way in which the political parties chose to voice some aspects of criminological concern. While criminology and criminal justice policy have always been intertwined with one another, it is important to develop an appreciation of the complexities of the links between the two, especially in the contemporary context. The chapters that follow will attempt to highlight the complexity of such links.

Conclusion: what are the key features of criminology?

This chapter has endeavoured to highlight a number of features about criminology:

1 As a discipline it is held together by a substantive concern: crime.
2 This means that it is multidisciplinary in character rather than being dominated by one discipline. As a consequence, in order to make sense of what criminologists might be saying it is important to understand the conceptual apparatus with which they might be working.
3 Thus criminologists frequently disagree with each other.
4 Despite such disagreements, it could be argued that there is some consensus around some features of what constitutes the crime problem, although much less agreement on how to 'solve' that problem.
5 Nevertheless criminologists have been historically (and still are contemporaneously) concerned to offer some form of intervention in the policymaking process.
6 These features of criminology sometimes resonate with popular (common sense) thinking about crime and sometimes challenge such thinking. Such tensions are a perpetual challenge for the discipline.
7 These debates are taking place in a 'late modern' society increasingly preoccupied with crime, risk and insecurity.

These features of criminology render it both stimulating and frustrating as an area of study. They also reflect the more general strengths and weaknesses between theoretical and practical concerns of any applied area of study.

It has already been said that this analysis of criminology is premised on the view that it is at the level of the social that criminology can best formulate an answer to the crime question. What such an answer might look like, however, will be highly dependent on which variables comprising 'the social' are privileged. In the chapters that follow, we shall be examining the different ways in which different strands of criminological thought privilege different variables and concepts in their endeavours to understand crime, explain crime and capture the policy domain. One of the particular concerns of this book will be to unpack how criminology over the last 20 years has endeavoured to address the question of 'what works' in the context of preventing and reducing crime. We shall also be concerned to explore what might constitute the inherent weaknesses in the foundations of the discipline itself that might militate against providing any effective answers to that question.

So, the claims made in the title *Understanding Criminology* are considerable indeed. In some respects there is little agreement about the nature of the subject matter of this area of study, how it might best be studied and how its findings might best be translated into policy. Nevertheless in each of the chapters that follow, we shall be concerned to map such competing claims to knowledge and the differential influence they have had.

In order, therefore, to contextualize the developments that have occurred within criminology since the mid–1970s, Chapter 2 will offer a brief but critical introduction on the nature of criminology and the competing theoretical perspectives within criminology, prior to that time. In Chapter 3, we shall consider those varieties of 'conservative criminology' that can be found in different ways in right-wing thinking about crime. In Chapter 4, we shall consider the emergence of 'left realism' as a response to those ideas. Each of these different ways of theorizing crime displays criminology's continued attachment to the modernist project and to the production of an associated policy agenda. It in interesting to note that some of the keenest criticism of 'left realism' has emerged from those working within a post modernist framework, so it is in Chapter 4 that we shall also consider some features of that critique. Post modernism emerges as a relevant theme again in Chapter 5. That chapter will map the various ways in which the question of gender has been rendered more or less visible within the criminological enterprise and what questions remain unanswered for a criminology that does not have a gendered lens. Chapters 6 and 7 share a common concern. The view of both chapters is that there is much left to be addressed within a criminology with a modernist heart. They argue for a criminology that has at its centre a concern with social justice and they endeavour to demonstrate the extent to which debates about the underclass or young people and crime, for example, might be better formulated by a criminology so informed. Chapter 8 offers one way of furthering the conceptual apparatus of a criminology that is willing to engage in a self-reflexive critique of its modernist and gendered presumptions. In that chapter we shall consider how an understanding of the concepts of risk, trust, social capital and the underlying relationship between the citizen and the state may affect the criminology of the future.

Further reading

A range of textbooks now endeavours to offer a feel for crime as a social problem and the response of criminology to that. Such texts provide a useful introduction to what criminologists know and do not know, as well as a sound foundation for more theoretical concerns. A good example is Felson (2002). Those wishing to pursue a more detailed understanding of the changing nature of wider society should look to Young (1999). Those wishing to explore the ideas around risk and their relevance for criminal justice mentioned here might find Stenson and Sullivan (2001) interesting.

chapter two

Perspectives in criminological theory

The behaviour of criminals
The criminality of behaviour
The criminality of the state
Conclusion
Further reading

It has been established so far that criminology as an area of study is a diverse discipline characterized by competing theoretical perspectives. However, before we proceed to examine the developments within criminology since the 1970s, it will be useful to identify in a little more detail some of the key themes embedded in earlier criminological debate. It is possible to identify three recurrent themes within criminological theory: a concern with the *behaviour of criminals*, a concern with the *criminality of behaviour* and a concern with the *criminality of the state*. Each of these themes has been more or less popular at different historical moments and each directs the criminological agenda, in theory and in practice, in quite different ways. We shall discuss each of them in turn.

The behaviour of criminals

A focus on the behaviour of criminals directs our attention to a central concern with the individual and the role of individual differences in producing crime. As Chapter 1 suggested, different writers have endeavoured to construct different historical connections for the emergence of criminology as a discipline. If a broad view of that history is constructed, a concern with the behaviour of individual criminals can be traced to early religious talk about crime. That view implied that criminals were possessed by demons and as a consequence they were subjected to different kinds of trials to rid them of such influences. For some religious sects, this way of thinking about crime is still considered to be appropriate today. Here, however, we shall be concerned primarily with two different ways of thinking about the individual behaviour of criminals: the classical school of thought and the positivist school of thought. Both of these have a resonance with the later criminological concerns discussed in Chapters 6 and 7. Throughout this chapter it is important to remember that criminology is a modern discipline. As Lea (2002) has observed, people have done nasty things to each other throughout history, what is different in the modern period, as opposed to the Middle Ages, is that these acts have been criminalized. As Lea (2002: 24) states: 'crime is not a form of action which exists prior to the institutions and social relations that deal with it.' In order words, crime, and our ability to make sense of it, is intimately connected with the processes of modernization and the concomitant developments of capitalism that inform the ever increasing sophistication of mechanisms designed to ensure social control and, in this particular context, crime control. Different criminological theories make sense of these interconnections in different ways, some focusing attention on the responsibility of the individual, others offering differing emphases on the responsibility of the social in producing criminal behaviour. Some of these differences in emphasis will become apparent in the discussion to follow.

Classical criminology

The key feature of classical criminology is its central presumption that individual criminals engage in a process of rational calculative decision making in choosing how to commit crime. This view is underpinned by two further assumptions: that individuals have free will; and that individuals are guided by hedonism, the maximization of pleasure and the minimization of pain. These ideas, in their initial formulation, were important in that they shifted attention towards punishing people's offending behaviour rather than 'punishing' the individual's social or physical characteristics in and of themselves. This shift consequently had an enormous influence on changing attitudes towards punishment and towards the purpose of the law and the legal system.

Classical ideas about crime and punishment can be found in the works of a number of different writers. The writings of Cesare Beccaria (1738–94) and Jeremy Bentham (1748–1832), however, were especially influential. Of the two, Beccaria is frequently cited as being the more influential in the subsequent development of the criminological agenda.

Put simply, Beccaria argued that there was a contractual relationship between the individual and the state. This relationship existed to prevent chaos. As a part of this contractual relationship individuals gave up some of their liberties in the interest of the common good, with the purpose of the law being to ensure that these common interests were met. For Beccaria, this meant that the law should be limited in scope and written down so that people could make decisions on how to behave. Importantly, punishment was to fit the crime not the individual and was to be certain and swift. Offenders were to be seen as reasonable people with the same capacity for resisting offending behaviour as non-offenders. The guiding principle of the criminal justice process, it was argued, was the presumption of innocence; and in this general framework punishment was to be seen as a deterrent to criminal behaviour. The central concern of the law and the criminal justice process was therefore the prevention of crime through this deterrent function. From within this way of thinking the push to extend imprisonment as a form of punishment was extended and as a disciple of Beccaria, Bentham is well known for his design of the prison called the Panopticon. This circular construction facilitated constant surveillance of inmates, making chains unnecessary. In such a structure regimes of discipline and hard work would change the behaviour of prisoners and it was aspects of this model that were put into place in a number of prisons built in the late nineteenth and early twentieth century.

These ideas were very influential in reforming criminal codes and informing legislative changes in a number of different social contexts. They were particularly influential in France at the time of the French Revolution and, it is argued, informed the formulation of the American Constitution. However, despite the significant ways in which these ideas underpinned major changes in different legal frameworks, these changes did not accommodate the issue of the differences in individuals' offending behaviour in general neither did it accommodate children's criminal behaviour or that of the insane. In addition, the policies that derived from this view of the criminal did not solve the rising crime rate. This led to what Hopkins Burke (2001) calls the 'neo-classical compromise'. This view tried to take account of the fact that the insane or children might not be as responsible for their actions as was presumed by the rational actor of classicism and permitted 'experts' (doctors, social workers, psychiatrists) to speak for these offenders. Thus neo-classicism draws on a model of the individual that suggests that their actions are predetermined in some way; hence the neo-classical compromise. Thus this is the view that draws on the concepts of free will and determinism simultaneously.

It should be noted however that the classical school of thought has had an enduring influence as many legal systems are built on some of its key precepts. The idea of 'intent' for example, emphasizes the importance of the state of mind of the individual and their capacity for making choices. Moreover notions of proportionality in relation to punishment, and equal punishment for the same kind, are clearly traceable to the ideas of classicism. Indeed the idea of the rational offender underpins many contemporary debates and policy responses to crime and the criminal as popular conservatism has taken a hold in the UK and the USA especially in the last 25 years (see Chapter 3).

Despite these intellectual and policy interventions, crime was still becoming increasingly problematic. Consequently, as social conditions worsened for many sections of different societies after the Industrial Revolution, the idea of individuals being motivated by hedonism and free will lost some of its popularity. In its place a more controlled image of the human being was constructed. This image reflected one of the ideas that contributed to the birth of positivism within criminology.

Positivist criminology

Many reviews of the development of criminology begin with reference to the influence of positivism. While the specific meaning to be attached to this term is open to some debate, in the context of criminology it is usually used to refer to a scientific commitment to the gathering of the 'facts' that distinguish offenders from non-offenders in order to aid the process of understanding the causes of crime. It is this search for 'facts' which most clearly delineates one of the differences between this version of criminology and classical criminology. The other main difference between these two different versions of the criminal individual was the commitment of the early positivists especially to search for the cause of crime within individual biology rather than individual free will. Cesare Lombroso (1835–1909) is frequently considered to be the founding father of this version of criminological thought.

Lombroso's ideas about crime are clearly influenced by Charles Darwin's ideas on evolution, which so challenged the religious principles of the nineteenth century. Most easily identified as an anthropologist, Lombroso embraced what was referred to as the law of biogenetics. This 'law' articulated a particular view of evolutionary development in which it is posited that every individual organism revisits the developmental history of its own species type within its own individual history. The phrase 'ontology recapitulates phylogeny' captured this view of the developmental process and introduced an important concept, that of recapitulation, to Lombrosian criminology. The idea that every living organism, as it develops, undergoes each stage of its own species history provided a mechanism for explaining both the normal and the abnormal (the pathological). This was achieved through the related concept of atavism.

It was clear, even to those committed to Darwin's ideas, that every individual member of a species type did not always possess all the characteristics of that species type; in other words, abnormalities were produced from time to time. These abnormalities, it was argued, were a product of that individual member being a throwback to an earlier stage of the developmental history of the species: that is, atavistic. In this way the concept of atavism permitted the law of biogenetics to retain its universal status; aberrations were explained as being reversions to an earlier species type. The idea of atavism appealed to the criminal anthropologists, especially Lombroso.

Lombroso assumed that the process of recapitulation usually produced normal individuals. Someone who became criminal, therefore, must constitute a throwback to an earlier stage of biological development – atavistic degeneration. For Lombroso, such biological degenerations manifested themselves in the peculiar physical attributes possessed by criminals – sloping foreheads, receding chins, excessively long arms, unusual ear size, etc. – resulting in the view of the 'born criminal'.

This commitment to the biological origin of criminal behaviour led Lombroso to construct a fourfold typology of criminals: the born criminal (true atavistic types); the insane criminal (including those suffering from a range of mental illnesses); the occasional criminal (opportunist criminals who commit crime because they possess innate traits that propel them in that direction); and criminals of passion (who commit crime as a result of some irresistible force). For all these criminal types, their behaviour is a result of their abnormality, determined by forces out of their control, rather than the consequence of freely chosen action.

The legacy of Lombrosian criminology has been profound. While the notion of the 'born criminal' might appear simple and naive in the early twenty-first century, Lombroso's commitment to a science of the criminal, and the search for a universal explanation of crime located within the individual, laid the foundation for much subsequent criminological work. Moreover, the search for the cause of crime within the individual and individual differences continued, albeit focusing on different biological and/or psychological factors. This has ranged from work on heredity (Goring 1913) and body type (Kretschmer 1926) to the notion of a criminal personality (Eysenck and Gudjonnson 1990).

Latterly, this way of thinking about crime has become theoretically more sophisticated, with the biosocial theory of Wilson and Herrnstein (1985), discussed in Chapter 3, and has become technologically more complex in the increasingly controversial world of neuroscience. Here, using advanced technology to construct images of the brain, the view that individuals are merely negatives waiting to be developed is beginning to reopen the whole debate about whether or not human beings possess free will and where and how an understanding of criminal behaviour might be situated. Thus the tension remains between classical and positivist views on the nature of human beings.

Each of these ways of focusing on the behaviour of the criminal carries with it different policy implications. As was suggested earlier for the classical criminologist, if individuals had a calculative, hedonistic approach to crime, then the purpose of the criminal justice system was to punish in order to deter them from committing crime. For the positivist, by way of contrast, if individuals' criminal behaviour is to be understood as being determined by their biological and/or psychological make-up, then the purpose of the criminal justice system is either to incapacitate them or, if appropriate, to offer them treatment until they are no longer a threat to society. In more current policy debate the influence of these different ways of thinking about and using the criminal justice system is still evident, standing as some testimony to the importance of these ideas.

Positivistic approaches to explaining crime are not only to be found within the search for the individual roots of criminal behaviour. They are also to be found in much more sociologically informed approaches to criminology. These approaches take as their focus of concern the wider socioeconomic and cultural conditions which may or may not propel individuals into criminal behaviour and it is these more sociologically informed approaches we shall consider under our next thematic heading: a concern with the criminality of behaviour.

The criminality of behaviour

A concern with the criminality of behaviour focuses attention on factors external to individuals that might result in their behaviour either being lawbreaking or being defined as lawbreaking. These ways of thinking about crime have also been influenced by positivism in the sense that they are approaches that have been equally concerned to identify the 'facts' that result in criminality. The way in which that concern has been addressed can be discussed in a number of different ways. For the purposes of this discussion four central ideas can be identified: the concept of social disorganization, strain theory and its derivatives, social control theory and labelling theory.

Social disorganization

The concept of social disorganization emanates from the Chicago School of Sociology of the 1920s and 1930s. It reflects one of two main strands of theoretical work emanating from Chicago which were to influence quite profoundly the later development of both criminology and the sociology of deviance, namely, social ecology and symbolic interactionism. The concept of symbolic interactionism is discussed on pp. 27–8. The concept of social disorganization is associated with those theorists concerned to understand the social ecology of the city.

Social ecologists drew parallels between the way in which it was thought living organisms maintained themselves and the maintenance of social life. In other words, just as it was possible to identify patterns in the processes of development and adaptation to the environment in the animal and plant world so it was possible to identify similar patterns in the growth and development of the city. This led theorists to suggest that it made sense to think of the city as a series of concentric zones radiating from the city centre, with each zone having different social and economic characteristics and the people living in those different areas adapting differently to those social circumstances. These general presumptions, when overlaid on the substantive data available about city life, led to a much more detailed appreciation of these differing patterns of adaptation. In particular, attention was focused on the 'zone of transition', the area nearest the city centre.

The 'zone of transition' became the focal concern since this was the area in which new immigrants to the city settled (as it was inexpensive and near to places of work), but it was also the area that appeared to manifest more social problems (according to official statistics), from incidences of ill health to crime. The manifestation of problems such as these was explained by the social ecologists as being the result of the breakdown of primary social relationships in this area, with the highly mobile and transitory nature of social life breeding impersonality and fragmentation.

In general terms, then, this theoretical perspective suggested that the processes of industrialization and urbanization create communities in which, as a result of immigration and subsequent migration, there are competing norms and values. The consequence of this is the breakdown of traditional norms and values: social disorganization. It is within this general context that crime is most likely to occur. Through the notion of cultural transmission it was also argued that these modes of adaptation to different social conditions in the city were likely to be passed on from one generation to the next as new immigrants enter that part of the city and adapt to those social conditions.

This way of thinking about and explaining the patterning of criminal behaviour (as it was officially recorded) was one of the first to consider the social origins of criminality as opposed to the individual roots of crime. As a result, it not only influenced subsequent generations of sociologically informed criminological work, but also carries with it clear policy implications. In theoretical terms, the concept of social disorganization led later theorists to work in different ways with the interaction between social structure and the social production of norms and values. In policy terms, it has led to a focus on how to 'reorganize' socially disorganized communities, to a desire to understand the ways in which the environment might contribute to crime (designing out crime), and to a concern with how general neighbourhood decline (rising incivilities) might contribute to the crime career of a community, to name several recurring and contemporarily relevant policy themes. The extent to which this is a legitimate evidence-based policy concern is a moot point, as the work of Walklate and Evans (1999) demonstrates. However, this kind of focus is clearly evident on the contemporary policy scene, evidence of which can be found in the establishment of the Social Exclusion Unit in 1997 and some of its subsequent publications – see, for example, Social Exclusion Unit (1998). Nevertheless, it is clear that the focus on the way in which social conditions produce social pathology is a common thread between the social ecologists and those who took up the ideas of strain theory.

Strain theory

Strain theory emanates primarily from the work of Robert Merton (1938, 1968). His theoretical work was concerned more with the way in which the tensions between the legitimate and illegitimate means of acceding to the norms and values of a particular society resulted in deviant (rather than just criminal) behaviour. The influence of these ideas on criminology has been profound. Merton's ideas can be situated within the theoretical tradition of functionalism. Largely informed by the work of Emile Durkheim and Talcott Parsons, functionalism views society rather like a finely tuned biological organism. In order for society to work effectively its component parts must be in balance and there must be some consensus or agreement concerning the appropriateness of that balance. Put simply, this balance produces social order. Any imbalance results in social disorder.

Merton's work endeavoured to address the social and cultural norms and values that underpinned social order and/or disorder. His central concern was to identify the circumstances in which, while there might be socially approved ways of achieving success, not everyone by definition had access to those socially approved means. How did those who lacked such opportunities adapt to the strain which that produced?

In order to understand the conflict generated between acceptance of the norms and values of mainstream society and the ability to succeed within those norms and values, Merton constructed a fivefold typology. This typology contrasted those people who accepted the cultural norms and values and the institutionalized means of achieving those norms and values (the conformists) and those people who rejected both and put new ones in their place (the rebellious). This schema was intended to convey the ways in which the structure of society in and of itself produced deviant behaviour, some of which would also be criminal behaviour, at all levels in the social structure.

However, the primary implication of this schema was a focus on those in the lower classes since, given the strains of their structural location, it was presumed that they were the most likely to engage in non-conformist behaviour. There are two important theoretical developments which arguably follow on from Merton's concern with the production of deviant behaviour: Cohen's notion of the delinquent subculture and Cloward and Ohlin's concept of differential opportunity. This focus on the lower classes constitutes one of the common strands between Merton's theoretical work and those who followed. We shall discuss each of these in turn.

Drawing on both Merton's work and the notion of cultural transmission embedded within social disorganization theory, Cohen (1955) developed a framework in which to understand why delinquent subcultures seemed to be formed primarily within deprived inner-city areas. Cohen's argument, following Merton, was that lower-class youth strove to embrace the norms and values of mainstream society but lacked the means to achieve success. They thus suffered from status frustration: they were denied the status of respectability because they did not have the means to achieve such respectability. Delinquent subculture provided an alternative, sometimes oppositional, means of achieving such status. So the strains produced as a consequence of social disorganization result in the formation of norms and values through which lower-class youth can achieve status and success.

One question, however, remained unanswered within this framework: how was it that not all lower-class youth embraced the delinquent subculture or chose the same kind of deviant solution despite being subjected to similar strains of social disorganization? It is at this point that the notion of differential opportunity structures associated with the work of Cloward and Ohlin (1960) became important.

Again embracing Mertonian strain theory, Cloward and Ohlin argued that there is more than one way in any society to achieve success. There are both legitimate and illegitimate pathways. In their view, the upper and middle classes have greater access to the legitimate opportunity structure, with the lower classes having greater access to the illegitimate opportunity structure. In a community where these two different kinds of opportunity structure are poorly integrated, there tends to be greater social disorganization. The greater the social disorganization, the more likely that the illegitimate opportunity structure, especially organized criminal gangs, will become dominant. This kind of opportunity structure, it was suggested, provides an alternative route for status and success for those who join it.

Cloward and Ohlin's theory facilitates an understanding of the ways in which different kinds of delinquent subculture come to be prevalent in different kinds of urban locations – from the retreatist gang (those primarily engaged in drugs) to the conflict gang (those most concerned with violence) – the outcome-predicting variable factor being the level of integration between the different opportunity structures. Thus, rather like Cohen, Cloward and Ohlin were endeavouring to weave together the work of the Chicago School on social disorganization with the strain theory of Robert Merton. This concern with the relationship between criminal (delinquent) behaviour and subcultural processes spawned a generation of studies with these ideas as their focus and it was not until the intervention of Matza's (1964) work that this focus took on a more subtle mantle.

Matza, with his concept of drift, challenged the presumption that subcultural norms and values defined an individual's identity and that those same norms and values meant that all those exposed to them would ultimately engage in criminal (delinquent) behaviour. His view was that young people (although these theorists were almost exclusively concerned with young males; see also Chapter 5) drifted in and out of delinquent behaviour and even when engaged in 'lawbreaking' activities used 'techniques of neutralization' to justify their actions; it wasn't me, I didn't mean it, he deserved it, they always pick on me, you have to stand by your mates. In other words, they were not simply determined by their subcultural involvement but actively understood and made choices about it. Put simply, Hopkins Burke (2001) suggests that Matza encouraged criminologists to think about deviancy as fun. The work of Matza set the tone for the development of more critical criminological work of the late 1960s and early 1970s that recognized the adage adapted from Marx, that people make choices but not in circumstances of their own choosing. Thus Matza offered a way of integrating an understanding of criminality as part of general behaviour more conventionally understood as deviant. In a different vein but equally concerned to offer an integrated approach to understanding behaviour that would cover both deviance and criminality is to be found in the social control theory of Hirschi (1969).

Social control theory

Equally concerned with social processes rather than individual ones, Hirschi (1969) developed what he called a 'social bond' thesis of social control. So this approach was as much concerned to offer a theory that could explain why people conformed to the norms and values of society as much as why they might deviate from them.

So rooted in trying to understand the nature of social control, Hirschi (1969) argued that there were four components to social bonds that might sustain or threaten social relationships. These were attachment (the strength or weakness of relationships); commitment (the level of investment an individual makes in a relationship); involvement (the amount of time an individual spends in conforming or non-conforming behaviour): and beliefs (the extent to which an individual has been socialized into being a law-abiding citizen). Aspects of these components clearly link with the discussion of common sense understandings of involvement in crime discussed in the Introduction. (For example, the adage that 'the devil makes work for idle hands' is not that far from the concept of involvement.) However, the strength of Hirschi's concepts lies in the ability to test them empirically and they have resulted in some sound support in this respect. (Again the reader might like to review Braithwaite's facts, listed in the Introduction, in the light of the discussion here.) Hirschi's social control theory has, inevitably, been subject to some criticism. For example, it cannot explain why lack of social bonds might lead someone to take drugs and another individual to engage in shoplifting. Criticisms such as these led Hirschi, along with Gottfredson (Gottfredson and Hirschi, 1990) to formulate a 'General Theory of Crime', in which they introduced the concept of 'self-control' to address some of the original theoretical weaknesses, although the extent to which this development overcame the kinds of criticisms alluded to earlier is a moot point.

What strain theory, social control theory and its derivatives achieved was to centre the importance of structural variables, external to the individual, as a way of understanding the nature of criminal behaviour. In particular, what both Cohen and Cloward and Ohlin and others were concerned to address was the question of subculture. Many criminologists accepted the Mertonian proposition that some people were disadvantaged in their efforts to achieve success and what required explanation was the resulting deviant behaviour. These conditions were mediated by the formation of different subcultural responses. This focus on the interrelationship between structural condition and subcultural response remains relevant today. Some would argue that the ultimate testing ground for this relationship lies within the more current concerns and debates on the underclass (see Chapter 3). Understanding the relevance of subculture is not solely the preserve of those on the right. It is also a concern of those on the left (see Chapter 4). In the 1960s this work certainly laid the groundwork for the further development of a second strand of thought emanating from the Chicago School. That work, largely associated with symbolic interactionism, placed much greater emphasis on the social processes involved in becoming deviant and came to be called labelling theory.

Labelling theory

Labelling theory returns us to the second school of thought that characterized the Chicago School of Sociology during the 1920s and 1930s: symbolic interactionism. Originating with the work of George Herbert Mead, symbolic interactionism was concerned to understand the processes underpinning social life and the mechanisms by which meanings are assigned to those processes. As a theoretical perspective symbolic interactionism centres the creative capacities of human beings and their ability to share understandings with one another. These general propositions direct attention towards the quality of the interactions that take place between people, how those interactions are understood and how they become modified, refined and developed. This perspective, then, shares common concerns with strain theory in addressing the general question of how behaviour comes to be understood as deviant (rather than criminal) and the role of shared norms and values in that process. In the latter respect, the work of Howard Becker, with what came to be called labelling theory, has been particularly influential.

There are two strands to Becker's (1963) labelling theory: a concern to address how a particular behaviour is labelled as deviant and a concern to understand the impact of that labelling process. As Becker states:

> Social groups create deviance by making the rules whose infraction constitutes deviance, and by applying those rules to particular people and labelling them as outsiders. From this point of view, deviance is not a quality of the act the person commits, but rather a consequence of the application by others of rules and sanctions to an 'offender'.

> The deviant is one to whom that label has been successfully applied; deviant behaviour is behaviour that people so label.
>
> (Becker 1963: 9)

In understanding deviance, then, importance lies in the reaction to the behaviour not the behaviour itself. This led Becker to construct a fourfold typology of possible labels (reactions) to perceived deviant behaviour: the falsely accused, the pure deviant, the conformist and the secret deviant.

This focus on the labelling process led criminologists and sociologists to think about criminal behaviour in quite a different way. For instance, while officially recorded crime data identified young, lower-class males as the key criminal group, labelling theorists wanted to explore what it was about the criminal justice agencies that led them to focus attention on this particular group of people (as opposed to others who might be secretly deviant, that is, not publicly labelled as deviant). Other theorists became more concerned with the impact of being labelled deviant and explored the notion of a deviant career.

Labelling theory had a major impact on criminology, which led to a closer examination of the way in which the criminal justice system operates and processes individuals. In policy terms, it connected most directly with those policies concerned to divert (potential) offenders from crime and/or the criminal justice system. But, both in theory and in practice, labelling theory has its limitations: the key problem being the question of power and power relationships.

Underpinning the theoretical strands of thought discussed here is a common image of society. That image presumes, for the most part, the normatively predominant view of society as comprising a democratic and consensual process. Largely as a consequence of this presumption, attention is implicitly focused on those who deviate from this normative view, which for the most part results in a concern with the deviant and/or criminal behaviour of the lower classes. There is, however, an alternative way of thinking about the nature of society, which results in quite a different focus in relation to thinking about crime. That view is subsumed in the third theme to be discussed here, the criminality of the state.

The criminality of the state

There is a clear connection between a critical analysis of labelling processes and their impact and the development of a close interest in those who have the power to label. However, once theorists were moved to consider the question of power and power relationships it also became clear that the implicit view of society previously held could not accommodate these newer concerns. In theoretical terms, it made much more sense to turn to

Marx and a view of society as rooted in conflicting interests than to retain the Parsonian image of consensus.

General Marxist presumptions about the nature of society direct attention to the way in which the powerful in society use the various resources available to them (including the law) to secure and maintain their dominant position. In particular, this means that the law and the processes that underpin the formation of the law are placed under scrutiny, alongside the way in which the law is used to criminalize particular social groups in the interests of the powerful. Consequently, the law and its enforcement are seen as particular sites where the legitimated powers of the state are exercised. Those powers, it is argued, express themselves especially along class, race and gender lines.

There are a number of different writers whose work can be located under this general heading of concern with the criminality of the state, although many would argue that its criminological lineage can be traced to the work of Bonger (1916) who squarely situated the propensity for criminal behaviour within the changing conditions of capitalism and the resultant and variable effects this had on individual economic circumstances. Here particular attention will be paid to three varieties of this interest: Marxist criminology, radical criminology and critical criminology. These labels are certainly not mutually exclusive. They are used here primarily as a heuristic device in an effort to address that range of work within criminology that has been of a more radical theoretical nature.

Marxist criminology

Strands of Marxist theorizing can be found in the writings of a number of different criminologists, although the work of Chambliss (1975) and Quinney (1977) has arguably been particularly influential.

Chambliss's work is a clear attempt to use Marxist theorizing to construct a political economy of crime. Marx himself had little to say about crime or the law, but the general tenor of his views on society and social relationships can be translated into the criminological context. As Chambliss argues, capitalism creates the desire to consume and it has to be recognized that not all members of society are able to earn enough to match the levels of consumption induced by the capitalist process. There are the owners and the non-owners, the bourgeoisie and the proletariat, all of whom have different capacities at different points in time both to produce and to consume.

Moreover, the underlying logical development of the capitalist process, it is argued, inevitably results in more and more situations where those who have and those who have not are put in conflict with one another. Sometimes that conflict is violent; more often it results in the behaviour of those who have not being labelled as criminal. As Chambliss (1975) puts it:

> The criminal law is thus not a reflection of custom . . . but a set of rules laid down by the state in the interests of the ruling class, and resulting from the conflicts that inhere in class structured societies; criminal behaviour is, then, the inevitable expression of class conflict resulting from the inherently exploitative nature of economic relations.
>
> (abridged in Muncie et al. 1996: 225)

In this sense, then, crime is to be understood as a reaction to the general life conditions in which individuals find themselves as a result of their social class position.

Within this general framework, of course, there is no necessary presumption that only the relatively powerless are likely to engage in criminal activities. Indeed, the general proposition would be that all people in all social classes are capable of committing crime. What is central to this argument is to understand why only some behaviours are so targeted as criminal. To quote Chambliss (1975) again:

> Criminality is simply not something that people have or don't have; crime is not something some people do and others don't. Crime is a matter of who can pin the label on whom, and underlying this socio-political process is the structure of social relations determined by the political economy.
>
> (Muncie et al. 1996: 228)

So for Chambliss the underlying cause of crime lies not with individuals, or their greater or lesser acceptance of cultural norms and values, but with the state and the political and economic interests that are necessarily served by the law and its implementation. (This observation returns us to the links to be made between modernization, capitalism and the processes of criminalization.)

In some respects, there is still a rational image of the human being embedded in this theoretical framework offered by Chambliss. Crime is to be seen as a rational response to social conditions for some individuals. It is a way of managing the material reality of their lives. This is a variation on Marx's observation that men make choices but not in circumstances of their own choosing. This rationality is consequently circumscribed. It is not the rationality of free will but that which is rationally dictated by the political economy of social relations. As Chambliss argues: 'The state becomes an instrument of the ruling class enforcing laws here but not there, according to the realities of political power and economic conditions' (Muncie et al. 1996: 230). A similar theoretical feel is found in the work of Quinney (1977).

It can be argued that Quinney's ideas were as heavily influenced by the work of the phenomenologists as they were by Marx. Consequently, different readings of his work can and do emphasize these different theoretical inputs. In general terms, however, Quinney talked about the 'politicality of law' and the 'politicality of crime'. By the politicality of law, he was referring to the extent to which social relations are reflected in the law and the lawmaking process – social relations which rendered some issues visible and ensured that others remained invisible or, in other words, reflected political interests.

In talking about the politicality of crime, Quinney was referring to criminal behaviour as a 'conscientious' activity: not the produce of poor socialization or a deficient personality, but a political expression. In other words, it is not the behaviour that is criminal but the action taken against it that renders it criminal; the process of criminalization.

There is a particular view of society that underpins these twin concerns. This view of society emphasizes the social construction of social reality. In its extreme form, this view of society presumes that social reality is simply a reflection of an individual's state of mind. In its milder versions, it is intended to draw attention to the way in which our understanding of social, political and criminological issues (to name but a few) is constantly subject to changing perceptions and interpretations. This theme links Quinney's general theoretical framework with that of critical criminology (discussed on pp. 34–6).

In this particular context, however, Quinney was endeavouring to draw attention to the ways in which definitions of what is and what is not problematic become taken for granted and embedded in social relations, a process which serves the interests of the powerful much more readily than those of the powerless. This, he argued, was a structural rather than a conspiratorial relationship.

Quinney went on to construct a typology of crime that could form the central focus of a criminology informed by these ideas. In this typology he talks of crimes of domination (police brutality, white-collar crime, governmental crimes), accommodation and resistance (theft and homicide produced by the conditions of capitalism) and terrorism (a response to the conditions of capitalism). Essentially, this position reflects a view of the causality of crime as being an expression of the desire for social change, that is, as a political act.

Both of these versions of criminology have two themes in common. Put simply, they both see crime as a product of the behaviour of the authorities rather than as a product of individuals. In other words, this kind of Marxist theorizing endeavours to further the labelling perspective's concern with the power to label. In addition, they both see crime as a relative phenomenon rather than an absolute one. In other words, there is nothing inherently wicked or sinful in criminal behaviour; it is simply behaviour that is so targeted.

The policy implications of work informed in this way are clearly neither simple nor straightforward. They ultimately imply a different social and economic order. Indeed, in many respects little practical work ensued from these theoretical developments as a consequence. However, these ideas were valuable in drawing criminological attention to the role of the law in defining the criminality that is seen and not seen and in establishing a much sharper critical focus on those processes. Moreover, these general ideas were also influential in contributing to what has been called radical criminology.

Radical criminology

The radical criminology of Taylor et al. (1973), which will form the basis of the discussion here, did not emerge in a vacuum. Although largely taken as the starting point of more radical work in the UK, the ideas contained within *The New Criminology* had their origins in the work of earlier labelling theorists as well as versions of Marxist criminology (discussed earlier). This work remains influential largely because it was one of the first to offer a wide-ranging critique of the (then) dominant form of criminology. This dominant form was peopled mostly by psychologists and psychiatrists concerned with the behaviour of the criminal, looking for the cause of crime within the individual.

Taylor et al. not only offered a thoroughgoing critique of criminology, but also endeavoured to offer a theoretical perspective to replace this focus on the individual with a focus on the social construction of crime. In so doing they offered a theory synthesizing labelling theory with Marxism as a means of retaining a concern with the value of appreciating individual meaning and action (the question of authenticity) alongside the power of state agencies to control and define (the question of the role of the state). It will be valuable to examine this framework in a little more detail.

The New Criminology has seven elements to it. The first argues that in order to understand a crime (or a deviant act), it is important to locate it within wider social processes. In other words, individual behaviour must be placed in a social, political and economic context. There must be a political economy of crime. Second, having situated a behaviour in this way, the immediate circumstances and origins of criminal behaviour must be kept in mind – in other words, how and why individuals choose to respond to their structural location in the way that they do. This is expressed as a requirement for a social psychology of crime. Third, people may choose to behave in a particular way, but may for various reasons not carry out their choices or their choices may become modified in the process of interaction. Recognition of these processes means that it is necessary to offer an account of the social dynamics of crime: what were the interactive processes that led to one outcome rather than another?

Fourth, people may behave in a range of different ways, some of which may be labelled deviant while others may not. In other words, it is important to understand the social reaction to crime. That social reaction may be rooted in the social psychology of what passes between the witnesses to a particular behaviour, but it may also be located in a wider audience. That wider audience will include professionals working in the criminal justice agencies as well as other people significant to the offender. Their response to different behaviours requires an understanding of what Taylor et al. call a political economy of social reaction, the fifth proposition. The sixth concern is with the relationship between the social reaction to the deviant and/or criminal behaviour and the impact of that social reaction. In other words, how might this impact or not on an individual's future criminal career?

The final proposition of what these authors call a fully social theory of deviance is an implicit acceptance of the dialectical nature of social reality:

> The central requirement of a fully social theory of deviance, however, is that these formal requirements must not be treated simply as essential factors all of which need to be present (in invariant fashion) if the theory is to be social. Rather it is that these formal requirements must all appear in the theory, as they do in the real world, in a complex, dialectical relationship to one another.
>
> (Taylor et al. 1973, abridged in Muncie et al. 1996: 237)

This last requirement demands that account be taken of the nature of the criminal process as a whole and how its component parts produce the whole.

Thus this way of talking about the criminality of the state, while offering a differently nuanced theoretical emphasis than that which was to be found in Marxist criminology per se, certainly shares some of its concerns. Of course, this version of criminological theory has not been without its critics. Moreover, in the years that followed the publication of *The New Criminology*, there was a marked move away from the grand theorizing attempted in this work. Perhaps most importantly, developments in Marxist theory, especially in relation to the state, rather left this version of criminology stranded. Some of these developments were embraced by the work of those based at the Centre for Contemporary Cultural Studies at the University of Birmingham. One of their seminal texts, *Policing the Crisis* (Hall et al. 1978), constituted an effort to make sense of the construction of 'mugging' as a social problem, but especially as the archetypal 'black' crime. It was a controversial analysis, but in terms of criminological theory, and in its use of the concepts of hegemony, culture and ideology, its value to the development of critical criminological work should not be underestimated. In relation to radical criminology in particular, it encouraged an understanding of the law, and the process of its implementation, as a much more differentiated concept. It also encouraged criminologists to think more carefully about the role of the state in the criminalization process, though this concept, with the exception of that work produced by those who call themselves critical criminologists, has remained largely marginal in much mainstream criminological thought contemporarily.

Nevertheless radical criminology, as a result of the emphasis that these theoretical concerns placed on understanding the processes of criminalization, certainly served to challenge the individualistic correctional stance of earlier criminologies. It also laid the foundation for later theoretical developments, particularly from those wishing to pursue the differing ways in which the power associated with the political economy of the state asserts itself. This is the central focus of the last of the themes to be discussed here: critical criminology.

Critical criminology

The label 'critical' is employed by different writers intending to invoke differing frames of analysis. It is used here to identify those who have concerned themselves with the multiplicity of ways in which the state uses power. The work of Foucault (1977) has been very influential in encouraging a more careful and detailed analysis of the concept of power and how power is asserted. Foucault was interested in the ways in which knowledge and power are constituted in each other and especially in the ways in which this mutual interdependence effectively exercised social control. In some respects, then, critical criminology is concerned to unravel the ways in which taken-for-granted talk about social problems simultaneously serves to define those problems and control them. In this sense its focus stems not only from the work of Foucault but also from those of a more traditional Marxist persuasion for whom the state is more explicitly implicated in rendering some issues visible and others invisible. Critical criminology seeks to develop this concern in a more subtly nuanced fashion.

Put simply, critical criminology seeks to explore the ways in which the variables of class, race and gender are played out in the criminal justice system. This version of criminology argues that each of these variables articulates a different structural relationship with the interests of the state. This is more than just a concern with (the potential for) discriminatory practices. It reflects a concern with the ideas that underpin discriminatory practices and consequently contribute to their perpetuation: how they become institutionalized. As Scraton and Chadwick state:

> Once institutionalised, however, classism, sexism, heterosexism, and racism become systemic and structured. They become the taken for granted social histories and contemporary priorities which constitute state institutions, informing policies and underwriting practices, and which provide legitimacy to interpersonal discrimination. Through the process of institutionalisation, relations of dominance and subjugation achieve structural significance.
>
> (Scraton and Chadwick 1991: 168)

Critical criminology, therefore, not only reflects a concern with myriad mechanisms whereby the state reaffirms its power and the underlying structural relations that support that power, as our last quote implies, but also in its more recent affirmation, centres the relationship between structure and agency as found in the work of Giddens (1984):

> What this discussion has pursued is the central argument that critical criminology recognises the reciprocity inherent in the relationship between structure and agency but also that structural relations embody the primary determining contexts of production, reproduction and neocolonialism.
>
> (Scraton and Chadwick 1991: 166)

These contexts do not determine outcome. That is the product of the complex interplay between structure and agency in which human beings are not seen either as the sole determiners of what they can and cannot do or of how they are seen or not seen. This use of the term 'critical' is certainly redolent of the way in which it has been used in more recent victimological concerns, which are discussed in Chapter 7.

Critical criminology, then, is concerned to unpick the ways in which ideas that support the state and state practices serve to marginalize and consequently criminalize some groups and not others. In addition, it represents a set of theoretical ideas designed to situate the significance of history to these processes. Of particular importance is the way in which this theoretical perspective centres the questions of not only class but also race and gender. In this latter respect, it constitutes an important development from the radical criminology of Taylor et al. (1973).

It is evident that the notion of the criminality of the state shifts the criminological agenda away from seeing society as essentially consensual towards seeing it as essentially rooted in conflict. This fundamental shift not only locates the explanation of crime squarely in the social domain, but also centres the practices of the powerful, both the seen and the unseen, as legitimate concerns for the criminological agenda.

This shift in concern also seriously challenges for the first time the presumption contained within much criminological work: the fundamental belief in the objectivity of knowledge. One common thread between those seeking to address the criminality of the state is the implied critique of this view of knowledge and the knowledge production process. In general terms within this perspective, knowledge is understood much more meaningfully as ideology – ideology that more or less supports the state and its practices. This view of knowledge seriously challenges the hold of positivism on criminology. It is a hold that is nevertheless still present and still significant in the criminological debates that have followed.

There are clearly some quite significant variations in the way in which this focus on the criminality of the state has been expressed, as this discussion has demonstrated. These variations notwithstanding, the importance of these concerns has remained relevant, if differently developed, in more contemporary theorizing. Indeed, it is against the backcloth of these theoretical developments, perhaps rather pejoratively labelled by Young as 'left idealism', that the more contemporary theorizing of the left needs to be situated. However, before proceeding to discuss those more contemporary developments it will be of value to reflect on the competing criminological perspectives addressed here.

Conclusion

Obviously it is very difficult in one chapter to do justice to the range of ideas that have been touched on here. What is significant for this book, however, is to consider the extent to which the ideas that have been discussed here still have some relevance for the criminological agenda. A recurring theme in this respect is the whole question of the relative importance to be attached to social factors and individual factors in constructing a theory or an explanation of crime. This tension remains. As the following chapters unfold the continuing importance of this tension will become increasingly apparent.

In addition, it is useful to reflect on what has remained unspoken in these competing perspectives. Indeed, until the later developments within critical criminology, questions of race and gender are barely articulated in the criminological world. Interest in these issues is certainly much more to the fore in current criminological concerns than these perspectives would suggest. The whole question of gendering criminology is discussed in Chapter 5.

However, what clearly remains present within these and subsequent criminological theories is the attachment to the modernist project in which both the production of crime as a problem and the production of the institutions designed to manage crime are intimately connected to the processes of modernization along with the kind of criminological knowledge that is produced to make sense of these issues. The desire to work towards the effective implementation of change, whether that be micro policy changes or macro societal change, is deeply embedded in the criminological agenda. The extent to which that continues both to manifest itself and to limit the criminological worldview will be of interest again in the chapters that follow.

Further reading

A range of general introductions to criminological theory are now available and will offer a more detailed appreciation of the competing perspectives than can be discussed here. See, for example, Gibbons (1994) or Williams and McShane (1994). A particularly interesting approach is offered by Lilly et al. (1995), which locates the different theories it discusses in the different social and political contexts in which they emerged. More detailed coverage of the theories discussed here is offered by Hopkins Burke (2005). Finally, there is no doubt that reading Taylor et al. (1973) and Walton and Young (1998) is a must for anyone seriously wanting to appreciate the unfolding nature of criminological theory. For a fuller appreciation of the relationship between crime and modernity see Lea (2002).

chapter three

Understanding 'right realism'

Socio-biological explanations: the work of Wilson and Herrnstein
Rational choice theory
The routine activity approach
Administrative criminology
Right realism: a critique
Ways of thinking about the family and crime
Conclusion
Further reading

The commitment to the welfare ethic of the 1950s in the UK reflected an underlying belief that social problems could be solved socially – that is, through the provision of adequate social and economic conditions. If such conditions were provided then social problems, including the problem of crime, would disappear. The continuing rising crime rate, combined with worldwide recession, however, called a halt to this way of addressing social problems and paved the way for a different manner of thinking and talking about crime and the crime problem. This different manner of thinking was characterized primarily by the re-emergence of a focus on the causes of crime as lying within individual processes rather than social ones. Centring the individual, and the notion of individual responsibility, in this way became embedded in a whole range of political and policy imperatives, including crime, associated in Britain with the Conservative Party of the 1980s: a focus that, as we shall see, has been perpetuated by the Labour Party of the late 1990s onwards.

The political shift to the right in the UK paralleled similar developments in the USA. It is arguably there that a range of criminological ideas which might be loosely labelled 'right realism' first emerged. While such ideas are largely associated with American writers, they resonated politically with some aspects of the law and order debate which ensued in the UK. The concern of this chapter, therefore, will be to try to untangle the political and intellectual connections that can be made between criminological right realism and changes in direction in criminal justice policy.

So what kind of theoretical work might be considered to constitute right realism? Here we shall discuss four different theoretical and/or policy strands under this heading: socio-biological explanations, rational choice theory, the routine activity approach and that which has been called administrative criminology.

Socio-biological explanations: the work of Wilson and Herrnstein

James Q. Wilson is an enormously influential figure in American criminology. While his book *Thinking About Crime* (1975) influenced political and policy thinking considerably, his work with Richard Herrnstein *Crime and Human Nature* (1985) offers a more definitive theoretical account of what, in their view, constitute the underlying causes of crime. This account has three elements to it: constitutional factors, the presence and/or absence of reinforcers and the nature of conscience. Each of these will be discussed in turn.

According to Wilson and Herrnstein:

> Crime is an activity disproportionately carried out by young men living in large cities. There are old criminals, and female ones, and rural and small town ones, but to a much greater degree than would be expected by chance, criminals are young urban males.
>
> (Wilson and Herrnstein 1985: 26)

This statement can be read in a number of different ways. In one sense, it can be argued that it articulates a very clear understanding of what constitutes the central problem for all those in the criminal justice industry: the highly problematic nature of the behaviour of young (urban) males. As such it could be said that it resonates very well with the work of those concerned to 'gender' criminology (see Chapter 5).

However, while those concerned to gender criminology problematize the issue of young men in relation to the expression of their masculinity as a socially constructed process, Wilson and Herrnstein proceed to explain the behaviour of young men by reference to their being just that: young men. In other words, they prefer to foreground in their explanation of the differences between the criminal behaviour of the sexes what they call constitutional factors. Such factors are not necessarily genetic but certainly have some biological origin. So, as Wilson and Herrnstein state:

> It is likely that the effect of maleness and youthfulness on the tendency to commit crime has both constitutional and social origins: that is, it has something to do with the biological status of being a young male

and with how that young man has been treated by family, friends and society.

(Wilson and Herrnstein 1985: 69)

So, as we shall see, their explanation is not solely rooted in biology, but reflects a concern to construct an explanation of criminal behaviour in which factors such as sex, age, intelligence, body type and personality are inserted as potential biological givens (although not necessarily determiners of action) of human beings projected into a social world – a social world in which the individual learns what kind of behaviour is rewarded under what circumstances. This is the second element of their theory.

Drawing implicitly on the work of psychologist B.F. Skinner, Wilson and Herrnstein place themselves squarely within psychological behaviourism. In simple terms, according to this theory, individuals learn to respond to situations in accordance with how their behaviour has been rewarded and punished on previous occasions. According to the Skinnerian approach, the environment can operate (hence the term 'operant conditioning') to produce the kind of behavioural response most wanted from an individual. In order to understand the propensity to commit crime, therefore, it is important to understand the ways in which the environment might operate on individuals, whose constitutional make-up might be different, to produce this response. Within this general learning framework, then, Wilson and Herrnstein locate the influence of the family, the school and the wider community.

This general learning environment is always very carefully explored by these authors, keeping in mind the important influence that individual differences can have on the learning process. So while certain family backgrounds might potentially spell trouble in relation to crime that is not always a determined outcome. The constitutional factors just mentioned might serve to make a difference, as might the power of the third element to their theory: the conscience.

In this last respect Wilson and Herrnstein (1985: 125) support the statement made by Eysenck that 'conscience is a conditioned reflex'. In this sense they are asserting that some people during childhood have so effectively internalized law-abiding behaviour that they would never be tempted to behave otherwise. For others, breaking the law might be dependent on the particular circumstances of a particular situation, suggesting less effective internalization of such rules. For yet others, the failure to appreciate the likely consequences of their actions might lead them into criminal behaviour under any circumstances. In other words, the effectiveness of something that is called 'the conscience' may co-vary with the individual's constitution and learning environment.

These three elements then – constitutional factors, the presence and/or absence of positive and negative behavioural reinforcers, and the strength of the conscience – provide the framework in which Wilson and Herrnstein offer an explanation of crime. For them the interplay between these factors can explain why crime rates may increase both in times of prosperity and of recession since the equation between the social and the individual is a complex one:

> Long term trends in crime rates can be accounted for primarily by three factors. First, shifts in the age structure of the population will increase or decrease the proportion of persons – young males – in the population who are likely to be temperamentally aggressive and to have short time horizons. Second, changes in the benefits of crime . . . and in the cost of crime . . . will change the rate at which crimes occur, especially property crimes. . . . Third, broad social and cultural changes in the level and intensity of society's investment (via families, schools, churches, and the mass media) in inculcating an internalized commitment to self control will affect the extent to which individuals at risk are willing to postpone gratification, accept as equitable the outcomes of others, and conform to rules.
>
> (Wilson and Herrnstein 1985: 437)

Given the complex interplay of these factors, and given the variables that these authors wish to highlight as constituting the key underpinning causes of crime, it might be possible to conclude that such a framework merely adds, in a fundamental way, to the view that nothing can be done about crime. This is not the conclusion reached by Wilson and Herrnstein. Their view is that while not enough may be known about what works under what conditions, marginal gains can be made by targeting what is known about crime. This might take the form of, for example, tougher sentences for repeat offenders, and/or working in a concentrated way in high-crime areas still deemed to be rescuable, or any combination of policies like these, so long as such policies are focused and 'doable'. In this respect, as Young (1994) argues, their concern is primarily with maintaining social order rather than necessarily delivering justice and their focus is on what can be done rather than on trying to achieve Utopia. However, their theory also marks a revitalization of ideas that some criminologists would regard as unfortunate, especially the sympathetic way in which constitutional (read biological) factors are dealt with.

However, it should be remembered that a concern with the potential contribution of biological factors to criminal behaviour never really disappeared from the criminological agenda. That a concern with such factors re-emerged during the 1980s is, arguably, a product of the cultural and economic processes of that time: the heightening of possessive individualism. This has been more colloquially expressed as the emergence of the 'me generation', in which the individual, and the pursuit of individual success, became the centre of all kinds of activity, including crime. It is no surprise, then, that within such wider cultural processes a view focusing on the individual and individual potentialities for criminal behaviour should also become popular. Those same circumstances also proved to be the context in which a view of the individual criminal as an economic decision maker became increasingly attractive. Such a view underpins the second variety of right realism to be discussed here: rational choice theory.

Rational choice theory

Gibbons (1994) argues that rational choice theory constitutes neither a new nor a general explanation of crime since elements of attributing the ability to make choices and decisions to criminals and criminal behaviour are present in a range of criminological perspectives. However, in contrast to earlier concerns with the rationality or otherwise of the offender, the concerns of rational choice theory are framed to address the central question of crime prevention. It is in this respect especially that Young (1994) argues that rational choice theory (in its embodiment within administrative criminology to be discussed later) refuses to address the causes of crime but is more concerned with its management. Indeed, in support of this view, Clarke, one of the main proponents of this version of criminology, accuses earlier criminological perspectives as suffering from 'predispositional bias':

> Criminological theories have been little concerned with the situational determinants of crime. Instead, the main object of these theories (whether biological, psychological, or sociological in orientation) has been to show how some people are born with, or come to acquire a 'disposition' to behave in a consistently criminal manner.
>
> (Clarke 1980: 137)

This bias, he goes on to argue, has had unfortunate consequences for the issue of crime prevention:

> These difficulties are primarily practical, but they also reflect the uncertainties and inconsistencies of treating distant psychological events and social processes as the 'causes' of crime. Given that each event is in turn caused by others, at what point in the infinitely regressive chain should one stop in the search for effective points of intervention?
>
> (Clarke 1980: 138)

For Clarke (and later Cornish and Clarke 1986), effective intervention can be established by understanding the criminal as an economic decision maker.

The idea of treating human beings as driven by the motive of profit maximization is one that has a longstanding tradition within the discipline of economics. This idea presumes that individuals make rational decisions on the basis of the costs and benefits that alternative courses of action have for them:

> Offenders seek to benefit themselves by their criminal behaviour; . . .

> that this involves the making of decisions and choices, however rudimentary on occasion these processes might be; and . . . these processes exhibit a measure of rationality, albeit constrained by the limits of time and the availability of information.
>
> (Cornish and Clarke 1986: 1)

This rational process of decision making is used to account for not only the decision to commit crime but also the time and the place in which such crime is committed. However, some effort is made to recognize that such decision making may be limited by the availability of information or inaccurate information. So, as can be seen, the rational choice model of criminology, while influenced by the assumed rationality of the economic human being, contains within it an appreciation that such rationality is limited.

The value of this perspective, as was suggested earlier, has been argued for within the context of its crime prevention potential, usually referred to as situational crime prevention. As Gibbons states:

> If many offenders, and predatory offenders in particular, weigh at least some of the potential risks against the gains they anticipate from lawbreaking, criminal acts may often be deterred by making them riskier or harder to carry out.
>
> (Gibbons 1994: 125)

By implication, then, the harder the target of criminal behaviour, the more likely the criminal is to choose another target. This, of course, illuminates the central problem of the rational choice model formulated in this way: displacement. What happens to the motive for profit maximization once the decision to commit crime has been made? Is it transformed into something else?

Of course, since the rational choice model is not centrally concerned to address the underlying causes of crime, this question is of little consequence. It is a question, however, which is not easily sidestepped given the practical implications of this way of thinking about crime. Every crime prevention policy carries with it some costs – whether quantitative (resource led) or qualitative (social), or a combination of the two – and these need to be weighed against the potential gains of the kinds of situational measure Clarke and Cornish propose.

In any event, this way of thinking about crime has been very influential in reorienting crime prevention policy towards victimization prevention policy (Karmen 1990). In addition, it has served to fuel political debate about the crime problem by focusing attention on preventing the behaviour of the individual criminal at a time when alternative policy initiatives might be considerably more expensive.

Of course, crime does not only occur because there is an offender with a motive to commit it. What rational choice theory also presumes is that there must be the opportunity for it to be committed. Routine activity approach takes the appreciation of this relationship between the offender and the opportunity to commit crime a stage further.

The routine activity approach

This version of right realism takes our thinking about crime beyond the individual per se and endeavours to locate individual behaviour in a wider social context. It has its origins in the work of Cohen and Felson (1979) and argues that crime is the product of three factors coming together in particular times and places: a motivated offender, a potential victim and the absence of a capable guardian. These three factors can be identified in people's daily, routine behaviours and their patterning may alter the times and places in which crime occurs, but their conjunction provides the framework within which crime takes place.

Indeed, the work of Felson (2002) has been particularly important in encouraging the acceptance of the normality of crime. Offenders are ordinary people who commit ordinary crimes who respond to the 'supply' of criminogenic situations in which they find themselves. So the different consumer goods available contemporarily, for example, offer different opportunities for criminal behaviour. Criminals are much like the rest of us, from this point of view, making rational decisions about the routine opportunities being presented to them. They are not abnormal, neither do they possess any special sense of motivation. The response to crime, in policy terms, then, is simply to make the opportunities for lawbreaking behaviour more difficult. We shall explore the contemporary implications of this version of criminology in more detail at the end of this chapter.

It must be remembered that routine activity theory does not purport to explain the motivation for crime, neither does it offer an explanation of the broader social framework that may facilitate some patterns between the three variables with which it is concerned – the motivated offender, the potential victim, and the absence of a capable guardian – rather than others. Moreover, it does little to explain why some guardians might prove to be more capable than others. Neither does it endeavour to say much about why it is that some individual behaviours render them more susceptible to victimization than others. However, as a theory it does recognize that there is a systematic patterning to crime, redolent of the social ecology approach discussed in Chapter 2. (Interestingly enough Felson (2006) has explored these connections with ecology and/or nature in a more detailed and a rather analogous fashion).

In this sense, it is an approach that has generated empirical findings that have been used to support a largely conservative orientation to criminal justice policy. Indeed, its limited conceptualization of the social does allow for the possibility of including variables other than just the individual offender into the criminological equation. This has been especially the case with respect to understanding the nature and extent of criminal victimization. It is primarily in this latter respect that the influence of the routine activity approach can be found within 'administrative criminology'. This influence has been felt most through the concept of lifestyle.

The connections between 'administrative' criminology and the routine activity approach are to be found in the influence of the work of Hindelang et al. (1978). The parallels between these ideas and those of Cohen and Felson have been discussed by Garofalo (1986). Focusing more on the routine activity elements to the question of lifestyle, they state that, for personal victimization to occur:

> First, the prime actors – the offender and the victim – must have occasion to intersect in time and space. Second, some source of dispute or claim must arise between the actors in which the victim is perceived by the offender as an appropriate object of victimization. Third, the offender must be willing and able to threaten or use force (or stealth) in order to achieve the desired end. Fourth, the circumstances must be such that the offender views it as advantageous to use or threaten force (or stealth) to achieve the desired end. The probability of these conditions being met is related to the life circumstances of members of society.
>
> (Hindelang et al. 1978: 250)

These authors go on to offer eight propositions designed to cast light on why some individuals are much more likely to be subject to personal victimization than others as a result of variations in exposure to different levels of risk reflected in their lifestyle. These propositions draw attention to the importance of variables such as age, sex and race, but also address the different routine patterns of behaviour that potentially expose people of different ages, races and sex to different levels of victimization. These patterns would include the amount of time spent in public places, how often people use public transport and at what time of day people find themselves in such circumstances. Of course, in all of these circumstances there may be an appropriate guardian absent or present. This will feed into overall levels of victimization, as Cohen and Felson's schema suggests.

A detailed critique of the work of Hindelang et al. (1978) can be found in Walklate (1989). The value of this way of thinking about crime in this context is the particular relevance it has in understanding the last of the variations in right realism to be discussed here: the administrative criminology of the UK Home Office.

Administrative criminology

In some respects it is doubtful whether or not such a criminology, as a coherent set of propositions, exists and/or whether indeed it counts as a variety of right realism in the same sense as the work of Wilson and Herrnstein. However, since this label for the work emanating from the Home Office was first coined, it has gained some considerable currency and for the purposes of clarity it has been adopted here. First of all, it will be useful to summarize what Young (1994) has characterized as administrative criminology since it is his label that has had such a powerful impact.

Young (1986) squarely locates the emergence of administrative criminology as following from the failure of what he calls 'social democratic positivism'. That position, both academically and politically, had endeavoured to centre the idea that crime was caused by social conditions and that what was necessary to combat crime was to change those conditions. Yet, despite efforts to change those social conditions, the crime rate still rose. And while some might have argued that such a rise in crime rate was no more (and no less) than an artefact of changing policing practices, administrative criminology at least took seriously the problematic nature of the rising crime rate. This is the clear point of convergence between this work and the other versions of right realism discussed here.

However, administrative criminology, as suggested earlier, sidesteps the question of what the underpinning cause of that rising crime rate might be. In Young's words, it fails to address the aetiological crisis within criminology – another similarity with other versions of right realism discussed here (perhaps, in fairness, with the exception of Wilson and Herrnstein). As a result of sidestepping this issue, the work emanating from the Home Office during the 1980s was characterized as 'administrative' insofar as its central concern became administering, that is, managing the crime problem, rather than working to explore its underlying causes.

Young (1994) identifies the main theoretical input of this work as being rational choice theory. Indeed, Clarke, a proponent of rational choice theory discussed earlier, was a central figure in the Home Office during the early 1980s. However, if the underlying presumptions of the British Crime Survey are explored a little more carefully it is also possible to see that routine activity theory, particularly through the concept of lifestyle, had its part to play in the formulation and the subsequent dissemination of these survey findings.

The British Crime Survey has been a vital source of political and policy information since the first survey was carried out in 1982. Conducted at regular intervals since then, the British Crime Survey has provided a very valuable database for both estimating the 'dark' figure of crime and informing the policymaking process. Its questions, especially in relation to the patterning of criminal victimization, very much reflect the routine activity lifestyle concerns of Hindelang and others. In this respect it has been possible to construct images of who is most likely to be criminally victimized which challenge conventional media images: the young male who uses public transport and goes out drinking two or three times a week as opposed to the elderly female, for example. However, the findings of the

British Crime Survey have not only been used to challenge media images of victimization. They have also been used more or less explicitly for political purposes. It is perhaps in this latter respect that the work emanating from the Home Office is best described as a version of right realism.

Mayhew and Hough describe the initial thinking behind the formulation of the first British Crime Survey in the following way:

> It was thought within the Home Office that distorted and exaggerated ideas of crime levels, trends and risks were widespread among the public, information on crime risks would demonstrate the comparatively low risks of serious crime, and puncture inaccurate stereotypes of crime victims. In other words, the survey was envisaged in part at least as a way of achieving what might be called the 'normalisation' of crime – to help create a less alarmist and more balanced climate of opinion about law and order.
>
> (Mayhew and Hough 1988: 157)

That more balanced climate of opinion was intended to address not only what were perceived to be the exaggerated fears of the public about crime, but also the question of how to resource law and order issues. Thus that same database could be used, and has been used, to bolster the campaign for the development and refinement of crime prevention initiatives (in the fashion of situational crime prevention) rather than necessarily finding funds for more police officers. This strategy was clearly adopted in the mid-1980s with a commitment and vigour not previously experienced by the police as a public institution.

In this sense, then, this kind of criminological work clearly lent support to a government committed to cuts in public expenditure via the mechanisms of demanding 'value for money' and 'efficiency' in a general political and economic climate working to recast the citizen as a consumer of public services – a consumer of public services in a social context in which there was 'no such thing as society'. This last comment and its implied denial of the importance of underlying social structures, famously made by the then Prime Minister Margaret Thatcher, leads us to a more careful consideration of what is both 'right' and 'real' about right realism.

Right realism: a critique

As Lilly et al. (1995) argue, there is no necessary connection between the theories discussed here and the adoption of conservative policy implications. However, the focus on the individual that is embedded in all these theories lends itself most readily to such an interpretation in particular social contexts. So it is easy to see how, at times of economic stringency, there might be an easy match to be made between holding the individual, or individual deficiencies, responsible for social problems and the drive to cut public expenditure. This view, of course, contains within it an inconsistency (as we shall see later), but focusing on that which goes on within the individual presumes that society, with all its inequities, is given and non-problematic (there is no such thing as society!). Thus this kind of criminology can avoid considering the potential interrelationship between individual 'deficiencies' and social 'deficiencies'.

In commenting on Wilson and Herrnstein's work, for example, Lilly et al. (1995) have this to say:

> Wilson and Herrnstein's work implied that certain biological dispositions, found frequently in the poor, may be responsible for excessive criminal behaviour. . . . The historical record teaches that attempts to root crime in human nature exempt the social fabric from blame and lend credence to the idea that offenders are largely beyond reform and in need of punitive control.
>
> (Lilly et al. 1995: 215)

These ideological implications result regardless of how carefully the authors themselves may frame their argument.

The resurgence of the idea that offenders are largely wicked or beyond control, of course, results in policy inconsistencies, if not contradictions. On the one hand, the economic and political conditions that render such ideas popular demand a withdrawal of the state. On the other hand, the policy initiatives that flow from taking these ideas imply deterrence from criminality in the form of incapacitation of various kinds, which by implication also requires the greater involvement of the state as an overseer and/or deliverer of incapacitation. The extent to which successive home secretaries have campaigned for tougher prison sentences as an answer to the crime problem stands as testimony to this, the successive election of Labour governments in the UK notwithstanding. Yet this is also the most expensive form of state intervention possible within the criminal justice arena, which at the same time has little empirical support as being an effective measure against the crime problem. A conservative would argue, however, that it is more than effective against particular criminals since it keeps them out of circulation; as Wilson (1975: 235) says: 'Wicked people exist. Nothing avails except to set them apart from innocent people.' So this perhaps demonstrates what is 'right' about right realism; but what is 'real' about it?

The question of what is 'real' about right realism raises a similar dilemma to that with left realism. Put relatively simply at this juncture, the use of the term 'realism' in this context is more political than it is philosophical. In this sense, one feature that binds these different theoretical perspectives together is that they all take the rising crime rate as a real problem to be tackled. In other words, the crime rate is not to be seen simply as a product of either changes in reporting behaviour, changes in the recording practices of criminal justice officials or a product of changes in implementation of the law. It is to be seen as a real indicator of a real social problem. It is in this sense that right realism and left realism share a common starting point.

This usage of the term 'realism' is, however, political, in the sense that it attempts to claim the territory of crime and criminal justice policy as a real issue to be addressed by the political domain. A philosophical use of the term 'realism' would be much more concerned to identify the underlying causes (or as Bhaskar (1978) would say, the generative mechanisms) which serve to produce the surface manifestation of, in this case, an increasing crime rate. This use of the term 'realism' arguably locates any analysis of a social problem with the realm of the social rather than the individual. As we have seen, the theories discussed here resist such an interpretation.

Hopkins Burke (2005: 37–8) adds a stronger political feel to the criticisms that can be made of right realism. His list of problems includes the inevitable focus on street crime to the exclusion of what is known about other forms of criminal behaviour and the resultant targeting of marginalized areas and disadvantaged groups. He concludes by stating that:

> 'Finally, the right realist rediscovery and adaptation of the rational actor model, with its central proposition that criminal behaviour is simply a rational choice made by those brought up in a world bereft of correct moral values, has led to the targeting and demonisation of whole groups of people – such as New Age travellers, drug users and groups of "marauding" males – by, it is argued an intrusive and punitive "law and order" state response with all the aforementioned categories of humanity deemed worthy of severe and vindictive punishment'.
>
> (ibid.: 38)

This is nowhere more the case than in targeting the family as the source of all our crime-related ills and at this juncture it will be of value to reflect on how such targeting has manifested itself in UK government policy over the last 25 years.

Ways of thinking about the family and crime

Arguably, any debate concerning the family is always tinged with political interest, since such debate is also always embedded in some notion of what counts as 'normal' family life. As Stone's (1995) historical analysis of divorce serves to remind us, families in earlier centuries were often not the 'ideal types' politicians would wish us to believe they were, being frequently 'broken' by death in childbirth, absent fathers, much reduced life expectancy and so on. Nevertheless, during the 1990s in particular, the public political debate on both the nature of crime and lawbreaking behaviour centred on the role of the family. We shall therefore consider the criminological evidence on the role of the family as a contributory factor in lawbreaking behaviour, the differing political interpretations that have been placed on that evidence and the policy implications that flow from those interpretations. In so doing, we shall pay particular attention to the ideological assumptions underpinning the images of family life that have become embedded in this debate. But first, why is the family important?

Why is understanding the family important?

Just as family structures have undergone considerable change, so the importance given to the role of the family in criminological research has varied. As was suggested earlier, influenced by sociology, that criminological work which has considered the role of the family in contributing to lawbreaking behaviour can be summarized under four main headings: the influence of the 'broken' family; family tension; the quality of parenting; and the 'abusive' family. Much of the work concerned with each of these factors has focused primarily on their relevance for understanding juvenile delinquency and the way in which that concern has manifested itself has varied.

For example, from the end of the Second World War until the 1960s, a popular thesis connecting family life with juvenile delinquency was to be found in the work of Bowlby (1965). Sponsored by the World Health Organization, Bowlby's work was initially concerned to address the effects on children of evacuation during the war years. His findings, however, while highlighting a number of different circumstances in which parental loss and/or separation resulted in behavioural or psychological problems for the children concerned, have been most remembered for the introduction of the notion of 'maternal deprivation'.

One of the factors identified by Bowlby as contributing to behavioural problems (including delinquency) in children was the deprivation of the mother or mother figure in the early years of life, especially before the age of 5. In political and social policy terms, this was interpreted as meaning that in order to rear problem-free children it was necessary for the mother to stay at home. For many families, of course, economic reality dictated that the woman of the house worked (at least on a part-time basis) as often as the man did. However, this notion of maternal deprivation served to fuel ideological beliefs about the role of women, beliefs that Wilson (1983) argued contributed to the 'Observer Wife' syndrome and helped sow the seeds of support for the feminist movement of the 1960s. It was, of course, out of that movement that a very different image of the family life of women and children was brought to the surface.

Recasting the family in terms of power relations between men and women led much feminist work to consider the ways in which those power relationships manifest themselves. It is from this work that one notion of the abusive family can be constructed. Understanding the private domain as one in which much criminal activity can occur in the form of rape and violence certainly both broadened and deepened the criminological agenda, although it was not (and is not) an image of family life which is much in evidence in political rhetoric on the family in general more recent commitments to centre issues such as 'domestic' violence notwithstanding.

Despite the evidence emanating from the feminist movement that the intact family might constitute just as much of a breeding ground for criminal behaviour as the maternally deprived family, it is not difficult to see why concern with the notion of the 'broken family' would lend itself more readily to political use. Whether or not this constitutes a valid interpretation of Bowlby's work in particular, or of work that followed in this vein in general, is, however, a moot point. As Currie states:

> The belief that the 'brokenness' of the home itself is of crucial importance in creating delinquency derives mainly from a tradition of studies of the supposed pernicious effects of 'father absence' or of 'maternal deprivation' on the growing child, especially at very early ages. But it has not held up well under the lens of careful research. . . . This isn't to say that family disruption is a benign or neutral event in the lives of children; it usually isn't, and many studies show that it can be damaging, at least in the short run – and for some children in the long run as well. But as a precursor of delinquency and other developmental problems, it is overshadowed by the effects of family conflict.
>
> (Currie 1985: 195)

The general empirical findings appear to support Currie's (1985) interpretation of the data. In other words, it is the presence or absence of family discord that has been found consistently to be associated with delinquency rather than the absence or presence of a mother or father. Other factors have also been found to be relevant, such as the changing material conditions of the child and the quality of the parenting. What is interesting, at a political level, is that, despite the empirical evidence, the intact nuclear family was accorded unprecedented importance during the 1980s and 1990s, especially in the call for a return to 'family values' and more recently exemplified in the parenting orders of the Crime and Disorder Act 1998. This political focus on the family has been particularly centred on those at the lower end of the social hierarchy and perhaps could be most readily identified in debates as to the importance of the 'absent father'.

One particular version of the 'absent father' debate gained especial political prominence in the late 1980s and early 1990s. That version focused on the notion of 'families without fathers' and the possible connections that could be made between rising rates of illegitimacy and rising crime rates. Of course, centring the importance of the nuclear family in this way neglected not only to address the version of family life proffered by the feminist movement, but also to consider the way in which the presence of a father, particularly one with a criminal record, might produce equally problematic effects for the child. However, the concern to consider the relationship between illegitimacy and rising crime arose from a wider debate that focused on the question of whether or not there was an 'underclass' in Britain.

The underclass and crime

The underclass debate and its connection to the production of dysfunctional families and crime provides link with those distinctions that have always been made historically between the deserving and undeserving poor – that is, between those who are genuinely poor and those who bring poverty on themselves. Such distinctions have always carried with them a certain amount of value judgment and social stigma as to what counted as proper (deserving) conduct. Historically, of course, there have always been lawbreaking means through which people dealt with their poverty. Indeed, in Marx's discussion of the Lumpenproletariat, he used somewhat pejorative terms to describe the 'social scum' of the criminal underclass. More recent debate on this issue has been little different in both the kinds of analytical distinction theorists have endeavoured to make in identifying the underclass and the value judgments that have accrued to those so stigmatized. An attempt will be made here to separate these issues and to consider the relevance of this debate in talking about the family and crime. The ideas of Murray (1990) have been particularly influential in this respect.

Murray defines the underclass not only by economic position but also by behaviour: 'When I've used the term underclass I am indeed focusing on a certain type of poor person defined not by his condition e.g. long term unemployed, but by his deplorable behaviour in response to that condition' (Murray 1990: 68).

For Murray (1990) there are three predictors of membership of the underclass: illegitimacy, crime and labour market behaviour. Murray takes illegitimacy to mean two things: first, when a child grows up without two parents from the moment it is born; second, when it is associated with a particular set of attitudes to marriage – that marriage is not important and has no value. Murray's argument is that this 'pure form' of illegitimacy is rising, especially in the lower social classes and in those communities where fathers are absent the children run wild.

Murray's second predictor of membership of the underclass is crime. Again Murray's argument is that crime is rising rapidly (he cites evidence to show that England has higher burglary and car crime rates than the United States) and that the rise in violent crime in particular (although lower in England than in the United States) reflects one measure of the development of the underclass. In his view, habitual criminals are by definition members of the underclass. In those areas inhabited by habitual criminals what results is, alongside the general rising crime rate, fragmented communities and the disruption of the norms of socialization. The final definitive indicator of the underclass is reflected in labour market behaviour. This is not simply a measure of unemployment, although that status is obviously a key factor, but it is defined in relation to the number of healthy young males on low incomes who refuse to take jobs.

So for Murray the presence of an underclass is defined; by the rate of 'pure' illegitimacy, the level of crime, and the attitude of young males to work. He states that:

> When large numbers of young men don't work, the communities around them break down, just as they break down when large numbers of young unmarried women have babies. . . . Men who do not support families find other ways to prove that they are men, which tend to take various destructive forms.
>
> (Murray 1990: 22)

The UK version of this thesis can be located in the work of Dennis and Erdos (1992). They focused their attention on what they call the 'dismembered family' within which it is possible to understand and explain the rising crime rate since the 1950s. They accept the view that crime is an activity overwhelmingly engaged in by young men, but their argument is that this is largely the result of the way in which childrearing practices have moved outside of 'normal' family structures. This is evidenced in a number of ways.

The first of these is the increase in the number of divorces. They argue that there is now much more freedom for a father to leave his spouse or children than there was in the 1950s. More liberal divorce laws now mean that, according to their figures, England and Wales have the highest rate of divorce in Europe. At the same time there has been a significant increase in the freedom to cohabit. Cohabitation, they argue, is much more likely to lead to lone parenthood. These factors, they argue, separate the act of impregnation from pregnancy. In other words, they are changes that permit young men to escape the consequences of their acts. In particular, a significant number of young males are growing up in families without fathers, so that they are not experiencing any training in fatherhood and have no conception of the obligations fatherhood entails. The outcome of these effects is increasing crime, echoing Murray's assertion that children in female-headed single parent households run wild.

This line of argument fitted in particularly well with the debate occurring in the political arena at that time. It struck a chord with a government already committed to a reassertion of family values. Fuelled by the civil disturbances of 1991 that brought to the fore the behaviour of young white, men living on council estates as a key social problem, the targeting of families without fathers in social policy terms proceeded relatively unabated. This concern was given added impetus with the murder of James Bulger in Merseyside in 1992. So this public focus on the disintegration of the nuclear family lent weight to the arguments of a government that had consistently denied that unemployment was connected with rising crime. For here was a view, rooted in a particular reading of the empirical evidence, which gave legitimacy to the already well-asserted political view that it was not unemployment or poor social conditions that resulted in a rising crime rate, but the changing nature of family structure and family life. Mooney (2003) expresses these processes in this way:

> So, the neo-liberal explanation was that the welfare state had created a dependency culture of single mothers and feckless fathers, which had, in turn, created a maladjusted population. Thus, the social democratic diagnosis is reversed – the welfare state causes rather than prevents delinquency. And free will, and thus responsibility, enter the equation: the feckless underclass chooses not to work and consequently generates a culture that schools its children in delinquency.
>
> Mooney (2003: 105)

In this way, as she goes on to comment, the underclass 'was demonized and blamed for the troubles of society' (ibid.). This welfare turnaround marked the beginning of a continuing concern with not only the family as the cause of criminality but also the question of the offending behaviour of young people in general (see Chapter 4) and young males in particular (see later).

At the start of this turn some attention was paid to the kinds of family circumstances that might contribute to persistent offending behaviour. Utting (1993) listed these factors as being: poor parental supervision, harsh or erratic discipline, parental discord, a parent with a criminal record, low income, family size, being a low achiever at school and behaving aggressively at school. As a result Utting concluded that there is no evidence that family structure per se contributes to persistent offending behaviour, but that perhaps more attention should be paid to families intact and the style of fathering that children are subjected to rather than freed from. This echoed Currie's (1985) assessment of the evidence on this issue. Of course, this latter point returns us to the importance of locating an understanding of young men's criminal behaviour within the context of young men's behaviour in general rather than just within a particular family structure (see Chapter 5). This theme raised questions about men and their relationship with and expression of their masculinity. From this point of view, the key criminological question lies in understanding not the presence or absence of fathers, but the presence or absence of different ways of being a man and how young men explore that for themselves in what might be criminal behaviour but might also be quite pleasurable risk-taking behaviour (Jefferson 1993). As Chapter 5 argues, it is relatively new for criminological work to explore criminal behaviour and its underlying motivation in this kind of gendered way.

There is, of course, an alternative viewpoint on this. As suggested earlier, many feminists might say that the number of petitions for divorce being made by women (and evidenced by Dennis and Erdos) potentially reflects a range of positive outcomes to the process of challenging traditional family structures, especially for women. This is nowhere more the case than for those women and children leaving traditional family structures in which violence or rape has been a routine feature. From this point of view the modern nuclear family and its inherently patriarchal structure has never served the interests of women as human beings.

In other words, underpinning some aspects of the debate we have addressed here lies an acceptance that it is within the nuclear family that produces individual and family harmony and consequently social order. This myth is a very powerful one in popular and political consciousness. The fact that this does not always resonate with people's everyday experiences does not render the myth any the less powerful. It is important, however, to recognize that while the provision of stability in relation to childcare is one factor on which all commentators might agree can produce the optimum circumstances in which a child may avoid getting into trouble, such stability is not necessarily guaranteed by only one kind of family structure.

However, in the policy arena the focus on the family and young offenders has persisted, as evidenced by the Home Office White Paper, *Respect and Responsibility – Taking a Stance Against Anti-Social Behaviour* (2003) in which the lack of respect found in dysfunctional families is highlighted as a key threat to safe communities. As Mooney (2003) observes:

> So, there we have it: governments . . . have attempted to disconnect the wider social and economic situation from the facts of crime, locating the weak family as the prime cause of criminality. Yet the supposed weakness of the family, although a constant theme, is recast at each political change, seen as isolated patches of dysfunction in social democracy, welfare dependent and excluded under neo-liberalism and welfare dependent yet redeemable through work and self-discipline under New Labour. Nowhere are the deep inequalities that stretch through our society mentioned – nowhere is class or patriarchy – the wider structural problems – allowed to enter the equation.
>
> (Mooney 2003: 107)

So this political move to the right over the last 25 years has resulted in the powerful influence of these kinds of criminological ideas and along with this influence there has been less attention paid to the role of the state in these processes. The importance of taking the long view of this move to the right has been eloquently explored by Garland (2001) as the 'culture of control'. The view draws our attention to the remarkable level of cultural acceptance of not only the normality of crime but also the language of control: social control, self-control, situational control (Garland 1999) alongside who is responsible for what and when that has notably resulted in a continued targeting of the dangerous classes (the underclass). This theme is revisited in Chapter 6.

Conclusion

While there are varieties within what might be called 'right realism', the common ground between them lies in their commitment to accepting that crime is a real problem and in their focus on understanding the individual and the role of individual differences as the key to tackling that crime problem. These common concerns render their policy focus as primarily concerned with the maintenance of social order. The politically conservative implications of this work are clear. The recognition of this intertwining of the political and academic highlights a further source of criticism for this kind of criminology.

As was observed in Chapter 1, the emergence of criminology as a discipline was intimately connected with the policymaking process: the desire to manage social change. In this sense, criminology, it has been argued, is intimately connected to the modernist project. This interconnection is clearly demonstrated in the work of the right realists and the use to which their ideas have been put in the policy arena. Crime in this context is used both to signify a social problem and to unify support for dealing with that problem. Assumptions such as these are challenged by the work of the postmodernists. They would argue that the presumption of such unity is highly problematic given the increasing importance attached to difference and diversity in the (post)modern world. Recognition of difference and diversity, therefore, renders the traditional relationship between criminology and the policymaking process a highly problematic, if not a dubious, one. From this point of view right realism makes little sense at all. It will be necessary to return to these issues in the next chapter.

Both this chapter and the one that follows lay bare the political interconnections between criminology and criminal justice policy. These interconnections have become more transparent, arguably, as the needs of the (capitalist) state have become more demanding. The underlying drive of 'possessive individualism', whether articulated in the Marxian sense or in the more liberal tones of the work of Bell (1976), celebrate the power of the individual in both positive and negative ways. In this sense, there is perhaps little to take issue with in some aspects of Wilson's arguments in which he asserts that crime and a rising crime rate are the price to be paid for (American) capitalism. There is, however, no necessary corollary between this assertion and the drive towards incapacitation as a way of solving the problem, although it does point to the view that it is highly unlikely that such processes can be reversed. It is out of recognition of the reality of this and out of the increasingly powerful influence of right realist thinking that left realism was born.

Young (1994) argues that there are four points of convergence between right realism and left realism. It is worth quoting Young at length on this:

> 1 Both see crime as really being a problem; both see the public's fear of crime as having a rational basis, in contrast to left idealism and administrative criminology.
> 2 Both believe that the reality of crime control has been misconceived, particularly the centrality of the public–police relationship.
> 3 Both are realistic about what can be done about crime and the limitations of our present-day knowledge. Neither disdains marginal gains, while both discount utopian solutions.
> 4 Both emphasize the need for closely monitored research and intervention and are critical of the widespread tendency to 'throw money' at the crime problem without attempting to measure cost-effectiveness.
>
> (Young 1994: 102)

The extent to which these points of convergence are more apparent than real will become more evident in Chapter 4, in which left realism will be discussed in detail. As we shall see, both also need to be situated within an understanding of the 'culture of control' referred to earlier, a point made by Young himself on the sleeve note of *The New Criminology Revisited* (Walton and Young 1998):

> Crime has moved from the rare, the abnormal, the offence of the marginal and the stranger, to the commonplace part of everyday life; it occupies the family, the heartland of liberal democratic society, as well as extending its anxiety into all areas of the city. It is revealed in the highest echelons of our economy as well as in the urban impasses of the underclass. The meta-narrative of progress has as its almost unspoken assumption the decline of crime and incivilities. Yet the highest living standards in the history of our species have been accompanied by a steady rise in the crime rate, while crime itself occurs in all the places it should not as well as being more frequent in all its traditional haunts.

To summarize: the emergence of right realism within criminology was a result of what was perceived to be the failure of more liberal stances on criminal justice process, a view which in and of itself was also clearly connected to changing social and economic circumstances. Out of these circumstances, it is no great surprise that in some respects a resurgence of interest in the more classical criminological ideas (discussed in Chapter 2) should occur. Certainly, a focus on the individual absolves governments of responsibility, on the one hand, and expects greater responsibility of individual citizens, on the other. The changing nature of this relationship between the citizen and the state will be a recurring theme throughout this book, but especially in Chapters 6 and 7.

Further reading

As this chapter has demonstrated, there is no easily identifiable body of knowledge called 'right realism'. However, those interested in pursuing this line of thinking could do worse than read Wilson and Herrnstein (1985). It can certainly pay to read material in its original form and this book provides a very sound empirical and theoretical basis from which the term 'right realism' has been constructed. An explication of rational choice theory and its relevance to criminology is best found in Cornish and Clarke (1986). Students will also find Felson (2002) a very persuasive and enjoyable read and the more ambitious would gain much from Garland (2001).

chapter four

Understanding 'left realism'

What is 'left realism'?
Left realism UK style: a critique
Left realism US style
The modernist dilemma
Left realism and New Labour: politics, policy and process
Conclusion
Further reading

One way of appreciating the relevance of any social theory is to locate the emergence and development of that theory in its political and social context. The 'left realist' approach to criminology is no exception. Chapter 3 has already indicated the presence and influence of a 'conservative criminology' promoted under the auspices of right realism that arguably informed some Home Office policy thinking during this time. So, it is against this general background of social, policy and political events that the term 'radical left realism', later to be referred to as simply 'left realism', was coined by Young, to connote an alternative way of talking about the crime problem to that offered by the general conservatism of the early 1980s.

Arguably, it is not until 1985 onwards (Matthews and Young 1992), in the aftermath of the Merseyside and Islington Crime Surveys formulated and conducted under the umbrella of left realism, that this theoretical position really emerged as espousing a relatively coherent set of ideas with a concomitant policy agenda. Since that time there has been both a consolidation and a critique of these ideas. Their presence and influence has extended beyond the UK as they have been modified and applied in different international contexts.

This chapter will endeavour to analyse and trace the development of these ideas since 1979. In so doing, particular attention will be paid first of all to the conceptual development of the central left realist ideas found primarily in the work of Lea, Matthews and Young. Second, these ideas will be compared and contrasted with other versions of left realism, paying special attention to the work of Elliott Currie. Third, we shall examine the methodological and policy agendas that flow from 'left realism'. Fourth, an overview of the various critiques of these ideas will be offered, with special reference to the relationship between left realism and feminism. Finally, we shall consider the relative merits and achievements of this strand of criminological work. But first, what is 'left realism'?

What is 'left realism'?

> The central tenet of left realism is to reflect the reality of crime, that is in its origins, its nature and its impact. This involves a rejection of the tendencies to romanticize crime or to pathologize it, to analyse solely from the point of view of the administration of crime or the criminal actor, to understand crime or to exaggerate it. And our understanding of methodology, our interpretation of the statistics, our notions of aetiology follow from this. Most importantly, it is realism which informs our notion of practice: in answering what can be done about the problems of crime and social control.
>
> (Young 1986: 21)

This desire to reflect the reality of crime and the crime experience, for Young, distinguishes 'left realism' from what he has labelled 'left idealism' as well as from the administrative criminology of the Home Office. In his view 'left idealism' neglected the problem of the cause of crime. In 'left idealism' the cause of crime was constituted as either an artefact of the state's need to criminalize in order to sustain itself consequent to the crisis of capitalism or was so obvious that it required no further explanation (the notion that poverty obviously causes crime, for example). On the one hand, the first assertion reflected a remarkably simplistic view of the state, how it operates and the relationship between individual citizens and the state. On the other hand, the second assertion assumed a rational economic view of human action that fails, at a minimum, to resonate with the empirical evidence.

In addition, Young argued that administrative criminology also sidestepped the problem of the cause of crime: for the administrative criminologists the key problem is how to manage the crime problem, not how to explain it. The lack of concern with aetiology (causes) rendered both of these positions similar for Young. Both reflected a concern with the mechanisms and management of the social control and/or social construction of crime rather than a concern with the potentially much more complex processes that feed into and generate the 'crime problem'.

So, in part, the left realist agenda emerged as a reaction to dissatisfaction with the (then) state of criminological theorizing. However, left realism set itself up, not just reactively but also proactively, as a way of thinking about the contemporary reality of the crime problem that pointed to an increasing awareness of the nature and extent of criminal victimization. Indeed, it was the Home Office-sponsored 'administrative' research in the form of the development of the criminal victimization survey that had contributed to the need for greater awareness of and sensitivity to the complex ways in which crime impacts on both individuals and communities. It is the complexity of these processes that left realism claims to address.

Left realism starts from a position that centralizes the need to address 'problems as people experience them' (Young 1986: 24). It 'necessitates an accurate victimology', it 'must also trace accurately the relationship between victim and offender' and must note that 'crime is focused both geographically and socially on the most vulnerable sections of the community' (Young 1986: 23). These concerns form the fundamental basis to the realist position, echoing what was later called a focus on the 'square of crime' (Young 1992: 27):

> The most fundamental tenet of realism is that criminology should be faithful to the nature of crime. That is, it should acknowledge the form of crime, the social context of crime, the shape of crime, its trajectory through time, and its enactment in space.
>
> (J. Young 1992: 26)

This tenet provides for four elements to understanding crime (hence the 'square of crime'): the victim, the offender, the reaction of the formal agencies of the state and the reaction of the public. Thus, for example, the crime rate needs to be understood as a product of the interaction of all these four points: changes in the offending population, changes in the victim population, policy changes within the formal agencies and changes in the reactions of the public to different kinds of crime. All these may, of course, vary independently of each other and may differ for different crimes (what Young refers to as understanding the 'shape of crime'). Thus any explanation of crime needs to be fourfold in character – in other words, it makes little sense to privilege an explanation that centres police activity, for example, over that of criminal activity. What, then, is the key explanatory concept employed by left realism?

The key explanatory concept employed by left realism is that of 'relative deprivation'. This concept has a substantial history in both sociology and social psychology and it refers to conditions in which people may not only be (or indeed may not at all be) objectively deprived, but also may feel so deprived and perceive themselves to be so deprived in comparison with either others in the same social category or others in a different social category. As a cause of crime Jock Young (1992) argues that relative deprivation is very powerful for three reasons: it can apply to circumstances throughout the social structure; it can be applied to all kinds of crime, not just those that may be deemed economically motivated; and it is a concept that is not dependent on identifying some absolute standard of deprivation or poverty. Utilizing the concept of relative deprivation in this way is not intended to suggest that there is one causal explanation for crime, but serves as a conceptual framework for understanding the social circumstances in which crime is likely to occur. In other words, it is important, left realists argue, to understand the ways in which the experience of relative deprivation may be differently constituted under different circumstances: the principle of specificity.

Jock Young (1992) argues that there are three major problems associated with the question of specificity that have both underpinned and undermined criminological thinking: a presumption that understanding male working-class crime equates with understanding all criminal behaviour; a presumption that understanding crime in advanced industrial societies equates with understanding crime in general; and a presumption that American criminological theorizing (produced in a very atypical society in terms of criminal behaviour) provides theorizing that is applicable elsewhere. In other words, while the concept of relative deprivation might be powerful, what it reveals about social and personal processes in one society needs to be quite tightly articulated and differentiated (that is, specified) from what might be revealed through its application in a different social context. For left realism, understanding the specific circumstances in which crime occurs can be achieved through the 'principle of lived realities'.

Focusing on 'lived realities' implies two concerns. The first addresses the potentially complex ways in which key socio-structural variables may interact with each other to produce differential experiences of crime. So, for example, there is evidence to suggest that differences in young white and black males' experience of being stopped by the police are lessened when social class is controlled for. Appreciating the complex ways in which variables interact with each other implies, of course, that simply to assert the importance of one variable over another might result in the distortion of not only the empirical data but also the reality of people's everyday experiences. The second concern foregrounds the need to place behaviour in its social context, whether that be criminal behaviour or police behaviour. It is important, for example, to appreciate that police behaviour is not merely the product of a 'macho cop culture' but the end result of understanding the specific nature of the task in hand alongside the strategy chosen to deal with that task.

'Realism, then, does not deal in abstractions: the principle of specificity demands that explanation be grounded' (J. Young 1992: 40). In other words, there may be different underlying causal and motivational factors contributing to different types of crime in different types of setting – an appreciation of which may require different kinds of response from the agencies of social control. This takes us to the next principle of left realism: how crime might be controlled and the role of the social control agencies in that process.

'The control of crime must reflect the nature of crime' (J. Young 1992: 41). This has a number of implications. First, it involves activity on each side of the square of crime. That is, the control of crime requires a response from both the formal and the informal agencies of social control for both the victim and the offender. Second, the control of crime involves appreciating that crime occurs in both a spatial and temporal setting, both of which are considerations that need to be built into crime prevention policy. Third, while realism favours structural intervention to prevent crime, this does not preclude proceeding with a whole range of different crime prevention strategies provided that they are put in place in settings and circumstances in which they have been shown to have some demonstrable effect. Fourth, while realists favour the retention of criminal justice sanctions for some crimes, crime control for the left realist involves recognizing that the process of criminalization is politically informed and that it is both possible and desirable to find means through which that process can be more widely and effectively democratized.

Recognizing that some crimes are more difficult to control than others, and recognizing the need for a much more careful debate on the role of the police in the crime control process, Jock Young states that:

> It is not the 'Thin Blue Line', but the social bricks and mortar of civil society which are the major bulwarks against crime. Good jobs with a discernible future, housing estates that tenants can be proud of, community facilities which enhance a sense of cohesion and belonging, a reduction in unfair inequalities, all create a society which is more cohesive and less criminogenic.
>
> (J. Young 1992: 45)

If this is the case, it is both misplaced and foolish to overemphasize the role of the police in contributing to the process of criminalization and to crime control. What is necessary is a concerted and coordinated response by all those agencies that potentially have an impact on crime: the principle of multi-agency intervention.

Left realism argues that it is only through multi-agency intervention that the reality of crime can be tackled. This is because of the variable nature of crime itself and the multifaceted nature of social control. A commitment to the principle of multi-agency intervention does not imply a blanket application of that principle. Different crimes may require the cooperation of different agencies at different points in the commission of those crimes for both the victim and the offender. They may require the formation of different types of relationship between the relevant agencies, and may require different levels of participation from the public. Much of the work to date around multi-agency intervention has neglected to pay attention to the complex processes that may inhibit or facilitate such working, under what conditions, and with what kind of support from the public. For left realism such initiatives need to be much more carefully and finely tuned to the reality of crime in order for them to work.

An effective relationship with the public is seen to be one of the elements of multi-agency intervention that can facilitate or hinder its working. Indeed, the public has a crucial role to play in formulating a policy response to the crime problem. This alludes to the next principle of left realism: the principle of rational democratic input. Democratic input recognizes the need to take people seriously. At one level, this is economic: the public pay for public safety, so in that sense they have a right to be consulted on how that public safety is constructed. At another level, it is also important to recognize that the public also have a range of worries and concerns about their safety. In this sense, there is also a voice to be heard on the way in which such worries may or may not be alleviated. Such democratic input is to be achieved through the social survey:

> The social survey is a democratic instrument: it provides a reasonably accurate appraisal of people's fears and of their experience of victimization. . . . Social surveys, therefore, allow us to give voice to the experience of people, and they enable us to differentiate the safety needs of different sectors of the community.
>
> (J. Young 1992: 50)

Social surveys, then, used locally, are a key mechanism for measuring the extent of criminal victimization, people's concerns about that criminal victimization and how policy responses might be formulated in order to respond to those concerns. For left realism, using the social survey in a geographically focused and local way provides a mechanism for contextualizing people's fears without either downplaying them through the production of aggregate statistical representations or making any necessary prior presumption concerning the level of rationality to be attributed to those worries or concerns. Such surveys also provide a database from which to construct some notion of democratic output.

Social surveys offer the opportunity of gathering some measure of understanding of the public's priorities with respect to crime work. Of course, those priorities will not be expressed as universal concerns. However, without such an input, left realists would argue that policymakers have no clear sense of direction around those initiatives for which public support can be mobilized and those initiatives for which public support might need to be differently harnessed, and for which sections of the public. The principle of democratic output recognizes that the public has a role to play not only in formulating and shaping crime policy but also in its effective implementation, alongside both the formal and the informal agencies in any particular community. In other words, the process of crime control policy and its implementation is complex, the success of which may be dependent on the quality of the relationships formed among policymakers, members of the crime control industry and the general public.

Consequently, looking for simple cause and effect solutions in relation to crime prevention may be misguided; the best to be hoped for in the short term may be marginal gains rather than dramatic changes (a clear point of convergence between left realism and right realism). Taking the needs of local people seriously may produce immeasurable but nevertheless qualitative improvements in the local quality of life none of which may be ultimately reflected in the crime statistics. This does not mean that a locally constructed and locally informed intervention has not worked. It does mean, however, that it may make little sense to use crime statistics as a measure of effectiveness. This view reflects a further left realist principle: the principle of democratic measurement.

For the left realist, as for many other strands of criminology, criminal statistics, as a source of information about the nature and extent of criminal behaviour, are hugely problematic. Moreover, the data derived from criminal victimization surveys do little to overcome the underlying problems associated with criminal statistics. It is necessary to appreciate that:

> If Quetelet pointed to the existence of a dark figure of crime, realist and feminist studies have pointed to how this dark figure is qualitatively structured. The dark figure varies with what type of crime committed by whom against which victim. Such an analysis takes us one step further. The dark figure expands and contracts with the values we bring to our study: recent studies of the extent of marital rape or changes in child abuse over time clearly indicate this.
>
> (J. Young 1992: 58)

However, the fact that we cannot measure the nature and extent of crime precisely as an 'objective' problem out there does not mean that there are not some features of that problem around which people are, or can be, unified and/or mobilized. So as J. Young (1992: 58) goes on to state, realism sees crime as a unifier, as a social democratic issue, rather like health and education, around which some democratic principles can be constructed, since, as with health and education, the poor suffer the most from the problems associated with criminal behaviour. Such a 'unity of interest allows us the possibility, both of a common measuring rod, and a political base which can argue for taking crime seriously' (J. Young 1992: 59). This leads us to the final principle of left realism: the principle of theory and practice.

Left realism challenges the conventional social scientific presumption that what takes place in academia can be and should be separated and separable from what takes place in the political and policy domains. Left realism recognizes that the practice of doing research is imbued with the personal theoretical and political preferences of the researcher, if not the funder of such research. This is as much the case for qualitative as for quantitative research. This being the case, it should be recognized and built into the research process. Moreover, as Jock Young argues, the same issues of political and personal commitment inform the policymaking process and that nowhere is this more the case than in the realm of crime prevention. At the same time, very few crime prevention initiatives are monitored for their effectiveness.

Recognition of these features of the reality of the research and policy-making processes foregrounds the political commitments that underpin those processes and opens them up for further evaluation and debate. This view of these processes constitutes a further expression of the political views that underpin left realism: that of social democracy. The commitment by left realists to the principles of the social democratic process arguably informs all the other 'points of realism' outlined here. It is also arguably this direct espousal of such a commitment that has served to provoke the debate that left realism has generated and which is discussed later.

Taking crime and people seriously, then, involves acceptance not only of the value of a particular explanatory framework at a theoretical level and the more specific propositions that might flow from this, but also of a particular political view of social reality and how the crime problem might best be prioritized and managed in the light of that political commitment. The extent to which this theory, practice and the linking methodological strategies proposed by left realism knit together has been subjected to relatively close critical scrutiny. It is to a consideration of that critical scrutiny that we shall now turn.

Left realism UK style: a critique

The overtly political stance adopted by those committed to the principles of left realism, evidenced by the clearly stated desire to reclaim the law and order debate in the 1980s for the Labour Party, constituted one of the more obvious critical starting points for some commentators on these theoretical developments. There are, however, three problematic issues for left realism: methodology, policy and feminism.

The question of methodology

The way in which any researcher presumes to connect their theoretical perspective with a particular method of exploring that theoretical perspective empirically, either implicitly or explicitly, adopts a way of thinking about how and what kind of knowledge can be gathered about social reality. These ways of thinking about the knowledge gathering process structure, in a fundamental way, what we think can be known about the world and the possibilities of accessing that knowledge. The label 'positivism', much criticized within criminology (see, for example, Taylor et al. 1973) articulates one set of presumptions about the knowledge gathering process. Realism articulates another.

What is meant by realism, like what is meant by positivism, is open to interpretation. It is possible, however, to construct an understanding of the central features of a realist project by drawing on the work of Bhaskar and

Giddens. In a fairly clear and succinct definition of realism, Outhwaite offers this illustration from the work of Bhaskar:

> The conception I am proposing is that people, in their conscious activity, for the most part unconsciously reproduce (and occasionally transform) the structures governing their substantive activities of production. Thus people do not marry to reproduce the nuclear family or work to sustain the capitalist economy. Yet it is nevertheless the unintended consequence (and inexorable result) of, as it is also a necessary condition for, their activity.
>
> (Outhwaite 1987: 51)

What is explicit here is the way in which the routine activities of individuals, more or less consciously engaged in, are structured by and through underlying social processes. These processes can be both sustained and threatened in the way in which individuals, acting as individuals or in concert with others, engage in their routine daily lives, not always aware of the underlying structures that inform those routine activities themselves. These underlying structures are what Bhaskar refers to as generative mechanisms. Such mechanisms can be both unobserved and unobservable, yet are real in their consequences (like the notion of the nuclear family or an economic system called capitalism). Positing the existence of generative mechanisms implies that in order to engage in any empirical investigation of the social world, it is necessary to go beyond the 'mere appearance' of social reality. It is necessary also to make sense of the underlying structures that result in those appearances. If this constitutes a way of thinking about the knowledge production process that can reasonably be identified as realist, the question remains as to whether left realism resonates with such a view.

As has been stated already, left realism starts from the theoretical position that we should take seriously those issues which people define as being serious and develop an understanding of social problems as people experience them. This places the victim and/or the potential victim of crime at the centre of the criminological stage at least in relation to formulating an appreciation of the experience of crime. The way in which those experiences have, to date, been explored empirically is through the use of the criminal victimization survey. As indicated earlier, such surveys have been geographically focused. However, the question at issue here is not the manner of deployment of this measurement tool but its appropriateness. Put another way, if realism as a methodology is concerned to locate people's experiences within a social reality in which they will be more or less aware of the processes contributing to those experiences (as discussed already) then can the criminal victimization survey tap such concerns?

Criminal victimization surveys, whether used nationally or locally, face a number of difficulties in the process of implementation that challenge their accuracy as measuring instruments. This much is well known. However, the general difficulties associated with the utilization of the survey technique in this way are compounded when a claim is made, on the one hand, to take people's grievances seriously and, on the other hand, to locate those grievances within their material context. The social survey as a research instrument cannot achieve this. It can only capture the responses made by individuals to the particular questions asked at a particular moment in time. To claim any more from the survey method reflects a tendency to 'reduce agents to the bearers of structures' (Outhwaite 1987: 111). Yet this is precisely what left realism appears to do. Not only does this apparent conflation of the relationship between the individual expression of experiences and the underlying structural processes occur, it has also on occasion been presented as if this were non-problematic (see for example, Crawford et al. 1990).

The commitment to the social survey as a democratic instrument clearly conveys the methodological tension under discussion here. To elucidate, Galtung (1967) regarded the social survey as possessing one key vice: it suffered from an individualistic and democratic bias. Galtung's point was that, while social surveys do give everyone who participates in them a voice – that is, their individual responses are all given the same weight – social reality is not simply the sum of these voices. It will be useful, perhaps, to explore this a little more fully.

Surveys make several assumptions. Surveys assume that human beings are in a position to know social reality, that they can perceive that social reality accurately and that such perceptions can be accurately articulated through the questions asked by the survey. Moreover, it is further presumed that a policy agenda can be reasonably constructed from this process. All these assumptions point to the problem of not only how and what weight can be given to individual responses to a range of standardized questions, but also how is it possible to make sense of those responses when indeed the nature of the data hides the fundamentally unequal nature of the social world. In other words, the survey instrument cannot capture the generative mechanisms of which realism speaks. This is not intended to imply that left realism has no commitment to understanding social reality and the way it is structured by age, class, gender and ethnicity. At a theoretical level this certainly is the case. However, the question remains open as to how these variables are deemed to interact with each other.

The criminal victimization survey provides a range of empirical observations as to the effects of these variables; and indeed, those surveys conducted under the umbrella of left realism have more than served the purpose of reminding policymakers that criminal victimization is not evenly distributed across the population. They have also been successful at counting more incidents of the kinds of criminal victimization somewhat neglected by more conventional criminal victimization work (violence against women and racial harassment, for example). But an understanding of how these empirical findings have been generated has arguably been politically asserted rather than empirically so.

The argument presented here is not intended to convey that left realists are not themselves aware of the issues discussed earlier. As Matthews and Young state:

> Social positivism is imbued with a sense of the objective, the mechanical and the instantaneous. Realism, by stressing the role of human consciousness within determinant circumstances, as in the tradition of subcultural theory, denies all of this.
>
> (Matthews and Young 1992: 7)

What is more to the point, however, is that acceptance of these inherent difficulties associated with social positivism is not overcome merely by stating an awareness of them. How such difficulties have been overcome needs also to be demonstrated; although, as has been stated already and as will be demonstrated further later, some of the work associated with left realism has clearly shown that the survey instrument can be sensitively and usefully deployed in the study of criminal victimization.

Of course, what underpins this whole discussion is what is real about left realism, above and beyond its commitment to take crime seriously (like right realism) and its commitment to the reality of the political importance of crime. Young (1999) has endeavoured to address this question. His analysis attempts to explore the underlying generative mechanisms resulting in the surface manifestation of crime and responses to crime as we experience them in late modern society. This he does by drawing our attention to the development of the inclusive society of the 1950s into the exclusive society of the new millennium. This development is characterized by social change along a number of significant dimensions.

For Young (1999), the inclusive society of the 1950s was characterized by security and tolerance. In this set of social arrangements, the question of citizenship was considered to be largely resolved, the welfare state made provision for the least well off, social order was uncontested and the main thrust of criminal justice policy was the assimilation of offenders. This sense of social order began to change culturally during the 1960s and economically during the 1970s. Now we live in a world characterized by insecurity and intolerance generated by social and economic precariousness in which the reward system appears to be 'chaotic' in a society marked by increasing cultural diversity. No wonder that, in terms of public and policy discourse, there has emerged a strong 'criminology of the other' – that is, a view of the criminal as demon. This is, of course, in marked contrast to the 'criminal as ordinary' found in the work of Felson discussed in the previous chapter. How these two images coexist in contemporary policy terms will be revisited in Chapter 8.

So the underlying generative mechanism within this analysis is the move from the inclusive to the exclusive society, which for Young parallels the transition from the modern to the late modern society:

> The movement into late modernity is like a ship which has broken from its moorings. Many of the crew cry to return to the familiar sanctuary of the harbour but to their alarm the compass spins, the ship continues on its way and, looking back, the quay is no longer secure: at times it seems to be falling apart, its structure fading and disintegrating. The siren voices which forlornly, seriously, soberly try to convince them that going back is possible are mistaken.
>
> (Young 1999: 193)

Nostalgia is clearly present in this kind of commentary, a nostalgia that we shall come across again later in this chapter when we consider how, if at all, left realism has succeeded in the policy domain. But for Young it is within these processes of change that an understanding of the contemporary importance of relative deprivation is to be found. It is a moot point whether or not this kind of analysis has resolved the methodological concerns with which this subsection began or equips us well enough to understand contemporary policy concerns.

The question of policy

The methodological tensions just outlined raise general questions concerning what can be read legitimately from social survey data. Moreover, it is also clear that left realism has placed great emphasis on the use of social surveys as a major source of information from which (democratically) informed crime prevention policies might be formulated. Such a commitment to the policymaking process constructed in this way raises both specific questions concerning how such a process might be implemented and more general questions concerning the kinds of policies that might be put in place. We shall address each of these questions in turn.

As Matthews and Young (1992: 15) freely admit, they have been accused of political populism – 'of merely moving from a public "commonsense" attitude to one of policy' (Mugford and O'Malley 1990). This view of their commitment to the use of the social survey to inform the policymaking process is denied. It is argued that 'policy cannot be read off a computer print-out of public opinion' (Mugford and O'Malley 1990). As was suggested earlier, individuals may be more or less aware of the social process and/or problems that routinely structure their lives. Given this limitation, how are such data to be read?

> The expert, the social analyst, therefore, has a vital role in contextualizing the problem of crime. First of all in mapping the problems and then putting the problems in context. In short, the analyst uncovers problems and then gives weight to their severity. This is a basis for a rational input into the system of crime control.
>
> (Crawford et al. 1990: 161)

In order for priorities to be realistically assessed, it is necessary to take account of three factors: public priorities, the prevalence of each kind of crime and an assessment of each crime's impact (J. Young 1992: 43). And as Matthews and Young (1992: 16) go on to assert: 'On a political level this [process] involves a debate between the criminological expert and the public.'

It would be difficult to deny the importance of the need for public debate concerning appropriate criminal justice policy. Such a debate, appropriately informed, may provide the basis from which it is possible to construct a vision of what makes 'good' sense from that which is rooted in 'common' sense. In other words, 'victims are not always the best judge of an appropriate and just crime control policy' (Brogden et al. 1988: 189) and, moreover, are not the only consumers of the criminal justice system (Jefferson et al. 1992). Indeed, in a much earlier discussion of the realist project, Sim et al. remind us of the interconnections between social policy and criminal justice policy (a theme that we shall revisit in Chapters 6 and 7):

> What is clear, however, is that new realism has led to a political cul-de-sac where 'realistic' policies on crime, welfare, housing, wages, health and schooling predominate over a class analysis. Consequently policies accept rather than challenge the terrain of the powerful.
>
> (Sim et al. 1987: 59)

The impasse here lies not so much with the question of the need for debate, but with how that debate is to be constituted, by whom and under what circumstances the analyst might lend greater weight to whose views. There are more than a few hints here of the Comtean view of the role of the social analyst (or social physician, as Comte might have said), which is perhaps not surprising given the methodological tensions outlined earlier.

So the commitment to the use of the social survey as a social democratic instrument for informing the policymaking process raises further questions concerning how that policymaking process might be managed. Of course, what underpins these questions in a much more fundamental way is the left realist commitment to the integration of theory and practice – that is, a clear statement that ties the criminological enterprise to the policymaking process. As Matthews and Young (1992: 10) state: 'Ideas do not arise out of thin air, and . . . practical engagement, on whatever level, is a crucial component in forming, testing, and shaping ideas.' As a principle, this is not so problematic. As a practice, of course, it is not so straightforward. Indeed, in some respects it could be argued that the kinds of policy suggestions that have emanated from left realism – multi-agency cooperation, greater use of community alternatives for dealing with offenders, recognition of the need to reform the relationship between social rights and social obligations – did not need empirical evidence from expensive social surveys in order to make 'good' sense in particular circumstances.

Moreover, as Stenson and Brearly (1989: 3) argue: the 'Theoretical bias towards methodological individualism creates the risk that it will be increasingly drawn into the methodological individualistic, utilitarian discourses which have long dominated state sponsored criminology and crime control policy.'

As the policy proposals alluded to earlier illustrate and as Sim et al. (1987: 59) state, the policies that flow from the left realist position 'accept rather than challenge the terrain of the powerful' and remain 'politically conservative in [their] conclusions about what can be done about the state'. This leads Downes and Rock (1988: 309–10) to observe that many of the policy suggestions emanating from left realism are not that far removed from those emanating from the more liberal sections of the Home Office. (A fuller exploration of the relations between left realism and the law and order agenda of New Labour is offered later.) It is at this level that the tensions between what is politically valued and whether or not that is supported empirically re-emerge. It is also at this level that the question of whether or not left realism has captured or can capture social reality also re-emerges. These questions leave untouched the thorny issue of social power and how social power is both mediated by and hidden from individuals.

The question of feminism

While the party-political allegiances of left realism have constituted a contentious source of criticism for the realist project, it is arguably politics of another kind that raised much more fundamental questions about left realist concerns. There are (at least) two questions raised by feminist work for the left realist project – one conceptual, one methodological. Can the concepts employed by victim-oriented research adequately capture and convey women's experiences of criminal victimization and can the techniques chosen to measure those experiences adequately do so? Young (1988) claims that the local crime survey approach adopted by left realism takes on board the questions raised by the feminist movement concerning the nature and extent of the criminal victimization of women. This, he argues, is achieved in the following way.

It must be recognized that much of the actual impact of crime on women is trivialized and hence concealed. This concealment is then compounded by the levels of sexual harassment that women experience every day, which, given the relative powerlessness of women, makes them more unequal victims and therefore vulnerable. All these processes are framed by the way in which crime is ultimately constructed within a particular set of social relationships: patriarchy. These are the mechanisms, then, underpinning women's victimization and which the local, theoretically informed, crime survey, it is argued, can uncover. The question remains as to whether or not the kind of conceptual outline and research strategy offered here can achieve these aims.

Of course, surveys can and do uncover more incidents of whatever is being measured, dependent on how the questions are asked and of whom they are asked. So, as Stanley and Wise rightly suggest:

> If we wanted to 'prove' how terribly violent women's lives were, we'd go to women who live in violent places – run-down inner-city areas of large conurbations – who have actually experienced male violence and ask them about it. . . . However if we called this a 'survey', then, with exemplary motives and using 'scientific means', 'the problem for those women out there' could be generalized into 'the problem for all women everywhere'.
>
> (Stanley and Wise 1987: 110–11)

As this quote implies, it is not the method employed that guarantees feminist insight, but the conceptual framework in which that method has been utilized. This does not mean that social surveys and feminism do not mix. The work conducted by Russell (1990), Painter (1991) and Mooney (1993) clearly indicates that they do. What makes the use of the survey by these researchers feminist, is theory. Moreover, social surveys cannot capture social processes that arguably form the basis of understanding what women (or any other powerless group) see and experience as criminal victimization and what they do not. The question of feminism draws together in a rather neat way the two other tensions of methodology and policy discussed here and it will be of value to follow those tensions through with a particular example.

Kinsey et al. (1986) argue for a policy agenda of minimal policing based on what the public wants. In this argument, an exception is made for domestic disputes. The case is made, quite rightly, that there is a material base to the victimization of women that the criminal justice has a role to challenge. While such a material base for women's experiences might make sense for some women, if a policy strategy is to be formulated based on what the community wants, there is no guarantee that the community, made up of men and women, will necessarily recognize, define and agree with making an exception for domestic disputes and thereby argue for more police intervention in this particular area. This, arguably, is the resultant effect of the problem of 'standpoint' (Cain 1986: 259).

It was suggested earlier that left realism asserted the importance of the variables of class, race, age and gender and yet has failed to explore how these variables might interconnect with one another. For some (see, for example, Edwards 1989), this has resulted in the implicit (if not explicit) privileging of social class as an explanatory variable at the potential expense of other structuring relationships. The failure of left realists to engage reflexively in this way with their own practices makes it difficult for left realism 'to see or know from two different sites at once' (Cain 1986: 261) – that is, to also see gender. This is not to deny that empirically individuals, and/or individuals acting in concert, may occupy more than one empirical site, as Matthews and Young (1992) quite rightly observe.

Cain's point, however, is more than an empirical one. This is a question of how to theorize those interconnections through the strategies of reflexivity, deconstruction and reconstruction (Cain 1990).

These three sources of criticism reflect a major underlying tension deeply embedded in the left realist project. That tension has been articulated by a number of different writers in terms of the assumptions that underpin the left realist use of the concept of crime and the role of a discipline called criminology. It is a tension constituted primarily in the binary relationship that is presumed to exist between modernism and postmodernism, a relationship which, it is argued, fundamentally challenges the possibility of there being something called criminology at all. However, before considering the questions posed by this debate for left realism it will be of some value to examine the form and content of other strands of criminology that might claim the label 'left realist'.

Left realism US style

The ideas associated with left realism have generated considerable debate and criminological attention in countries other than the UK. Proponents of versions of left realist ideas can be found in Australia, Canada and the United States. These versions of left realism have been careful to maintain the need for a context-specific application of left realist ideas in different national and cultural settings. Brown and Hogg (1992) offer qualified support for the left realist project in Australia and MacLean (1992) provides a detailed empirical agenda and argument for the use of local crime surveys in Canada. While these developments carry with them explicit criticisms of the left realist project, they nevertheless adhere to the general political persuasion contained therein. However, perhaps the most clearly articulated of all these international versions of left realism is that found in the work of Elliott Currie.

During the 1980s the parallels between the UK and the USA in social and political terms were, in some respects, remarkable. The emulation and influence of American politics and policies was, of course, grounded in earlier decades, but that emulation arguably reached a new peak in the form of the political relationship which developed between Ronald Reagan and Margaret Thatcher during the 1980s. The similarity between these two leaders in the kinds of economic and political strategy adopted to respond to the world's changing economic climate contributed to what appeared to be an increasing desire to look for solutions to UK social problems in the USA. That same shared social and political climate also arguably contributed to the emergence of a similar debate to that found in the UK, both within academic criminology and within the sphere of criminal justice policy, as to how best to tackle the increasing crime problem. In the USA, a major exponent of a left realist response to the crime problem was to be found in the work of Currie (1985). It will be valuable to consider Currie's arguments in order to develop our understanding of both the similarities and differences in what might be called a left realist criminology.

Currie's work, rather like that of Young, emerged from not only the social and economic changes taking place in the USA and alluded to earlier, but also from a deep dissatisfaction with the (then) current mainstream criminological thought. He considered that the conservative explanation of crime was unhelpful for two reasons. The first of these is theoretical: to say that the propensity to commit crime is part of human nature, meaning that some people are just more evil than others, ignores the huge differences in crime rates in different areas. Second, in policy terms, to suggest that increasing the costs of crime (that is, locking more people up for longer) is desirable ignores the question whether or not locking people up actually makes a difference. Currie also argues that liberal criminology had offered no effective alternative to such conservative thinking, again for two reasons stemming from the failure of that criminological viewpoint to appreciate the depth of the social and personal impact that crime has. First, liberal criminology failed to appreciate the complexity of political economy and has thus avoided the difficult issue of just how jobs are created. Second, liberal criminology failed to appreciate the complexity of communities in which crime prevention strategies had been more often than not couched in individualistic terms.

From a thoroughgoing analysis and critique of the political and policy possibilities of both conservative and liberal criminology, Currie constructs his own analysis and policy agenda towards a better management of the crime problem. For Currie (1985), work is the central bond that links people to society. In a later piece, he argues that it is the economic problem of producing too much (overcapacity), sustained in the 1990s by what he calls the 'jobless recovery' (an economic recovery that did not involve creating more jobs), alongside the political expectation that there are private solutions to the consequences of these processes, that expresses the central importance of this bond. According to Currie:

> In the long run there can be no private sector solution to the crisis of overcapacity. Nor therefore a private sector solution to the inevitable social crises which that trend is already bringing and which will worsen in the future. Namely mass exclusion from meaningful work; the resulting declining income and social well being; rising poverty among increasing numbers denied access to livelihood, and a widening gulf between them and those who are able to cling to the remaining stable and well rewarded jobs; social pathology and social conflict on an unprecedented scale.
>
> (Currie 1995: 72)

Centring the need for work in this way, and identifying the underlying mechanisms that have changed the nature of work, fundamentally and on a worldwide basis, constitutes the key theoretical focus from which Currie's more specific policy agenda emanates. That agenda is worth focusing on in some detail.

Currie (1985: 275–6) recommends:

- a stronger response to domestic violence by the police and the courts
- greater attention to be paid to innovative policing practices
- greater use of more middle-range sanctions by the courts
- the development of intensive rehabilitation programmes for young offenders, preferably in the community or a supportive institutional setting
- community-based, comprehensive family support programmes
- improved family planning and support for teenage parents
- paid leave and more accessible childcare to ease the conflicts between work and home
- high-quality, early education for the disadvantaged
- an expansion of the community dispute resolution programme
- local services for victims of domestic violence
- intensive job training for the young
- upgrading low paid jobs
- a permanent job creation programme
- universal and generous income support for families headed by individuals outside the labour force.

The criminological thinking underpinning a policy agenda such as this involves taking seriously the impact of crime, especially the impact of violent crime on women. In addition, it involves taking seriously the fundamental features of a society that bind that society together, namely the world of work and the diversity of family structures which support and sustain individuals as they participate in the wider social order. Currie's agenda does not pathologize those who are not members of the labour force or those for whom the notion of the nuclear family has little resonance. But his agenda does involve taking seriously that evidence that connects family life and joblessness with the likelihood of engaging in criminal behaviour and constructing policy response that might (realistically?) tackle such issues.

In some respects Currie's realism, as wide ranging as it is, might, in a UK political context, look more like idealism. Nevertheless, there are specific points of overlap between this agenda and that proposed by left realism in the UK. In particular, the emphasis on the role of the police, community alternatives to punishment and a concern with violence against women are the obvious points of comparison. So, too, are the dissatisfactions expressed with the way in which the criminological enterprise has respectively understood and offered proposals on the crime problem, as is their respective concern to take the impact of crime seriously, especially the way that impact takes its toll on the socially disadvantaged. Currie's focus on understanding the changing nature of work and the differing ways in which individuals connect with that world, however, stands somewhat in marked contrast with the emphasis on relative deprivation found in the work of Young. These are not, of course, mutually exclusive concerns, but Currie's deeper concern with the role of political economy arguably equips us with a clearer conceptualization of his vision of the underlying generative mechanisms that produce a range of social problems. In this particular contextual evaluation of left realism, Currie's work also exposes the criminological left-wing continuities with the earlier radical tradition of Marxism. This commitment is not so easily identifiable in the writings of realists in the UK, though some have observed that the policy proposals emanating from the work of Young are discernible in the final chapter of Taylor et al. (1973). It is a commitment, however, that returns us to some of the more fundamental and uneasy tensions embedded in the left realist commitment to a fairly traditional interpretation of the nature of criminology and its subject matter: the modernist dilemma.

The modernist dilemma

Matthews and Young (1992) commit themselves unashamedly to the modernist project. This much is clear. Yet such a commitment does not offer a complete answer to those critics who draw attention to the problems of treating crime as a unified and unifying concept, treating the notion of the victim in the same way and the underlying essentialist and totalizing presumptions that these practices lead to. We shall address each of these questions in turn.

These problems, each in a different way, raise the explicit commitment to the interconnection between theory and politics found within the left realist project. In that commitment common sense, everyday understandings of crime are treated as if they were by definition non-problematic. In other words, taking seriously how people define and understand their experiences as the starting point of criminological investigation treats those definitions and experiences as though 'there is an easily recognisable reality "out there", known as crime, that can be understood through empirical investigation and in its own terms' (Carlen 1992: 59).

Not only is the presumption made that crime can be identified in this way, but also it is presumed that through understanding crime in this way consensual support can be galvanized for policy change. As Brown and Hogg state:

> The uncritical use of the concept 'crime' suggests that other purposes may underlie the realist project, or at least that it does not escape the effects of a certain essentialism – an essentialism that utilises crime as an ideological unifier: a mode for expressing the 'real' and common interests of working-class people.
>
> (Brown and Hogg 1992: 145)

This uncritical use of the concept of crime therefore has two problematic elements associated with it: one empirical, the presumption that there is some steadfast and easily identifiable empirical referent out there called 'crime'; and one political, that such an empirical referent resonates with the 'natural' supporters of the Labour Party whose attitudes towards criminal justice policy are also, coincidentally, progressive.

Invoking the concept of crime in this way not only overlooks the problems inherent in assuming that common sense articulates a social reality 'out there' rather than one which is socially constructed and commonly understood. It also overlooks the problem of how that common sense is to be transformed into something identifiably progressive. It takes little imagination to identify some aspects of common sense that could hardly be identified as progressive at all. So while left realism, on the one hand, within its basic principles reflects a concern with specificity – a desire to be locally sensitive to locally informed policy solutions – its underlying commitment to modernism, demonstrated by its unproblematic use of the terms 'crime', 'victim' and so on, clearly militates, on the other hand, against its ability to achieve this goal. Locally informed policy agendas might not be progressive at all.

The question of the left realist commitment to the modernist project, so deeply embedded in the criminological enterprise, raises questions about the nature of criminology as a whole. It is a question raised for all the social sciences by postmodernism. Put simply, postmodernism asks whether it is at all possible to talk in universal terms, to make claims concerning truth. Can there be anything deemed as 'knowledge' above and beyond experience? Expressed in this way, treating the notion of 'crime' as though it represented some unifying and essential concept is problematic indeed.

However, the relationship between left realism and the modernist project encourages us to think again about the relationship between left realism and politics. Are the 'natural' supporters of the Labour Party progressive and what input has left realism had, if any, on the law and order agenda of New Labour?

Left realism and New Labour: politics, policy and process

Left realism, as this chapter has been at pains to establish, is committed to the principle of community inclusion in both the formulation and the implementation of criminal justice policy. It has also been concerned not to ignore the intra-class and intra-racial dimensions to crime and criminal victimization and it has not been involved in minimizing the criminal victimization experience of women. This much is self-evident. The question remains as to the extent to which these ideas have had any influence in the political domain that it was so concerned to capture in the mid–1980s.

There are different ways in which we might begin to formulate an answer to these questions, some of which are addressed again in the chapters that follow. However that influence can also be traced in the flagship legislation of New Labour – the Crime and Disorder Act 1998.

Hopkins Burke (2001) argues that 'balanced intervention', characterized in the left realist policy agenda by the need to address all sides of the crime problem, is clearly evident in the oft-quoted Blair soundbite 'tough on crime, tough on the causes of crime'. Indeed, if one were to focus on the Crime and Disorder Act in relation to young offenders, for example (see also Chapter 6), then there is evidence of such 'balanced intervention'. Some, however, would call this the 'new correctionalism' (Muncie 1999). There are other themes in this legislation that also resonate with the principles of left realism, for example, the requirement for partnership working and the invocation of the importance of 'community'-based initiatives. Moreover, there also appears to be an implicit acceptance of crime as a unifier (an issue referred to earlier) along with the possibility of universally applicable policy packages. Much of this has permeated theoretical and policy agendas for a long time. Space inhibits a thorough analysis of links between this legislation, New Labour and left realism, but for the purposes of illustration we shall focus here on the extent to which a commitment to community inclusion endemic in all of these is a viable policy option. If we were to take an understanding of the *structure* of local communities into account in formulating crime prevention policies, what would that look like?

First, it would mean not assuming that there is an appropriate package which one can take off the shelf and apply to all communities. This is the case whether one is considering a particular crime prevention initiative, a focus on a particular crime problem or a particular style of implementation. If this first observation is the case then what follows is the requirement to develop quite a sophisticated understanding of how particular localities are structured; who is powerful and why; what kind of intervention might solicit support and why. This, of course, may result in quite different crime reduction agendas in different localities that might need to be differently negotiated between, for example, local businesses, young people and residents' associations. In some areas, this might also require the recognition of the role that organized crime might play in a locality. Such a role might be not only in terms of intimidation but also in providing an alternative job structure, for example, from (illegitimate) criminal gang activity to (legitimate) security work – a different understanding of access to employment than that implied by the Social Exclusion Unit (2001).

Crime prevention informed by such a structured sense of well-being would, as a consequence, take people's 'lived realities' (Crawford et al. 1990) very seriously indeed. This may mean transgressing debates about the relevance of the public and the private (though not necessarily ignoring them) and moving towards taking on board the things that concern people. This would require a genuine dialogue between those who are currently charged with policy implementation and those who are not. Such a dialogue might find it necessary, at a minimum, to understand the important role that is played within any community of the locally powerful and, at a maximum, targeting resources towards them. It may also mean recognizing and accepting that in some communities, increasingly marked by the withering away of the state, their vested interests might lie with their already well-established ways of managing their sense of security – recognition that is not nostalgic.

In other words, we need to look for ways of understanding how social capital works, or does not work, for communities in their own terms. Of course, locating an understanding of crime prevention in this kind of setting raises fundamental questions about the role of the state, its local legitimacy, social justice and democracy, questions that have quite a different feel to them now than they did in the era immediately after the Second World War, a theme that is developed in Chapters 6 and 7.

So, a genuine desire for policy to work for change needs to recognize the importance of the local context in which that policy is set. In some settings this might mean taking gender into account, in others it might mean that other structural variables are more important. But above all, policy needs to work with, rather than against, the historical and socioeconomic circumstances which structure any local context. It also requires the desire for policy to work to be both authentic and genuine for the communities themselves. Such a desire may also require a closer critical examination of what we understand by crime, community, prevention and protection, who is responsible for the delivery of these and how that might be implemented: questions that have been glossed over by New Labour and by left realism some of the problems of which have been recognized more recently by Matthews and Young (2003: 15). They offer this rather tempered statement about contemporary policies of social inclusion:

> The structural causes of crime are clearly delineated, but that is as far as it goes; rather than these being located in the deep structures of society, and its inevitable divisions of class, the concept of social exclusion carries with it the notion that the problem is that of inadequate management of society. The solution becomes managerial rather than transformative.

This clearly hints as the ever increasing presence and prevalence of neo-conservatism within UK criminal justice policy in the new millennium. We shall be returning to some of these themes in Chapter 8.

Conclusion

This chapter has offered a relatively detailed overview of both the form and the content of that version of criminological theorizing known as 'left realism'. In offering this overview, particular attention has been paid not only to its strengths and limitations in constituting a theoretical and empirical agenda for criminology, but also to its variant forms. Indeed, it is within those variant forms and some of the more fundamental criticisms of the left realist project that it is possible to catch sight of other ways of thinking about the criminological enterprise. For this author, there are two problematic issues endemic to the left realist project that demand reconciliation in one form or another if a genuine alternative (left-wing?) criminological agenda is to be constructed. The first issue relates to the question of what constitutes the real. The second issue is concerned with the relevance of postmodernism. We shall deal with each of these issues in turn.

Arguably, it is the question of what constitutes the real that, at a fundamental level, most clearly distinguishes the left realism of Currie from the left realism of Young. In this chapter, that has been most definitively articulated in Currie's concern with the relationship between the changing nature of the political economy and the impact that has on people's lives (including crime) and Young's focus on the concept of 'relative deprivation'. Here we are presented with two analyses, both claiming a left-wing position, with each arguably presenting the cause of crime as being constituted at different levels. These are, of course, not mutually exclusive positions. But in comparing the two, Currie's analysis comes closer to identifying a way of understanding how the real is constituted which resonates more readily with a Bhaskarian definition of realism. If Bhaskarian realism does offer a way of thinking about how the real is constituted, then such a framework provides a much more effective mechanism for exploring the ways in which the various sides of the 'square of crime' not only relate to each other but are also fundamentally constituted in and by processes outside the question of crime and the workings of the criminal justice system. There are different ways in which developing an understanding of those interconnections might be constructed. One way is offered in Chapters 6 and 7.

The second fundamental issue raised in this chapter is that concerning criminology's relationship with and intimate connection to the modernist project and the questions that postmodernism raises for this relationship. As was stated earlier, postmodernism poses a fundamental challenge to the domain assumptions of all the social sciences, not just criminology. Some of that challenge for criminology has been at its most pertinent in the work emanating from feminism, some of which will be discussed in Chapter 5. Others, however, have endeavoured to take the postmodernist challenge on board and to construct a 'criminology' informed by these ideas. The likely success of such an enterprise is open to dispute. A consideration of the relevance some of these ideas is, however, offered in Chapter 8.

To summarize: Young (1994) is correct to point out the clear points of agreement between right realism and left realism, especially in their starting point – the desire to take crime and the crime problem seriously. It is also useful to observe that, in the context of the UK at least, there is a much more clearly identifiable body of knowledge and work labelled left realism. In this respect, it may be that left realism has met some of its goals. However much remains to be done if this kind of criminology is ever to achieve the transformatory potential that its authors would wish for.

Further reading

The best sources for understanding left realism and the criticism it has generated are the collections of papers edited by Matthews and Young (1992) and Young and Matthews (1992). Young (1999) offers a more general theoretical overview of the issues addressed here. Young and Matthews (2003) endeavour to update the relevance of the themes addressed in this chapter to contemporary criminal justice policy concerns in the current political climate.

chapter five

Gendering the criminal

The gender blindness of criminology
Feminism and criminology
Feminisms and criminology: contradictions in terms?
Ways of thinking about men within criminology
Sex role theory and criminology
Categorical theory and criminology
Doing gender as criminology
Biography and the psychoanalytical turn
Reflections on masculinity and criminology
Summary: gendering the criminal or gendering criminology?
Conclusion
Further reading

One issue around which both criminology and common sense have been relatively blind is the question of gender. In this chapter, we shall explore the way in which gender issues have been hidden by criminology, the different ways in which feminists have attempted to make those issues visible and the more recent theoretical interest in the maleness of crime. It should be noted that the theoretical and empirical concerns of this chapter have emerged and developed largely independently of those concerns addressed by Chapters 3 and 4. But first we should explore how the question of gender (as opposed to sex) has been hidden within criminology.

The gender blindness of criminology

Braithwaite (1989: 44) suggests that the first 'fact' that any theory of crime should fit is that males disproportionately commit crime. In 2000, for example, 81 per cent of known offenders were male (Home Office 2001), a proportion that, for the most part, has remained relatively stable over the past 10 years. Moreover, it is possible to argue that if account is taken of the findings of feminist-inspired work on rape and domestic violence (crimes that are still frequently hidden and also disproportionately committed by men), then the maleness of lawbreaking behaviour is heightened. Yet the early incursions into criminology made by feminists were not as concerned to take account of or explain this maleness of crime as to talk about 'women and crime'.

This concern with 'women and crime' began with the seminal work of Smart (1977) and was continued by Leonard (1982), Heidensohn (1985), Morris (1987) and Naffine (1987). These texts shared a number of common concerns: first, to raise the visibility of women within criminological knowledge; second, to address women's relationship with crime not only as offenders but also as victims; and third, to understand crime as a male-dominated activity produced not as a result of sex differences but as a product of gender differences. However, many of these early texts tended to treat the 'woman and crime problem' as if it were a separate and separable issue within criminology. As Brown (1986) cogently argued, the more the woman question was treated in this way, the more mainstream (read *malestream*) criminology was left alone and presumed to have got its story straight on men. More recently there has been a tendency to equate gender and crime as constituting only a concern with women (see for example, Heidensohn 2002) and while there might be defensible policy reasons for this equation, gender, by definition, as we shall see in this chapter, means that we are concerned with men and women.

There is, however, a more fundamental question posed by a concern with just women and crime and that question raises the issue of the whole relationship between feminism and criminology. Gelsthorpe and Morris, for example, choose to talk of feminist *perspectives* and criminology, arguing that: 'Criminology has for many feminist writers and researchers been a constraining rather than a constructive and creative influence. Indeed, in a sense our task . . . is to fracture its boundaries' (Gelsthorpe and Morris 1990: 2). So what are these feminist perspectives of which Gelsthorpe and Morris speak, how have they influenced criminology, if at all, and how might they differently gender criminology?

Feminism and criminology

Gelsthorpe (2002) discusses six different feminist perspectives in her analysis of the relationship between feminism and criminology, but for the purposes of this discussion we shall focus on four, all of which have had different impacts on criminology: liberal feminism; radical feminism; socialist feminism; and postmodern feminism. We shall discuss the differential influence of each of these perspectives in turn.

Liberal feminism

Liberal feminism, stemming from the work of Wollstonecraft, Taylor and Mill, presumes that it is 'bad' or 'poor' scientific practice that produces the sexist bias in empirical research. In other words, it is a view of the scientific process which presumes that the rules of science and scientific inquiry are in themselves sound and that what is at fault is how they are applied. To alleviate this problem, liberal feminists align themselves with the view that more women researchers are needed and that any empirical investigation should include women in the sample.

In some respects, it is possible to argue that liberal feminism has had the longest historical impact on the study of criminology. This statement can be defended in a number of ways. There have always been women researchers looking at the problems associated with crime. There may not have been very many of them and the work that they produced may not have been particularly radical, but they were nevertheless present and they were examining the sex differentials associated with crime, especially delinquency (see, for example, Cowie et al. 1968; Glueck and Glueck 1950; Wootton 1959). In other words, there is both a history of women researching within criminology and a history of work addressing female offending behaviour.

It is possible to align much of that work with the liberal imperative of ensuring that females feature as a part of any empirical dataset – a question of good 'scientific' practice. There is a second theme, however, to that work that we might locate as being influenced by liberal feminism – a focus on the discriminatory practices of the criminal justice system. This strand reveals itself in different ways.

The work of Pollak (1950), concerned as it was with understanding the influence that chivalry might have in the under-documenting of women's criminality, is at the same time arguably a study of discriminatory practice. The presumption that women are discriminated against, either favourably or unfavourably, within the criminal justice system has informed a wealth of criminological research. Research has shown that factors such as type of offence (Farrington and Morris 1983; Hindelang 1979), home circumstances (Datesmann and Scarpitti 1980) and personal demeanour (DeFleur 1975) are contributory factors to the way in which women are processed by the criminal justice system.

This theme has been explored in ever more detailed and specific circumstances: in magistrates' courts (Eaton 1986), in prison (Carlen 1983; Dobash et al. 1986, Hedderman and Gelsthorpe 1998), and in women's experiences as victims of crime (Chambers and Millar 1983; Edwards 1989). That these factors simply represent sexist practices, however, is not easy to assert. Some studies suggest that the courts treat women more leniently, others suggest a harsher outcome. Such contradictory conclusions point to the complex way in which factors such as age, class, race, marital status and previous criminal record interact with each other. Moreover, Gelsthorpe (1989) found that there were organizational influences that affected the way in which females were dealt with by practitioners that were difficult to attribute to sexist or discriminatory practices alone.

Some writers have argued that the pursuit of this discriminatory theme, with its underpinning assumption of equality before the law, is no longer a fruitful enterprise for feminists interested in the crime problem (Smart 1990). What is clear, however, is that the work informed by these themes has yielded a wealth of information concerning the complex way in which factors interact to produce different outcomes for different female offenders and victims of crime. Indeed, it is the sheer weight of that evidence which renders a simplistic assertion of chivalry highly problematic and points to understanding women's experiences of the criminal justice system by reference to factors outside the operation of the criminal justice system.

Radical feminism

Understanding the ways in which such processes result in differential outcomes for victims of crime leads to a consideration of the value and impact of radical feminism on criminological concerns. In contrast to liberal feminism, radical feminism focuses more clearly on men's oppression of women rather than on other social conditions that might result in women's subordination. Crucial to the radical feminist analysis is the question of sexuality. The emphasis within radical feminism on women's oppression and control through their sexuality has had its greatest impact on criminology through the avenue of 'victim studies'. It must be said, however, that radical feminists display a far greater preference for the term 'survivor' than for 'victim', since that term implies a more positive and active role for women in their routine daily lives. These contentions over terminology, notwithstanding the work of radical feminists on rape (including marital rape and date rape), domestic violence, child abuse and sexual murder, have certainly constituted a challenge to criminology in what is defined as criminal, the extent of that criminality and its location (see, for example, Cameron and Fraser 1987; Russell 1990; Stanko 1985).

Understanding and embracing the 'safe haven' of the home as a place in which much criminal behaviour occurs, and is perpetrated by men towards women, is still a difficulty for some mainstream (malestream) criminological work, since taking this seriously means taking gender seriously. The campaigning voice of radical feminism that shouts 'all men are potential rapists' reflects both the power and the threat of feminist studies to a criminology informed in this way. There are difficulties, however, with accepting this stance uncritically.

Radical feminism presumes that all men have the same power and control over their own lives as they have over women. Moreover, the view that 'all men are potential rapists' presumes that all men have the same relationship with violence and the expression of their masculinity in violence towards women. This presumption is derived from the problem of essentialism of which radical feminism is frequently accused. Essentialism asserts the view that there are immutable differences between men and women shared by all men and all women. Despite the problems inherent in this position that results in the erasure of difference(s), radical feminism clearly placed men's violence towards women on the criminological agenda.

Socialist feminism

The complex ways in which variables such as sex, race and class might interact with one another has been the central concern of socialist feminism. Here some attention will be paid to the work of Messerschmidt (1986) as articulating one expression of this position.

Messerschmidt has this to say about his theoretical framework for understanding crime:

> My socialist feminist understanding of crime had two premises. First, to comprehend criminality (of both the powerless and the powerful) we must consider simultaneously patriarchy and capitalism and their effects on human behaviour. Second, from a social feminist perspective, power (in terms of gender and class) is central for understanding serious forms of criminality. It was theorised that the powerful (in both the gender and class spheres) do the most criminal damage to society. Further, the interaction of gender and class creates positions of power and powerlessness in the gender/class hierarchy, resulting in different types and degrees of criminality and varying opportunities for engaging in them. Just as the powerful have more legitimate opportunities, they also have more illegitimate opportunities.
>
> (Messerschmidt 1993: 56)

Of course, as Messerschmidt himself admits, as with all theoretical constructions, this framework has its limitations. For example, it denudes the criminal actor of a sense of agency, locating the motivation for crime within the social system. It also asserts patriarchy as being unitary and uniform in its impact on both men and women. Yet despite these problems, this framework does offer a starting point which posits an understanding of criminality located within socio-structural conditions – a way of thinking about the criminal behaviour of both men and women and the way in which those socio-structural conditions impact on men and women. Elements of these concerns are also found in the work of Carlen.

Carlen is very critical of feminist efforts to explain criminal behaviour and points to two major limitations in such efforts with respect to female lawbreaking behaviour in particular. First, she argues that an exclusive focus on women's lawbreaking behaviour presumes that women break the law for essentially different reasons than do men. This, for Carlen, reflects a reductionist and essentialising position similar to that adopted by the biological positivists. Second, when the historically and socially specific contexts of male and female offending behaviours are examined, the explanatory concepts that emerge rapidly merge with issues of racism, classism and imperialism rather than gender per se. She goes on to comment that women in prison represent those whose criminalization has been over-determined by the threefold effects of racism, sexism and classism. None of these variables is reducible to any other and all, for Carlen, point to connecting the debate around women and crime to the broader issue of social justice.

What is particularly striking about both the theoretical work of Messerschmidt (1986) and the range of work conducted by Carlen on female offenders and women in prison is the way in which both writers have drawn on conceptual formulations that take us outside mainstream criminological debates in order to understand the nature of criminality. This process of moving to debates outside criminology in order to understand women's and men's experiences of the criminal justice system is one of the features of what Cain (1990: 2) has called 'transgressive criminology'.

Cain's 'transgressive criminology' constitutes a call to move beyond what she defines as the 'binding web of co-man sense' (Cain 1990: 8). In order to do this, criminology must take seriously what actors themselves take seriously, yet simultaneously make visible what is taken for granted. This concern generates a criminological shopping list of women-only studies, that is, studies exploring the totality of women's lives, as well as studies of men. As Cain (1990: 12) states, criminology must take on board the question of 'what in the social construction of maleness is so profoundly criminogenic: why do males so disproportionately turn out to be criminals?'

Postmodern feminism

Of all of the feminism under discussion here it is perhaps fair to say that as yet postmodern feminism has had relatively little impact on criminology. Put rather simply, postmodern feminism celebrates difference. It is a position that is concerned to address the positive side of being the 'other', that is, outside mainstream thinking and concerns. This 'otherness' for postmodern feminism represents openness, plurality, diversity and difference and it is an emphasis that renders problematic any uncritical or universalizing use of the category 'women' or 'men' to denote all women or all men. In criminological terms, postmodernism attempts to give voice to those silenced by the discourses of modernism.

In order to do this within criminology, Alison Young (1992) argues that it is necessary to appreciate the power of criminology's 'semantic rectangle'. This reveals that the structure of the discipline of criminology is imbued with assumptions around two oppositional pairs: normal/criminal and male/female. These pairs subjugate the normal to the criminal, the male criminal to the female criminal, the female criminal to the criminal, the normal to the male criminal and so on. Thus, when the category 'criminal' is paired with the category 'male criminal' they are almost indistinguishable within criminology; and when the category 'female criminal' is paired with the category 'normal', normality is subjugated. As Young states: 'Woman is always criminal, always deviant, always censured. This condition is utterly normal' (A. Young 1992: 76).

So postmodern feminism demands that we go beyond the transgressive requirements of Cain. It demands not that we deny racism or sexual violence, but that we deny the view that the intellectual per se can devise any answers to these problems. This shakes not only the conceptual foundations on which criminology is based, but also its assumed relevance and ability to produce knowledge or truth on which to make policy claims. This renders the notion of traditional empirical work and any associated policy agenda very problematic for postmodernism. As a consequence, while this work has generated a highly provocative critique of criminology (see, for example, A. Young 1992) it has generated little generalizable empirical knowledge. Indeed, such a product stands in contradiction to the postmodernist project.

The resistance found to postmodernist ideas within criminology does not mean that such ideas in general have not been influential in encouraging the reconsideration of the relationship between the social scientific search for knowledge and the claims that can be attached to such knowledge. It is clear that giving voice to diversity is an explicit concern of the agendas of both Carlen and Cain, for example. Giving voice to that diversity has led not only to the reconsideration of the way in which feminism in general has presumed that the category 'woman' represents Women, but also to a re-examination of what is implied by the category 'man' and the way in which this has been used to delineate all men. The blossoming literature on masculinity/masculinities stands testimony to this. However, before considering the value of that literature to criminology, it will be useful to offer some assessment on the state of the relationship between the feminism outlined here and criminological knowledge.

Feminisms and criminology: contradictions in terms?

The extent to which it might be possible to argue that feminism(s) and criminology constitute contradictions in terms depends to a certain extent on which of the feminisms is being discussed. Certainly liberal feminism with its concern to practice good science and to address discriminatory practices sits most comfortably with mainstream criminological concerns. In this brand of feminism, the commitment to the central problems of criminology remains unchallenged; what criminology needs is more accurate knowledge about who commits crime and why. Radical feminism, contrariwise, sits much less comfortably with mainstream criminological concerns; indeed, radical feminist work that has relevance for criminology has largely emerged outside of the criminological domain, although its importance for criminology lies in its concern to address men and their behaviour towards women. So the tensions that exist between this brand of feminism and criminology are largely dependent on whether or not 'men' as men are considered the central concern of the criminological agenda.

Socialist feminism, however, takes us beyond a concern with just men and women towards addressing the ways in which a range of structural variables interact with one another to both enable and constrain the behaviours of men and women. Here again the tension with criminology lies not so much with the subject matter of crime itself but with how the exploration of that subject matter might be best conceived.

Postmodern feminism poses the most fundamental challenge for criminology. The strains within postmodernism against any universal explanations towards contextualizing and specifying the differences between people render the criminological implication in the policymaking process highly problematic indeed. These kinds of question become ever more pertinent in an increasingly diverse social world; ethnically, culturally, socially etc. that lends even greater weight to the expression by bell hooks (1999), 'Ain't I a Woman too'. This expression points to the increasing problematic of looking to the law (a universal response) as a means of fixing social/criminological problems (an individual circumstance).

So each of these feminisms poses different questions for criminology and genders criminology in quite different ways. More recently criminology has, arguably as a result of the work of both radical and socialist feminism, attempted to place men and masculinity more squarely on the criminological agenda. Before considering the extent to which the developments in criminological theory have or have not been influenced by the question of gender, we shall offer a brief overview of the differing ways in which the question of masculinity has been addressed and how that has been manifested within criminology.

Ways of thinking about men within criminology

Men certainly have not been absent from criminological thinking. Indeed, the activities of young, urban males have preoccupied criminologists since the delinquency studies of the 1940s and 1950s. What criminologists have paid little attention to, however, are the potentially different ways in which the behaviour of young, urban males might be informed by their understanding of themselves as men; or indeed, how criminological analyses might be better understood as a reflection of male understandings about crime. Here we shall offer a brief overview of how those understandings have become deeply embedded in the criminological literature.

Tolson (1977) explored the different ways in which dominant forms of thinking about masculinity constrained different men in different ways. In some ways, Tolson's work constituted a central moment in setting the further development of the exploration of masculinity. His work posed two key questions for that debate. Is there one overarching form of masculinity or are there many diverse masculinities? Is masculinity best understood as a product of sex role development or gender relations? These two questions clearly underpinned the debate on masculinity that ensued during the 1990s. Each of them informs the summary that follows.

Sex role theory and criminology

The concept of role is central to social psychology and some versions of sociology. As a concept it is used as a way of organizing people's behaviour into a meaningful whole. It acts as a mechanism for understanding the ways in which social expectations, actions and behaviour reflect stereotypical assumptions about behavioural expectations – that is, what should be done, by whom and under what circumstances. In the context of understanding gender relations, this leads to the identification of male roles and female roles. These roles are presumed to outline the appropriate behavioural sets and associated expectations for men and women (male(s) and female(s)). Sex role theory takes as a given the biological origins that define the differences between males and females. These biological origins constitute the raw material on to which specific behavioural sets, called sex roles, are painted through the process of socialization. As a theory, then, it is rooted in essentially *biological* assumptions concerning what count as the *defining* characteristics of being male and female. In the criminological context, the work of both Sutherland (1947) and Parsons (1937) embraced sex role theory. Indeed, these two writers have wielded a particular influence on criminology's grasp of the maleness of the crime problem, so we shall examine briefly the work of each of them in turn.

Sutherland's key premise was that criminal behaviour was learned behaviour like any other. Moreover, he argued that people learned criminal behaviour when exposed to an 'excess of definitions' favouring deviant as opposed to conventional (or rule-abiding) behaviour. This view of criminal behaviour focused on the importance of not only the socialization process in learning crime but also the values attached to the behaviour learned, meaning that it is not just a matter of whom the individual associates with but also the kinds of meaning those associations provide for the individual with respect to engaging in criminal behaviour. So an individual may know how to act criminally, but may not do so in the absence of the values, motives, attitudes and so on, which support such behaviour. The more an individual is exposed to such support, the more likely it is that that individual will share in that behaviour. For Sutherland, then, criminal behaviour was learned behaviour like any other behavioural response rather than being the product of some innate atavistic or degenerative drive.

Within this general framework, Sutherland commented that boys were more likely to become delinquent than girls. This, he suggested, happened for two reasons. First, boys are less strictly controlled by the socialization process in general than girls. Second, in that process they are taught to be tough, aggressive, active risk seekers, all characteristics that Sutherland considered to be the prerequisites for involvement in the criminal world. These two factors, taken together, mean that boys are more frequently exposed to the kinds of learning situation in which criminality becomes a possibility. This happens despite the fact that in other respects both boys and girls may be growing up together in the same economically deprived neighbourhoods – a view that clearly indicates that there is something more to be understood about boys' involvement in the criminal world than can be explained by reference to socioeconomic factors alone.

Sutherland labelled this general theory of criminality 'differential association'. When it is applied generally to an understanding of criminal behaviour, it can be seen to offer a framework substantially different in some respects than that proposed by the biological positivists. However, when applied specifically to understanding the differences between male and female involvement in delinquent behaviour there are a number of issues that this theory treats as being unproblematic.

As a theory it is rooted in the presumption of sex role theory and thereby a notion of biological difference. Being rooted in this way, it implicitly accepts that biological difference constitutes part of the explanation for any observed behavioural differences, despite the foregrounding of the importance of the socialization process. It must be remembered that in sex role theory the socialization process only provides the mechanism through which specific learning takes place. In other words, the fact that girls, not boys, get pregnant constitutes the basis for explaining both their different experience of the socialization process and their subsequent different rate of criminality. This is particularly evident in that work influenced by functionalism. Indeed, the work of Parsons added a further dimension to this way of thinking about the relationship between sex differences, the socialization process and the maleness of criminal behaviour.

The functionalist sociology of Talcott Parsons placed the family at the centre of the social learning associated with sex roles. In the family children learn that the expressive role, the role associated with nurturing, caring and keeping the family together, is what women do; the instrumental role, that concerned with achievement, goal attainment and breadwinning, is what men do. In the work of Parsons, these roles provide for the stability of society from one generation to the next. Moreover, society in general and the family in particular are presumed to operate most effectively in this form. This presumption is made on the basis of the fact that because women have the reproductive capacity to bear children they are deemed to be best suited for the expressive role, a role which is denied to men and which young men experience as being denied to them.

The process of learning these sex roles poses different problems for boys than for girls. Exposed to feminine care, girls have little difficulty in finding appropriate role models for themselves. Boys, by the same token, do not have a readily and routinely available male model to follow. Exposed to the female model as young children, they quickly learn that the feminine role model is not one for which they will be accepted as men. Parsons argues, therefore, that boys engage in what he calls 'compensatory compulsory masculinity'. In other words, boys reject any behaviour seen to be feminine. So tenderness, gentleness and the expression of emotion are rejected because they are not seen to be masculine. In their place, boys pursue that which they observe to be masculine: being powerful, tough, and rough. The pursuit of these masculine characteristics is engaged in vigorously, in order to avoid any doubt being cast on the boys' sense of themselves as men or being recognized by others as men. This pursuit of masculinity, and its approved forms of expression, results in boys engaging in antisocial behaviour much more often than girls. It is this greater likelihood to engage in antisocial behaviour that is subsequently related to their greater delinquency.

The work of Albert Cohen (1955) draws together the work of both Sutherland and Parsons and was very influential in the development of delinquency studies during the 1950s and 1960s. Following Parsons, Cohen viewed the process of socialization in the home as neither a smooth nor an easy process for boys. He accepted the view that the lack of a readily available masculine role in the home, alongside the availability of a feminine role associated with nurturing, raised anxious questions for boys. Given that the nurturing role in the domestic context is so readily identified with that which is 'good', boys are left unsure as to how to be good yet not be seen to be feminine. The resultant anxiety generated by this for boys is, according to Cohen, resolved in the street gang. Here the assertion of power through physical prowess rather than negotiation, the taking of risks rather than keeping safe, and the thrill and excitement of breaking the rules rather than accepting them all provide not only the avenues and the motivation for delinquent behaviour but also an expression of themselves as young *men*.

Cohen, however, did not really pursue his analysis of delinquency along these lines. He rather presumed that delinquency was primarily a working-class phenomenon. So his explanation of delinquent behaviour ultimately downgrades what he has to say about masculinity in favour of upgrading the emphasis on class and class conflict. For Cohen, the delinquent subculture is seen to be a consequence of a working-class collective response to the shared experience of being judged by middle-class values and the frustration that results from this. This does not mean that Cohen did not recognize other possible motivations for delinquent behaviour; he did. For example, he viewed female delinquency primarily in terms of the expression of deviant sexuality; and he viewed middle-class delinquent behaviour primarily in terms of 'drag racing' or 'joyriding' (in the 1950s' American sense of the term). Cohen saw this latter type of delinquent behaviour as masculine protest against female authority.

Connell (1987) gives three reasons why sex role theory in general constitutes an attractive starting point for explanations concerned with gender and gender difference. First, sex role theory presumes to move us beyond biology as a way of explaining sex differences in behaviour. As an approach it replaces biology with learned social expectations. Second, role theory in general, and sex role theory in particular, provides a mechanism whereby an understanding of the impact of social structure can be inserted into an understanding of individual personality. The process of socialization is obviously crucial in this and this facilitates a way of thinking about the contribution made by different kinds of institutions in mediating the effects of structure on individuals. Third, given the emphasis on the socialization process, role theory offers a politics of change. If men and women are what they are because of the oppressive experience and impact of the socialization process, then if this process can be changed, so can men and women.

As Connell argues, these virtues are substantial. There is, however, a central difficulty contained within them. This difficulty has been alluded to already in our discussion of the way in which sex role theory has been applied within criminology; that is, the difficulty highlighted by the fundamental resilience of the biological category of sex. Connell expresses this problem in this way:

> The very terms 'female role' and 'male role', hitching a biological term to a dramaturgical one, suggest what is going on. . . . With sex roles, the underlying biological dichotomy seems to have persuaded many theorists that there is no power relationship here at all. The 'female role' and the 'male role' are tacitly treated as equal.
>
> (Connell 1987: 50–1)

This tacit treatment of the sex roles as if they were equal has the effect of drawing attention away from analysing social reality in terms of power relationships. It also implies a concern with what should be the case as opposed to how people genuinely experience that social reality. In other words, it is a way of thinking about masculinity (and femininity) that cannot capture its fragile, tentative, and negotiated character.

So while sex role theory has had some influence on criminological thinking in some attempts to explain the maleness of crime, that influence has been limited. This limit is manifested not only by the failure of criminology and criminologists to reflect on its value (the downgrading of class over gender, for example), but also by the limitations inherent within the theoretical framework of sex role theory itself. Such limitations, as already highlighted, point to the need for a theoretical framework that can at least encompass an understanding of the power basis to gender relations.

It is in developing an understanding of masculinity in this respect that the influence of both radical and socialist feminism cited earlier can be found.

Categorical theory and criminology

Categorical theory (a label used by Connell 1987) refers to a range of theoretical perspectives, emanating primarily from the feminist movement, which promote an understanding of gender relations by reference to two opposing categories: men and women. Understanding gender relations in these terms identifies both a theory and a politics for action. The categories, men and women, constitute both the units of analysis in which to understand gender relations and the source of explanation for those relations. As was commented on earlier, the key concepts here are patriarchy, domination, oppression and exploitation. Within this conceptual apparatus men are deemed the powerful and women are deemed the other. Under this heading, it is possible to group the potential influence of a range of feminist perspectives from radical feminism and socialist feminism to cultural feminism.

In criminology, this kind of categorical analysis has had its most profound effect in the study of sexual violence. The compelling evidence for thinking about sexual violence in terms of power relations and particularly in terms of the power that men wield over women has been well argued by radical feminists in particular. The notion that all men keep all women in a state of fear was revolutionary not only in its public, personal and political implications but also in the avenue it provided for recognizing a further dimension to the maleness of the crime problem.

It must be remembered that sexual violence is not exclusively a male activity and the victims of sexual violence are not exclusively female. Nevertheless an ungendered understanding of sexual violence would only be a partial one and a criminology that failed to acknowledge the nature and extent of sexual violence would be incomplete. However, an analysis of sexual violence couched in categorical terms is severely limited as a way both of understanding the nature and extent of that violence and as a way of understanding the expression of either masculinity or of femininity. This occurs for two reasons.

First, a concern with the category 'man' produces statements that characterize the behaviour of typical men. In this context, this process equates the category 'man' with the potential for sexual violence. Hence the statement: 'All men are potential rapists.' Such a process does a disservice to any individual experience of being male and/or being female. As Connell states, it presents a 'false universalism' that does not resonate with lived social reality. In one sense, then, it could be said that categorical analysis takes us little further, theoretically, than sex role theory.

Second, a focus on the category 'man' equates that category with masculinity. This equation presumes that there is one universal form of masculinity (or, by way of contrast, femininity) that is static. In one sense, of course, this tendency towards universalism and quiescence in understanding gender relations present in radical versions of feminism was designed as much to serve political purposes as it was to serve theories of gender relations. However, it is the theoretical implications of these ideas that are of prime concern here.

These limitations, taken together, should not serve to undermine the profound importance that feminist work, which has been loosely identified here as categorical, has had on our understanding of the nature of gender relations in general and the expression of masculinity in particular. Without this work it would not have been possible for theorists to recognize the need to connect the emphasis on patriarchally rooted power relations with both individually and collectively negotiated identities of masculinity and femininity. But in a sense the question left unanswered by feminist work is the same as that posed by Brittain (1989).

Brittain (1989) identified the problem of trying to understand the relationship between masculinism, the ideology which supports male dominance, and masculinity(ies), the individually negotiated and fragile identities constructed by men. This is the gap left by feminist work in this area which Connell (1987) and Messerschmidt (1993) have attempted to bridge, the latter especially in the particular context of understanding crime.

Doing gender as criminology

In some respects the problem of 'doing gender' is the problem of understanding how any social action is constituted; how to find the balance between the impact of social structure and the choice of social action. In general sociological theory, the work of Giddens (1984) has been particularly significant in finding a way to avoid the determinism inherent in a structuralist position, on the one hand, and the voluntarism inherent in a position which gives primacy to freedom of choice, on the other. His work encourages us to think about the ways in which structure is constituted, reconstituted and changed by human actors through their everyday activities. These processes, which apply to the general construction of social action, also apply to the way in which gender relations are negotiated. The theoretical question to answer, then, to paraphrase Connell (1987), is how gender is organized as an ongoing concern.

Messerschmidt (1993), developing the work of Connell and influenced by Giddens, has offered one way of thinking about how gender is accomplished in the context of criminal behaviour. This analysis endeavours to identify the way in which expression of masculinities constitutes a continuous thread in criminal behaviour, from the use of violence in the street to involvement in white-collar crime. He suggests that there are three specific social structures underpinning gender relations from which such a continuity can be derived: the gender division of labour, the gender relations of power and sexuality. None of these is a constant entity. Their specific form varies through time and space but, taken together, they define the conditions under which gender identities are constructed. In other words, these structures define the conditions under which expressions of masculinity and femininity are constructed. Connell (1987) has coined this as 'hegemonic masculinity'. Jefferson (2006) defines 'hegemonic masculinity' in the following way: 'The set of ideas, values, representations and practices associated with "being male" which is commonly accepted as the dominant position in gender relations in a society at a particular historical moment' (Jefferson 2006: 199).

What does this mean?

Hegemony is a term borrowed from Gramsci referring to the way in which one class or group can dominate a society by consent. According to Connell (1987), in the expressions of masculinity to be found in late modern societies, those males who give expression to normative heterosexuality possess hegemonic power. This is achieved in the three domains of gender relations identified earlier in different but related ways. So, for example, it is found in the dominant notion of the male as the breadwinner (from the gender division of labour). It is found in the definition of homosexuality but not lesbianism as a crime (from the gender relations of power). Finally, it is found in the objectification of heterosexual women in the media (from the arena of sexuality).

Normative heterosexuality is that form of masculinity that is valued in all aspects of social life (as suggested by the examples offered here). In being so valued, it defines both the structure and the form of the struggle of any individual man to live up to the power of its expectations. At the same time it structures the lives of those who fail, or choose not to engage in such a struggle. As Messerschmidt (1993: 76) states: 'It defines masculinity through difference from, and desire for, women.' It also defines the kinds of possibility available for variations in masculinity.

So, if this version of masculinity (normative, white, heterosexual masculinity) possesses hegemonic power then it follows that it serves not only to provide individual men with a sense of themselves as more of a man or less of a man, but also to downgrade other versions of masculinity – homosexuality, for example – as well as downgrading femininity. Normative heterosexuality gives credence to a hierarchical structure that underpins the sense we have of ourselves as gendered subjects while simultaneously permitting an array of expressed masculinities and femininities. Such variations from the normative offer templates for individual action, which are differentially valued and differently expressed in relation to normative heterosexuality for both men and women. In this sense, as Messerschmidt (1993: 79) states, 'gender is an accomplishment', something we are all required to work at, and to provide some account of, in our relationships with others. In this sense, work within criminology rapidly moved on from a concern with hegemonic masculinity, as a unitary and unifying form, but with the masculinities 'variable sets of ideas, values, representations and practices associated with "being male" ' (Jefferson 2006: 245). From this starting point in understanding gender relations, Messerschmidt (1993) goes on to offer one of the most thoroughgoing descriptive accounts of the relationship between masculinities and crime, which we shall discuss briefly here.

'Research', according to Messerschmidt (1993: 119), 'reveals that men construct masculinities in accord with their position in social structures and therefore their access to power and resources'. This leads him to analyse a variety of social contexts in which differential access to power and resources produces differently emphasized constructions of masculinity. In the context of crime this results in the consideration of three key locations: the street, the workplace and the home. In each of these locations, Messerschmidt provides a detailed account of the variety of ways in which masculinity is expressed – the pimp on the street, the sharp business practice of the rising white-collar executive and various kinds of violence in the home. All these accounts are offered as a means of demonstrating the ways in which men display their manliness to others and to themselves. So while the business executive might use his position and power to sexually harass his female secretary in perhaps more subtle ways than the pimp controls his women, the effects are the same. In this particular example, the women concerned are subjugated and the men concerned are affirmed as normatively heterosexual men.

In his later work, Messerschmidt (1997) became much more concerned with not only how the lens of masculinities might provide us with a better picture of lawbreaking behaviour but also how class and ethnicity might differently focus that lens. Building on his own earlier work as well as that of Connell and Giddens, he states that:

> Specific forms of gender, race and class are available, encouraged, and permitted, depending on one's position in these social relations. . . . Accordingly, gender, race and class, must be viewed as *structured action* – what people do under specific social structural constraints.
>
> (Messerschmidt 1997: 6)

This is his way of recognizing the question of difference. In other words, people routinely enact and re-enact social structures in their everyday activities – activities that are mediated by a number of different socio-structural variables only one of which will be gender. They 'do' class and ethnicity as well. In this way this later work attempts to accommodate difference. As Connell (1997: 64) has argued, hegemonic masculinity is contested and in that contest groups of less dominant men (along with women) carry the burden for those men who benefit from the contest so: 'Gay men are systematically made targets of prejudice and violence. Effeminate and wimpish men are constantly put down. Black men in the

United States (as in South Africa) suffer massively higher levels of lethal violence than white men.' This emphasis on difference or masculinities has led to further work on masculine identity that draws on biographical studies and psychoanalysis.

Biography and the psychoanalytical turn

One source of interest in the relevance of psychoanalytical concepts in understanding crime and the experience of crime has been developed within the 'fear of crime' debate. In this context, Hollway and Jefferson (1997, 2000) have been particularly influential in developing the concept of anxiety. The particular problematic in this context was to make sense of the disparity between the risk of crime and the fear of crime, especially for young men, by placing that conundrum within a psychoanalytical frame of reference. However, the psychoanalytical focus within understandings of lawbreaking behaviour has been much more concerned to use the notion of the 'masculine defended subject' (Jefferson 1994) to facilitate an understanding of men's recourse to the use of violence. Gadd (2000: 431) defends this recourse to psychoanalysis as follows: 'By articulating the many emotional truths of men's "experience" we expose the disparity between what violent men feel, say and do, the interface of men's *psychic investment* in *social discourses* and *practices*' (emphasis in original). Exploring individual biographies through the use of the 'narrative interview method' (Hollway and Jefferson 1997) is the means through which these disparities are to be made visible. The concern to focus on men's 'psychic investment' is also pivotal to Jefferson's work on Mike Tyson (see, inter alia, Jefferson 1997, 1998).

However, this psychoanalytical turn within criminology is not without its critics. Hood-Williams, for example, has this to say:

> The psychic processes that psychoanalysis so cutely describes – projection, introjection, identification, cathexis, parapraxes, unconscious incorporation – are not, not one of them, 'gendered'. They are simply processes. They are certainly invested – cathected to – ideas about what it means for the subject to be a woman/man, but masculinity and femininity are what the psyche deals with. It is not what psyches are. This means recognising that masculinity must be understood phenomenologically, that is not the exclusive property of men, that it has no essential underpinning in sex nor in the intrinsic character of what is to count as masculine.
>
> (Hood-Williams 2001: 53)

This potentially damming critique is rescued by the recognition that the kind of work referred to here has forced a consideration of the subtly nuanced expression given to both masculinity and femininity in different contexts. Indeed, in a different way and suggesting a somewhat different agenda, Goodey (2000) develops a cogent argument for a return to biographical studies within criminology. These studies, however, would be concerned with 'epiphany', significant turning points in the lives of individuals that propelled them into crime against the structural backcloth of hegemonic masculinity. As Hood-Williams (2001: 44) remarks: 'The question remains, however, why it is that only a minority of men need to produce masculinity through crime rather than through other, non-criminal means?' It is at this juncture that it will be useful to develop a sense of the emerging critique of this masculinity-aware criminology.

Reflections on masculinity and criminology

It must be remembered that much of the work discussed over the last few pages is still, for the most part, on the edges of criminological theorizing and empirical investigation. The reasons for this are to do with the intransigence of the traditional concerns of criminology, on the one hand, and the (potential) inherent limitations of this kind of gendered work, on the other. These limitations are twofold in character and in order to explore these limitations we shall revisit some of the issues addressed earlier in this chapter.

First, while all men might be potential rapists (the radical feminist assertion), not all men do rape. Why they choose to rape, or not, can only be understood in part by reference to the available, socially acceptable styles of masculine expression. Another part of the explanation for their choice must lie with understanding the contribution of motivations such as desire, pleasure, risk seeking and so on. Raising concepts such as these may, of course, take us down the highly individualistic route of psychoanalysis; but they might also lead us to reconceptualize our understandings of criminality in terms of what Katz (1988) calls 'the seductions of crime'. As Jefferson (1993) argues, unless we understand the pleasures of crime as well as the opportunities for crime, we shall never really have a complete picture of criminal behaviour. So there may be some value in situating our understanding of motivations such as these within the framework of hegemonic masculinity: but to what extent and within what theoretical framework? As Hood-Williams (2001) comments, the defence mechanisms alluded to by those adopting the psychoanalytical frame of reference are not in themselves gendered. So what are these researchers tapping? It is his view that they are grasping a sense of the 'performative' aspects of masculinity, not the psychic aspects. He goes on to suggest that the puzzles this work leaves criminology with may lead to the erosion of the terms 'masculine' and 'feminine', in and of themselves. This kind of observation leads to a second different but related concern.

There is a tendency within some of the literature that centralizes a concern with masculinity to seek to explain all kinds of criminal behaviour by reference to that masculinity – from state terrorism to joyriding. This tendency runs the risk of being tautological and reflects the underpinning desire of many criminologists and criminologies to produce a universal explanation of crime. This desire betrays the discipline's inherent commitment to the modernist as opposed to the postmodernist project and its wish to generate a meaningful policy agenda implied by that commitment. It also betrays the discipline's inherent heterosexism. This kind of critical analysis of the discipline and some of its contemporary concerns is fully explored by Collier (1998). A third, though related, theoretical problem is pointed to by MacInnes (2004). He observes that the concern with identity (of which masculinity is one facet) has resulted in a social science that is both over-socialized and over-individualized all at the same time. As a result concepts like, masculinity, femininity, and gender come to mean everything and nothing and, consequently, may offer us a means of social comment but not social (or criminological) analysis.

Fourth, there is a political concern. At one level there has been much to commend to feminist interventions in the academic and policy arena. However, as MacInnes (1998) has argued, there may now be drawbacks to the focus on the 'personal is political' strategy, some of which are evident in the criminological concerns addressed in the latter half of this chapter. His concern is to 'reassert what politics is properly about: the collective struggle against material exploitation and inequality to achieve equal public rights for private citizens, using the sort of material which classic sociology provides' (MacInnes 1998: 136). The extent to which contemporary criminology reflects this kind of concern is the central theme of the two chapters that follow.

Summary: gendering the criminal or gendering criminology?

From the thematic overview presented here it is fair to say that in various ways criminology has both implicitly and explicitly addressed the question of sex and crime. In other words, there has been a tradition of work concerned to examine the differences between male and female offending behaviour, their experiences of the criminal justice system and to invoke the importance of sex as a variable in explaining those differences. Indeed, early feminist work gave a significant impetus to studies addressing those concerns. There has been less work generated – with the notable exception of the work of Carlen, Cain, Eaton and Worrall – within a theoretical framework that explicitly deals with the question of gender as it impacts both women and men.

Gender has remained implicit to criminology rather than explicitly explored by it. As Jefferson (1993) has argued, the view has been sustained that crime was men's work (and not women's) and that central criminological assumption has not been adequately explored. This raises the question not whether the criminal is gendered or not, but the extent to which criminology has, or can be, gendered or not.

Scraton (1990) observes that there is a 'pervasiveness of hegemonic masculinity' within the discipline, 'found covertly in the academic discourses which prevail within malestream criminology'. This statement sensitizes us to understanding the discipline not just as one peopled and dominated by men, but as one in which in the very fabric of its structure has taken as given views of men, women and crime. This has its origins in what Eagle-Russett (1989) has called the nineteenth-century 'sexual science' that laid the foundations for subsequent images of men and women. Those images have, according to Naffine (1987), associated female crime with activities surrounding sexuality and what is considered to be the normal expression of sexuality. They are images that have also most readily associated men with criminal activity. As Naffine has stated:

> Feminist theory is likely to dismantle the longstanding dichotomy of the devilish and daring criminal man and the unappealing inert conforming woman. The threat it poses to a masculine criminology is therefore considerable.
>
> (Naffine 1987: 133)

The threat is still there. Criminology has, as yet, done little to dismantle it. As Gelsthorpe (2002: 136) observes: 'Feminism may not now be "the great unspoken" in criminology, but in certain quarters it remains "the great unheard".' So while the criminal and criminal activity may well be gendered, criminology has yet to be. However, another issue remains: what primacy should we give gender?

In responding to critical review of their seminal work *Mean Streets* (1997), Hagan and McCarthy say:

> [W]e also assumed gender would play a more important role than it did. Together these findings suggest that we need to give more thought to the ways that gender's relationship with crime is conditioned and mediated by background and foreground variables.
>
> (Hagan and McCarthy 2000: 235)

Messerschmidt makes the same point:

> Gender, race and class are not absolutes and are not equally significant in every social setting where crime is realised. That is, depending on the social setting, accountability to certain categories is more salient than accountability to other categories.
>
> (Messerschmidt 1997: 113)

The work reported on by Walklate and Evans (1999) would make the same point about the mediating effect of community. The different ways in which researchers have endeavoured to conceptualize the sex/gender issue has been well summarized by Daly (1997). The point is well made, however. The complex ways in which different variables may interact with each other both in determining structural conditions for action and biographical responses of action demand critical reflection and examination.

By implication, this means exploring femininities as well as masculinities. It means exploring whiteness as well as 'blackness'. It means exploring class. It means exploring different sexualities and challenging normative heterosexuality (Collier 1998). It means exploring the real world as opposed to just the discursive one. Such a process may call into question all kinds of knowledge claim, including those made by feminists, and will certainly call into question any policy process that assumes that what works in one setting may work in another.

Conclusion

This chapter has explored the different ways in which assumptions concerning the concept of gender have been more or less visible within the criminological enterprise. Criminology, of course, has no special status in the way in which it has rendered questions of gender invisible. Such invisibility is, arguably, deeply rooted in conceptions of what counts as knowledge and who can know things – processes which all the social (and natural) sciences have been subjected to (Harding 1991). The question remains, however, as to how much there is to be learned about crime, its causation and the processes of criminalization, by rendering the question of gender more explicit.

It is clear that much has been learned concerning the locus of criminal behaviour, how it is manifested and by whom, from that feminist work that has exposed the nature and extent of broadly defined sexual violence against women and children. It is also clear that recasting an understanding of that kind of criminal behaviour in terms of masculinity has provided an increasingly perceptive insight into some aspects of its underlying 'causal' processes (see, for example, the work of Scully 1990, on convicted rapists). The question remains, however, the inherent hegemonic masculinity of the discipline notwithstanding, as to how and under what circumstances gender is the prevailing or key explanatory variable. Put more simply, is the opportunist burglar expressing his manhood or something else? As I have asked elsewhere: 'A gendered lens certainly helps us see some features of the crime problem more clearly perhaps; but under what circumstances is that clarity made brighter by gender or distorted by it?' (Walklate 1995: 192). If mainstream (malestream) criminology is to be persuaded to meet the challenge which much of this work on gender constitutes for it, then that work itself needs to consider its own assumptions in a reflexive and self-critical manner.

As was demonstrated within the critical evaluation offered of left realism, it is simply not enough to assert that questions of gender have been embraced or that it is through a gendered lens that a solution to the causation of crime may be found. These assertions do not in and of themselves equip us with the understanding of what underpins the circumstances in which gender matters more than any other variable and those circumstances in which it does not. Put another way by Jefferson (2006: 247) the questions remain whether masculinity is a necessary condition to explain a particular crime and 'whether it is *sufficient* as an explanation of *any* crime'.

Further reading

One way of mapping the changing nature of the way in which questions of gender have been addressed or not addressed within criminology would be to compare and contrast Heidensohn (1996) with Walklate (2004). Each provides a usefully different overview of the kinds of gendered question criminology might address. Those wishing to explore in greater detail the relationship between masculinity and crime will find Messerschmidt (1993, 1997) invaluable. For a different kind of critique of the criminological enterprise from a gendered perspective, Collier (1998) is a good choice. For a more North American feel to how these issues are addressed by criminology, see Morash (2005).

chapter six

Crime, politics and welfare

Understanding the welfare state
Why it is important to understand the relationship between the citizen and the state
New Labour, new policies? Young people and crime
Young people, crime and antisocial behaviour
Conclusion: questions for criminology
Further reading

So far this text has evidenced some of the key theoretical developments that have occurred in criminology over the last two decades. In the course of reviewing those theoretical strands, it has been shown that it is possible to forge different links between them and the world of politics. In other words, as theories, they may lend themselves to different uses and interpretations by those occupying the political domain. The question remains, however, as to what kind of relationship might exist between events in the political domain and the formation of an agenda for criminology. In this chapter, then, we shall be concerned to contextualize the possibilities for a criminological agenda by mapping the interconnections between criminology, criminal justice and social justice. But why make these connections?

Principles of social justice are fundamental to the organization of any society. An appreciation of the way in which any particular society believes rewards and punishments should be distributed reveals much about the fundamental (taken-for-granted) features of that society. Moreover, there are different ways in which such an appreciation might be developed. However, as Cook (2006: 30) cogently argues the relationship between criminal justice and social justice in fostering social inclusion or exclusion (mainly contemporarily exclusion) is crucial for four reasons. First, the criminal justice system by definition, renders the 'deviant' as the 'other', that is outside of the processes of inclusion. Second, much antisocial behaviour, (and it must be noted that such behaviour is not necessarily criminal), is resulting in the exclusion of increasing numbers of young people, as we shall go on to discuss in the rest of this chapter. Third, the ultimate punishment of the criminal justice system (prison) is in and of itself exclusionary. Fourth, those who are punished in this way are subjected to further exclusion in the problems that they face in reconstructing their lives after prison. So how the criminal justice system operates sends very important messages about social justice as well as real implications for the realm of social policy that might be concerned with social justice. In this chapter, in order to engage in an analysis of this kind we shall address the issue of social justice through three interlinked issues: first, the changing nature of what has been understood as the 'welfare state'; second, the ways in which that changing conception of welfare might facilitate an understanding of the criminalization process; and, third, the outcome of that process for questions relating to young people and crime.

Understanding the welfare state

As has already been indicated, the way in which any society organizes its social policies presupposes some notion of how the rewards and punishments in that society are to be distributed. In the UK, political views concerning the appropriateness of the distribution of such rewards and punishments have arguably changed in emphasis over a remarkably short period of time. That change has been encapsulated, some would say, in the creation of the citizen as consumer (Edgar 1991). Whatever terms are used to articulate the way in which the distributive process of welfare works, the principles on which it rests are underpinned by the notions of needs, rights and social justice and the role that the state might play in meeting these for its citizens. The concepts of needs, rights and social justice have been enjoined in different ways since the end of the Second World War and so our analysis will begin with the post-war era.

The Beveridge reforms, implemented in the first years immediately following the Second World War, were intended to provide protection against the five great social ills: disease, squalor, ignorance, idleness and want. According to Marshall (1981, writing in 1948), those reforms, while embedded in and arguably consolidating earlier social policy legislation, marked a development in extending the nature of citizenship. That extension moved the rights of the citizen from the realm of the civil and political into the realm of the social. In other words, it was considered that being a full member of society entailed the right to live the life of a civilized human being according to the standards currently prevailing in that society.

The key to the extension of citizenship into this social realm was the introduction of an insurance-based benefits system. This, it was argued, constituted a clear extension of such social rights since by implication this system put into practice the idea of a contract between the individual (citizen) and the state. Put simply, if as an individual citizen you paid into the system, the state offered you some guarantees in return.

This contractual basis to the post-war reforms, however, did not extend to every citizen automatically. It always contained within it a notion of less eligibility. In other words, if individuals did not pay into the system they were less eligible for rewards from it. In practical terms, this meant being subjected to a system of means testing. So, arguably, the Beveridge proposals always excluded those who were seen to be 'undeserving'. In some respects, therefore, this legislative package built on and consolidated the historical distinction that had always been made between the 'deserving' and the 'undeserving' poor – a distinction pervading not only the social security legislation but also thinking within the criminal justice system. The latter effect is best illustrated in the underlying philosophy of the Criminal Injuries Compensation Board (now called the Criminal Injuries Compensation Authority).

It has been argued that the formation of the Criminal Injuries Compensation Board constituted the last brick of the welfare state to be cemented with the post-war principles of Beveridge (Mawby and Walklate 1994). It was the groundwork of Margery Fry, a key criminal justice campaigner of the 1950s, which largely influenced its formation in 1964. Fry's argument was constructed in this way. Since all taxpayers could be potential victims of violent crime, and since the state forbade its citizens to arm themselves as a means of protection against violent crime, when individual citizens became victims of violent crime and it could be demonstrated that they were the innocent party, the state should assume some responsibility for having failed to protect them. Within this argument, it is possible to identify two key principles of the welfare state: the contractual obligation between the citizen and the state and the notion of less eligibility.

This way of thinking about the relationship between the citizen and the state lasted until the 1970s. It was a view in which the citizen had social rights and the state had obligations to fulfil those rights provided that the contract between the citizen and the state had been fulfilled – in other words, provided that those rights were deserved. So, arguably, even within the Beveridge ideal not everyone was included as a full social citizen: the undeserving were always excluded from full social citizenship. As Cook (2006: 33) states: 'Contemporary images and assumptions about poverty and crime, and about criminal and social justice, tap into a rich historical vein. From the "dangerous classes" of the nineteenth century to the "underclass" of the late twentieth century, the poor have been portrayed as in essence criminogenic, posing a threat to both law and the social order.' Thus echoing our discussion of family, crime and the underclass in Chapter 3, this thread joins the conceptions of social justice of the 1950s with more contemporary interpretations. It is in understanding this 'historical vein' that it is possible to understand how it was that a change of emphasis in the relationship between the citizen and the state was made possible during the 1980s.

To summarize: while the notion that the 1950s represented a period of political and social consensus is somewhat problematic, it is clear that Macmillan's adage, 'You've never had it so good', conveyed a powerful symbolic message at a time when the end of rationing, the extension of educational opportunities, the building of council houses and the achievement of near full employment became significant and taken-for-granted features of people's everyday lives. Crime itself, the caveats concerning the use of official statistics as a reliable indicator of crime rates notwithstanding, had declined from a post-war peak by 1955 (Wootton 1959), although recorded crime began to rise sharply again at the end of the decade, especially violent crime (Morris 1987; Rock 1990), with adolescents being increasingly identified as 'trouble'. Arguably, however, it really was not until the early 1970s that this sense of general comfort, associated with the 1950s (with some underlying tensions evident in relation to young people), began to be undermined.

The Labour government of the early 1970s presided over high rates of inflation that set the economic framework in which changes in public policy were likely to take place. Moreover, by the time the international recession of the mid-1970s began to take effect, the scene was set for a change in political climate as well as a consequent change in social policy and what was considered to be the appropriate relationship between the citizen and the state. Public expenditure was seen to be at the heart of the economic difficulties being experienced and the plan for reducing the rate of inflation by restoring incentives included removing what Margaret Thatcher referred to as the 'nanny state'. In 1977 she wrote:

> The sense of being self reliant, of playing a role within the family, of owning one's property, of paying one's way, [is] all part of the spiritual ballast which maintains responsible citizenship and a solid foundation from which people look around to see what more they can do for others and themselves.
>
> (Thatcher 1977: 97)

In this statement lies the embryo of the political ideas that were to change the direction of the relationship between the citizen and the state throughout the 1980s and early 1990s. These changes were also fuelled by the civil disturbances of 1981 and the concern that they generated (reiterated in the early 1990s) marks that continuing preoccupation with the undeserving; those dangerous classes who live in dangerous places. Those disturbances, while varied in their causes, marked the beginning of a decade in which the legitimacy of the criminal justice system was seriously tested. Indeed, it was within the criminal justice system, as well as in other areas of public policy, that the relationship between the citizen and state was given new expression.

Put simply, the change in direction in the relationship between the citizen and the state was primarily about reducing the obligations of the state to provide and increasing the obligations (as opposed to the rights) of the citizen to contribute to society and provide for themselves. Such a view was constituted within an overarching belief that giving a simultaneous free reign to market forces would increase competition, expand consumer choice and provide a way out of economic difficulties. For the individual, these expectations were encapsulated by 'active citizenship'. In other words, individual citizens no longer fulfilled their obligations to the state through the payment of their taxes or national insurance contributions. In these particular economic circumstances the welfare of the state, as opposed to the welfare of the individual, demanded more of them. In this case, the individual subjects of 'active citizenship' are the successful, enterprising, consuming, property-owning classes (the deserving) not those living on state benefits (the undeserving).

Again this view of citizenship, while evidenced in a range of policy initiatives, was clearly present within the world of the criminal justice system. It was perhaps found in its most definitive form in the massive growth of Neighbourhood Watch schemes (in which 'good' citizens become the 'eyes and ears' of the police), in the growth of Victim Support as a voluntary organization, in the increasing importance of the symbolism of the victim politically and in the generation of consumer charters and concerns with consumer satisfaction within policing. In all these developments, the poor in general (contemporarily more likely to be referred to as the socially excluded) are those most likely to be the objects of this active citizenship rather than its subjects simply because they do not possess the power to pay or make their claims count. Some would describe this as a re-articulation of the principle of less eligibility. Others would say that principle never disappeared.

The picture of this changing emphasis in citizen–state relationships is undoubtedly more complex than has been outlined here. It has been presented here as though it were a process that sustained historical divisions in a uniform fashion. However, as Lister has stated:

> The extent to which women and black people have always been the victims of exclusionary practices is all too often ignored by those who deplore today's retreat from supposedly universal rights. The point being that universal rights never existed in the first place.
>
> (Lister 1990: 27)

The rationale for such a view can be found in the extent to which in the formulation of the legislation of the late 1940s there are presumptions (understandable given the cultural and political norms of the time) concerning race and gender that have not been spelled out here. The Beveridge proposals worked with a notion of female dependency on a male breadwinner who was also implicitly white. Presumptions such as these, of course, (then as now), are always overlaid by issues of class and poverty.

Morris (1994), for example, has argued there is a strong historical continuity in those who find themselves defined as part of the 'dangerous classes'. In comparing Victorian England with the 1990s, she states:

> Dependency, then, as now, is largely explained as a defect of character, though there is also a fear that adequate provision for the poor could undermine the work incentive among lower paid workers. Even Marx, who saw poverty as an inevitable product of capitalism, with the poor as its helpless victims, identifies a depraved and decadent 'social scum'.
>
> (Morris 1994: 157)

Part of that historical continuity has also undoubtedly been the extent to which claimants on the state have never been free from moral condemnation and stigmatization and in this respect have always constituted part of that group excluded from full social citizenship from 1945 to the present day. Of course, in contemporary political terms it is much more usual to talk in terms of social inclusion and social exclusion with the policy emphasis on trying to include the excluded. These efforts are contemporarily referred to as the Third Way and given the increasing adoption of this approach throughout the European Community, it will be of value to say a little more about it at this juncture.

Giddens (1998: 66) lists the key components of the Third Way as being:

Equality
Protection of the vulnerable
Freedom as autonomy
No rights without responsibilities
No authority without democracy
Cosmopolitanism pluralism
Philosophic conservatism

These are grand goals and, as Cook (2006) observes, consist of politically useful vague and fuzzy concepts. Jordan (2005: 427) observes they reflect a 'liberal communitarian mix', the influence of which has been commented on elsewhere in this book, that appear to have a common appeal. However, as Jordan (2005: 428) goes on to comment: 'This raises fundamental issues about the role of government in general, and public services in particular, in the creation of a viable social order.' So how has this creation manifested itself in the Third Way especially in relation to social justice?

Cook (2006) points out that social justice, in this frame of reference, means equality of opportunity, (another continuity with the 1950s), along with social investment in children, education and skills. This social investment takes social inclusion as meaning the same as equality and social exclusion as being commensurate with inequality. In other words, (in)equality is not a systemic problem but an opportunity problem. This is a position that conflates economic and social issues. However, the policy possibilities that stem from this foster the 'restoring of order and disciplined personal behaviour' (Cook 2006: 72) especially, of course, for the socially excluded and as this chapter unfolds we shall see how this has manifested itself in particular in relation to young people. At this juncture, the question remains, however, why an understanding of this relationship between the citizen and the state should be of importance to criminology.

Why it is important to understand the relationship between the citizen and the state

A key question underpins the discussion so far: how much responsibility should we assume, collectively, for the most vulnerable in our society, however we might choose to define that vulnerability? As this discussion has highlighted so far, the answer to this question of the just distribution of rewards and punishments is linked with the question of citizenship: who is included and excluded in the relationship between the citizen and the state. It has also been suggested that, while that relationship has changed in emphasis since 1945, there are strong historical continuities underpinning the mechanisms of social exclusion in particular. Those mechanisms of social exclusion have been differently identified as the distinction between the deserving and the undeserving, the principle of less eligibility or the notion of the 'dangerous classes'. This last label provides the clearest clue to the importance of understanding these processes for criminology. The 'dangerous classes' provide the criminal justice system with much of its work. How they are variously and differently criminalized, and the changing social processes that feed the process of criminalization, constitute the stuff of criminology. The stuff of criminology, those defined as the dangerous classes living in dangerous places, leads us to revisit the systemic nature of social exclusion so denied in contemporary policy preoccupations.

One of the most striking features of the period since 1979 has been the overwhelming increase in the gap between the rich and the poor (Hutton 1995; Scott 1994). This has led Hutton (1995), in particular, to talk of the 30/30/40 society, emphasizing not only the gap between those securely well off and those who are not, but also the increasing number of people who are economically vulnerable. The impact of that increasing economic vulnerability for an increasing number of people has been felt nowhere less than in the criminal justice system. As Carlen states:

> The striking increase in inequality and wealth which has been a major feature of the last decade has been accompanied by a steady increase

> in the prison population. . . . This is not surprising. Whatever else prisons may be for, they have always housed large numbers of the poor, the unemployed, the unemployable, the homeless, the physically ill, and the mentally disturbed.
>
> (Carlen 1988: 8)

In other words, there is a relationship between the changing size in the ranks of the 'dangerous classes' and the levels of work likely to be facing the criminal justice agencies. While the nature of this relationship has been strongly contested (and denied) politically, it nevertheless points up the interconnections between the distribution of social justice and the likelihood of being subjected to the criminal justice system. This observation has increasing relevance as for example, the prison population has grown, the preoccupation with security has increased, the community safety industry has developed and so on.

This relationship also points to another problematic issue. If those people who come before the criminal justice system are increasingly likely to be the kinds of people identified earlier, then how might such people be treated justly by it? What does a socially just punishment for a mentally disturbed offender look like who becomes homeless following the implementation of policies designed to provide care in the community and what resources do they have as individuals to manage how they are being dealt with? Asking questions of this kind clearly conveys the very real way in which social justice and criminal justice are interrelated.

To summarize: a criminology concerned with questions such as these offers an agenda which neither subjugates its work to the vagaries of politics nor consigns its explanations to the realm of individual responsibility, both of which have been evidenced in earlier chapters. This kind of criminological agenda has as one of its central concerns the processes of criminalization, not just of individuals but of social groups, alongside an understanding of how those processes are structurally informed. For some on the left the definition of a criminological agenda in this way would be seriously limited by the lack of attention it would pay, by implication, to the crimes of the powerful – those who rarely have to face the attention of the criminal justice agencies. Arguably, it is only from a position that has such a relatively clear vision on the interconnections between criminal justice and social justice that the greater injustices of the activities of the relatively powerful can be most effectively exposed.

In order to develop such criminological concerns in greater detail, the rest of this chapter, then, will take as its substantive example one area in which such interconnections can be made: the relationship between young people and crime and policy responses to this issue as articulated by the Third Way. While there are clearly other issues that could have been explored as a way of exemplifying the importance of the relationship between criminal justice and social justice, this example affords continuity between the discussion of the family and the underclass in Chapter 3 and the discussion of restorative justice that is to come in the next chapter.

New Labour, new policies? Young people and crime

By the time the Labour Party came to power in 1997, the policy issues discussed earlier in this chapter had gelled into one focal concern: young people. Of course, attention to troublesome youth has ebbed and flowed in the political arena over the preceding decades. As Parton (1985) observed, young people have only ever been regarded as victims with respect to crime for a relatively brief historical moment around the turn of the twentieth century. Moreover, as Newburn (1996) observed, 'authoritarian populism' reared its head again with a vengeance in the early 1990s with the inner-city disturbances of 1991, the murder of James Bulger and the combined media and political coverage of these events. However, being 'tough on crime and tough on the causes of crime' prompted the then Home Secretary Jack Straw to pursue the tactic of 'demonizing young people' (Brown 1998: 75). This is not the place to offer an overview of the criminological and policy debates on young people and crime (for this see Brown 1998; Goldson and Muncie 2006); the concern here is to offer an understanding of some features of the contemporary policy scene. At centre stage in this scene is the Crime and Disorder Act 1998.

The 1998 Act stands as the flagship piece of legislation epitomizing New Labour's stance on law and order. As a piece of legislation it was very much influenced by the Audit Commission (1996) report, *Misspent Youth*. This report focused attention on the amount of crime committed by young people, the costs this crime incurred and the paucity of the criminal justice response to it:

> The current system for dealing with youth crime is inefficient and expensive, while little is done to deal effectively with juvenile nuisance. The present arrangements are failing young people – who are not being guided away from offending to constructive activities. They are also failing victims.
>
> (Audit Commission 1996: 96)

Moreover, as the findings from the 2000 British Crime Survey indicate, about one-third of adults reported that vandalism and teenagers hanging about in the street were a big problem in their local area. So there is some continued resonance with the government among the general public that young people are a problem. Part of the perceived solution to this problem was contained in the proposals implemented in the 1998 Act.

This piece of legislation is very broad in coverage; our central concern here, however, is with those aspects of the legislation that particularly impact on young people. There are a number of dimensions to this. Perhaps of greatest importance to this discussion is the establishment of the Youth Justice Board to oversee the youth justice system and, in particular, to monitor multi-agency youth offending teams. The legislation also introduced the final warning scheme to replace the police cautioning system, and made provision for parenting orders, reparation orders and antisocial behaviour orders as dispositions from the court.

There are a number of themes underlying these emphases, one of which marks a continuous thread between this discussion and the earlier concerns of Chapter 3. That is the concern to ensure that both parents and young offenders take responsibility, albeit in different ways, for lawbreaking behaviour. The principle aim of all this is to prevent young people from engaging in offending behaviour.

So the 1998 Crime and Disorder Act stands as a milestone in New Labour's governmental policy, designed to be tough on both the causes of crime and crime itself. In order to achieve this there appear to be two emerging effects of this legislation. On the one hand, young offenders might find themselves before the courts both sooner in their lawbreaking careers and more quickly under the final warning scheme. On the other hand, there are also strong elements of the 're-integrative shaming' approach favoured by Braithwaite (1989) and others, with the use of the reparation order. What is also clear is that there has been a proliferation of mentoring, parenting and other interventions all directed at youthful offending behaviour.

Pitts (2001) has expressed the view that the establishment of youth offending teams, and initiatives related to this development in youth justice, constitutes one feature of the 'new correctionalism' that has been identified by Muncie (1999). This seems to be a policy process whereby greater numbers of less problematic young people are being drawn into the criminal justice system and ultimately into custody, whether or not there is evidence for effectiveness of this as a crime prevention strategy. He argues this is 'because the prime target of New Labour's youth justice strategy is not . . . the criminal behaviour of a handful of young offenders, but the voting habits of a far larger and much older constituency' (Pitts 2001: 189).

However, in the process of putting a legislative framework in place characterized by such a correctionalism, New Labour has also established what Muncie (1999) has called 'institutionalized intolerance'. Such institutionalized intolerance connects to two other processes. The first of these Young (2001) calls the 'dynamics of essentialism': the repeated recreation of 'The Other' – a neat reminder of what is and what is not present in the New Labour agenda with respect to left realism. There is, however, a second thread underpinning this legislative approach. This is the denial of the reality of youth offending behaviour in high-crime areas (see, for example, Walklate 1998), along with the denial of young people's 'social capital'. This latter point requires further elucidation.

Putnam (2000) argues that social capital contributes to safe and productive neighbourhoods. He is primarily talking about 'civic engagement':

people's willingness or otherwise to participate in community life. However, as Hagan and McCarthy's (1997) celebrated study of youth, crime and homelessness clearly suggests, it is also important to treat young people as human beings with resources, that is, with social capital. It might not be that social capital of which people who find themselves in different circumstances approve, but it is nevertheless present. Some initial exploration of these matters in the light of the Crime and Disorder Act has been made by Pain et al. (2002). However there has been a further twist in the tail of policy responses to young people: the increasing focus on antisocial behaviour.

Young people, crime and antisocial behaviour

Burney (2002) reports that the government was 'very disappointed with what it considered to be a poor response to the use of this policy response made available under the Crime and Disorder Act 1998. Since then the Anti-Social Behaviour Act 2003 has both heightened the use of this order (the ASBO) and extended the range of constraints that can be applied in the interests of controlling unacceptable behaviour. Most notable here perhaps has been the use of the dispersal order that the police can invoke if two or more young people gather in a place and their behaviour is perceived to be problematic. The important point about these interventions is that the behaviour itself does not necessarily have to be criminal: just perceived to be problematic. However, failure to comply with the requirements of an ASBO is a criminal offence. Hence the concerns many have raised about more and more young people having criminal records for behaviour that in and of itself is not defined as criminal. If the Government Respect Task Force introduced in 2005 is added to this range of activity then it is difficult to sidestep the view that increasingly less legally (i.e. criminal) behaviour is being subjected to control and criminalization for more and more young people. The question is why?

Squires (2006) offers five reasons for this. First, he posits that the criminological preoccupation with crimes of everyday life and the neatness of fit that this has with the criminal justice policy concern with the 'broken windows' thesis of Wilson and Kelling (1982) set the backcloth against which this kind of agenda might emerge. We have seen some evidence of this in Chapter 3 in the elision between the right realism and the policy focus on crime, the family and the underclass that reflect a concern with young males in particular. However (and this is a second reason for the emergence of the ASBO), left realism also played its part in this emergent agenda as it married itself with New Labour and aspects of Etzioni's moral conservatism on responsibilizing the community. Third, they offer a space in which the other agencies charged with community safety under the Crime and Disorder Act 1998 can respond and operate in a meaningful way especially housing departments struggling with managing deprived housing estates. Fourth, he suggests that the rediscovery of unruly youthful behaviour as a sign of an incipient criminal career rather than something that they would grow out of took a stronger hold in the discourse on young people and crime. Finally, he suggests that the 'language of demonisation' (ibid.: 150) all added to the view that young people hanging about were by definition 'up to no good'. All this taken together has provided a stronger platform for agencies, other than criminal justice agencies, to engage in responding to perceived problematic behaviour in the interests of community safety. In the view of Squires (2006: 154): 'The enforcement activity aimed at tackling "anti-social behaviour" is one of the clearest instances of a process of criminalisation occurring within and across social policy programmes.'

This slippery slope has been well illustrated by the way in which those who wear hooded tracksuit tops (hoodies) have been handled in respect of antisocial behaviour by a number of shopping centres. As Cook (2006: 166) observes: 'But here it was not the thuggish or yobbish behaviour itself which generated such condemnation and exclusionary rhetoric, but the type of clothing (stereo)typically worn by many children, young men and women.' If the respect agenda is added to this, then as Jamieson (2006: 186) observes, 'it is clear that the marginalised poor are the prime targets' of these agendas and she goes on to say that: 'The danger of this strategy is that it not only encourages intolerance and hostility, but also serves to mask the often complex and diverse needs underlying "parenting deficits" and "anti-social" and "criminal" behaviour' (ibid.: 189).

It is true to say, of course, that other kinds of behaviour, most notably prostitution, have also been the subject of ASBOs. So this piece of legislation has not been solely deployed to widen the net on the young. However, if the focus on the family from Chapter 3 is taken along with the increasing use of restorative justice to be discussed in the next chapter are taken alongside ASBOs and the 'respect agenda' one could be forgiven for thinking that what is happening alongside the widening mechanisms of responsibilization is the ever increasing demonization of the young. Yet as was suggested earlier in reference to Hagan and McCarthy's (1997) it would be very unfortunate to consider the young, even those in very poor circumstance to lack any sense of how to manage themselves and those circumstances. However, this would mean recognizing that young people are people with resources and connections in their localities. As Squires and Stephen (2005) quoted by Jamieson (2006) state:

> Respect and responsibility is a two way street – it cannot be demanded of children (or of adults for that matter) who have not the wherewithal or the appropriate opportunities to demonstrate responsibility.
>
> Jamieson (2006: 189)

However, offering such opportunities or taking account of people's pre-existing coping strategies (social capital?) would also demand that we start in a different place in understanding the nature of the problem we are dealing with and its causal mechanisms. These are issues that have been absent from contemporary criminal justice policy. So it is important to recognize the fads and foibles of youth justice policy as it has become both the subject and the object of denial in a highly politicized process. But it is also important to consider whether policies work on or through individuals. If it is the latter, then it might be necessary to rethink how to make such policies work, for whom and under what circumstances. This might lead us to think quite differently about the problems and possibilities of the youth justice system.

Conclusion: questions for criminology

The preceding discussion has endeavoured to illustrate the ways in which conceptions of social justice – that is, what a particular society believes to be the fair and just distribution of the rewards and punishments in that society – can be and are connected with the processes of criminalization and the workings of the criminal justice system. Such conceptions reveal much concerning who is most likely to receive most attention from the criminal justice process – from policing the benefits system to receipt of prison sentences. These issues have been substantiated by exploring the extent to which key foundational aspects of social justice (how to deal with poverty, conceptions concerning the importance of the family and the problematic status of young people) are embedded in historical continuities identifying those groups in society as problematic. In addressing those foundational aspects of social justice and the ways in which they are translated into social policies that differentially target different segments of the problematic population at different points in time, several questions remain understated.

In exploring the potential relationship between conceptions of the underclass or young people and crime, it is clear that one explanatory variable has been privileged in each of those explorations. Yet, at the same time, it is also clear that to do this is highly problematic. In a traditional social scientific sense (that is, in a sense which requires a search for causes so that preventive policies can be formulated) the privileging of variables in this way is perhaps not so difficult to appreciate. In reflecting on this discussion one may be left, quite rightly, with the difficulty of deciding whether it is age, the changing nature of family structures or the changing nature of social deprivation that is the root cause of criminality. Indeed, it is probably impossible, other than heuristically, to separate these variables from each other. So the examples discussed in this chapter demonstrate just how difficult it is to make such causal connections and to devise policies accordingly. It may be, for example, that the policies that have been put in place are in themselves part of the 'causal' mechanism contributing to the criminalization process (think again about the discussion on young people and crime).

This chapter, then, demonstrates the importance, in criminological terms, of setting any criminological agenda in a broad social and political context. At a simple level this may mean devising research agendas that resist the temptation to privilege one variable over another. At a more fundamental level it requires a rethinking of the domain assumptions of the discipline; of what it can and cannot achieve. Certainly a criminology that fails to appreciate the complex interplay between the processes of criminal justice and social justice is one likely to be impoverished in its understanding of who is most likely to receive attention from the criminal justice system and the role that the state plays in contributing to who is made visible and who is made invisible in that process. This is not a simple call to revert to the radical criminology of the 1970s, but reflects a clear concern for us not to lose sight of the complex ways in which national (and international) agendas are reflexively constructed. This concern reappears in the next chapter in which questions of victimization, as opposed to criminalization, will be more squarely addressed.

Further reading

Some of the criminological work that endeavours to formulate the links between social justice, criminal justice and criminology is to be found in the writings of Carlen (1988, 1996) and more recently in an excellent exposition by Cook (2006). On young people and crime, see Brown (1998) and Hagan and McCarthy (1997). The collection of readings edited by Goldson and Muncie (2006) are also a must for anyone interested in the debates that the issues covered in this chapter raise.

chapter seven

Criminal victimization, politics and welfare

What is victimology?
A challenging victimology?
Rebalancing the criminal justice system
Feminism, policy and violence
Ethnicity and hate crimes
Conclusion: criminal victimization and social responsibility
Further reading

The previous chapter considered the way in which it is possible to map interconnections between notions of social justice and the process of criminalization. This chapter will be concerned to examine those same interconnections but with a differing focus, that of understanding the process of victimization. In order to achieve this aim, this chapter will offer an overview of the different strands of victimological thought that have influenced criminology since 1979 (namely positivist and radical victimology) and will consider the potential for a critical victimology as a way of constituting a better informed policy agenda on criminal victimization in the twenty-first century. It is via the latter concerns that the relevance of the question of the relationship between the citizen and state, considered in the previous chapter, will re-emerge. But first, what is victimology?

What is victimology?

The origins of victimology have been variously ascribed to Mendelsohn (1974), von Hentig (1948) and Wertham (1949). It was arguably von

Hentig who really focused attention on the relationship between the victim and the offender in contributing to an understanding of the perpetration of a crime. Indeed, it was the early conceptual work of both Mendelsohn and von Hentig which endeavoured to establish victim typologies (a means of identifying types of victims, mirroring in some way earlier criminological concerns with types of offender) and set the victimological agenda in two different ways. Von Hentig's work generated a concern with victim proneness, but located that concern primarily within the legal domain. Mendelsohn's work generated a concern with victim culpability, arguably setting in train the much more emotive and contentious exploration of victim precipitation, but located that concern within a framework that was concerned with all kinds of victimization. The legacy of each of these authors is to be found in what has been termed 'positivist' victimology, on the one hand, and 'radical' victimology, on the other. We shall discuss each of these in turn.

Positivist victimology

Miers identifies positivist victimology in the following way:

> The identification of factors which contribute to a non-random pattern of victimization, a focus on interpersonal crimes of violence, and a concern to identify victims who may have contributed to their own victimization.
>
> (Miers 1989: 3)

The grouping of these concerns under the heading 'positivist' parallels Karmen's (1990) identification of 'conservative' victimology and Walklate's (1989) concern with a 'conventional' victimology. All these labels capture different, but important, aspects of the kind of work being discussed here. This work focuses on that which is conventionally understood as criminal (street crime and burglary) to the neglect of the private world of the home and the private world of the business corporation and certainly marries well with conservative politics and understandings of what counts as the crime problem.

However, what underpins the surface manifestation of the characteristics variously identified by these authors is a concern with regularities, or patterns of behaviour, that can be identified objectively through a commitment to a traditional conception of being 'scientific'. Of course, as has been suggested elsewhere in this text, what counts as 'scientific' has become an increasingly contested terrain, especially in the challenge to traditional conceptions of science posed by feminist work (see, for example, Harding 1991) and others (see, for example, MacIntyre 1988). Despite this challenge, which largely accounts for the marginalization, and indeed alienation, of feminist work from victimology (for a fuller discussion of this, see Mawby and Walklate 1994; Walklate 2003), this concern with regularities has been immensely influential on the focus with victims found in the political domain. This has been manifested in a number of different ways.

Initially, it was the refinement and development of the criminal victimization survey, informed by the concept of lifestyle as articulated in the work of Hindelang et al. (1978), which exerted the most influence on victimology and its utility in the political domain. As earlier chapters have demonstrated, the criminal victimization survey as a research instrument has been harnessed by academic work on both the right and the left of the criminological political spectrum and their findings have been used by political conservatives to both downplay the risk of crime and to emphasize the risk of crime. Increasingly, of course, such surveys carry some weight on the international scene, especially with the development of the International Criminal Victimization Survey, first developed in 1989 and having completed its fourth round of data collection in 2004. Moreover, feminist informed work concerned with violence against women has used this kind of survey methodology more frequently to measure the nature and extent of 'crime behind closed doors'. Although it should be noted that significant modifications have been made to this technique to render it more sensitive to measuring this kind of victimization (see for example, Piipsa 2003; Walby and Myhill 2001).

So the patterns and regularities revealed by positivistic victimology have arguably been used both expediently and to some effect in the political arena. The connections between this kind of victimology and a more general political conservatism, however, run somewhat deeper than the mere political manipulation and utilization of survey findings. They are connections that emanate from the image of the victim and the presumptions about the nature of society that positivistic victimology makes, presumptions that gel quite nicely with the inherent functionalism in New Labour's embrace of communitarianism commented on in the previous chapter (see also Prideaux 2005).

The three characteristics of positive victimology offered by Miers (1989) with which this section began are underpinned by a presumption that the term 'victim' itself is non-problematic (with the exception, of course, of feminist-informed work). In various forms of victimological work conducted within this vein, the victim is taken to be a given either by the criminal law or by the self-evident nature of their suffering. Such a starting point enables the generation of data concerned with patterns and regularities since it presumes that what there is to be measured can, in fact, be measured and in itself is a static entity.

As has been argued elsewhere (Walklate 1989), this initial presumption conceals an inherently static and functionalist view of society in which the themes of consensus, equilibrium and incremental change are predominant. There is little sense in this image of society or the individual in which the law or the state contributes to the social construction of the victim, the processes of criminal victimization or processes of social change that may be unforeseen and/or dramatic as opposed to managed and incremental. So positivist victimology, and the survey work emanating from it, may provide snapshots of regularities of criminal victimization but cannot provide an understanding of the social and historical reproduction of those regularities through time and space. Such a concern demands at a minimum a different understanding of the term 'victim' and at a maximum a different theoretical starting point.

However, this non-problematic treatment of the notion of the victim offers one way of thinking through those other connections with political conservatism. Karmen expresses some of those connections in this way:

> Conservatives within victimology and the victims' rights movement see the criminal justice system as the guarantor of retributive justice – satisfying victims with the knowledge that offenders are being punished for their crimes.
>
> (Karmen 1990: 11)

It is to this end that the 'powerful motif' of the victim, commented on by Bottoms (1983), was put to most effective use in the UK during the 1980s and 1990s, and still has contemporary resonance, most recently articulated in the UK in the Home Office document *Rebuilding Lives* (2005) produced in the aftermath of the 7 July 2005 bombings in London. As Phipps (1988) has argued, the politicization of the victim led to a separation of the notion of criminal victimization from its *social* origins seeing it as something that interferes with the 'normality' of an ordered society. The argument developed by Phipps suggests that what conservatism does is to transform the harm caused to individuals as a result of criminal victimization into a harming of the social order, of the rule of law and of 'community'. In policy terms, this does indeed translate into a general commitment to repressive justice (see Garland 2001) that can take a number of different forms some of which are discussed later in this chapter and have been alluded to in the previous one.

Moreover, as Alison Young (1996) argues, the use of the term 'victim' in the political domain serves more purposes than just a need to generate support for a particular policy initiative or direction. Those other purposes serve to signify the ideological mechanisms whereby the term 'victim' acts as both a strategy for including 'all of us' while simultaneously excluding the criminal. Such purposes, however, are not solely the prerogative of conservative politicians. As Garland's (2001) analysis so aptly demonstrates, this process of including 'all of us' has led to a society in social, political and policy terms characterized by a 'culture of control'. Signifying the victim in this way is equally problematic for that victimology which sees itself as being of a more radical persuasion.

Radical victimology

Radical victimology arguably has its origins in the work of Mendelsohn (1974) who, despite the more conservative implications of other aspects of his ideas, argued for a victimology concerned with all aspects of victimization, not just those which could be defined as criminal. This concern can be traced through the work of radical criminology (Quinney 1972) as well as radical victimology (Elias 1986, 1993).

The common threads that bind these different strands of work together can be identified as a concern with the role of the state alongside the law in producing victimization. These threads connect this version of victimology to a concern with the question of human rights. As Elias (1985: 17) states:

> A victimology which encompasses human rights would not divert attention from crime victims and their rights, but would rather explore their inextricable relationship to more universal human rights concerns.

Such concerns readily connect the radical victimologist with the victims' movement through organizations such as Amnesty International, for example. However, in the more localized political domain of party politics in the UK during the 1980s it was arguably the ideas of radical victimology which underpinned some of the concerns of the radical left realists discussed in Chapter 4.

As that chapter discussed and as has been commented on elsewhere (Mawby and Walklate 1994; Smart 1990), radical left realism in particular and radical victimology in general fail to escape the chains of a positivistic conception of science. Thus while the underpinning focus of radical victimology on questions of human rights might be considered laudable, their translation into standards that can be measured objectively, as articulated in the work of Elias for example, remains problematic. Moreover, the recognition of the power of the state and the law to oppress, which offers a less than consensual image of the relationship between the individual and society, has had a more rhetorical impact on politics than a 'real' one.

As Chapter 4 demonstrated, radical left realism argues for what has been called an 'engaged' criminology. In England, this was reflected in an association between 'left realist' criminologists and some Labour-controlled local authorities, primarily in London, in an effort to reclaim the debate on law and order for the Labour Party. In very general terms these efforts present a different conceptualization of victimization. As Phipps points out:

> [C]riminal victimization is but one aspect of *social* victimization arising from poverty and disadvantage – in which people are harmed by *normal* social and economic relations, a process which in turn results in their harming each other.
>
> (Phipps 1988: 181)

The endeavour to reclaim the law and order debate in this way has in part led radical left realism to elide the concern with crime with a concern with criminal victimization. This issue is worth developing a little more fully.

As Chapter 4 illustrated, one of the criticisms made of left realism lies in its use of the notion of crime as a unified and a unifying category. One of the implications of this use is the idea that crime is a 'leveller'. As Alison Young (1996: 55) puts it, crime 'provides a sense of community. . . . But our belonging comes not from the fact that we are all criminals but from the shared fact of victimization.' This sense of common victimization providing a basis to belonging may be differently distributed by space, age, race or gender, but it is nevertheless the means through which 'all of us' as potential victims can be harnessed to participate in the democratic process. Thus our potential victimization acts as a mechanism whereby our activities as citizens can also be harnessed.

Of course, it is not only left realism that has connoted the term 'victim' in this way. The 1980s, characterized as they have been by Karmen (1990) as a move from crime prevention to victimization prevention, saw those of both a left- and a right-wing political persuasion collude in the construction of a notion of social responsibility in relation to crime control in terms of victimization reduction. Indeed, the intervention of left realism, albeit brief, into the debate on citizenship argued for a social individualism that considered not only the rights of the citizen but also of their obligations. Such a conception of citizenship marries with that discussed in the previous chapter.

Thus it can be seen that, while radical victimology of this persuasion tries to construct and work with a much more general notion of victimization and with a relatively subtle and nuanced understanding of the sources of such victimization, its failure to break free of positivism at a fundamental level results in a political agenda not that dissimilar in its presumptions from that of a more conservative political persuasion. However, the idea of a radical agenda for victimology has not been totally lost. Recently Kauzlarich et al. (2001) reopened the argument for such a victimology in proposing a 'victimology of state crime'. This framework defines crime victims as:

> Individuals or groups of individuals who have experienced economic, cultural, or physical harm, pain, exclusion, or exploitation, because of tacit or explicit state actions or policies which violate law or generally defined human rights.
>
> (ibid.: 176)

They go on to suggest that ratified international law, domestic law and human rights standards can be used to look to the criminal activities of the state and go on to produce a fourfold typology that might be used to iterate the nature of victimization by the state. As the authors acknowledge, taking this kind of victimization into account is not without its problems. As Box (1983: 17) observed some time ago: 'The majority of those suffering from corporate crime remain unaware of their victimisation – either not knowing it has happened to them or viewing their "misfortune" as an accident or "no one's fault".' A phenomenon Geis (1973) referred to as 'victim responsiveness'. Yet, the case for an understanding of the involvement of the state in criminal victimization remains a solid one and clearly recognizes the power dimensions to criminal victimization, the relative invisibility of some forms of criminal victimization (those associated with the workplace and those committed in the interest of the state, in particular), and by implication the highly problematic issues associated with measuring the nature and extent of such victimization. In addition, this version of radical victimology presupposes that an important causal mechanism underlying patterns of criminal victimization is the capitalist state and how its interests are maintained. This presupposition posits a different political relationship between the individual and the state that places greater responsibility on the state for the processes of criminal victimization.

Thus it can be seen that, while radical victimology tries to construct and work with a much more general notion of the nature and extent of criminal victimization and with a relatively subtle and nuanced understanding of the sources of such victimization, in many of its guises (with the possible exception of the propositions discussed earlier) it still fails to break free of positivism. It has either relied on the criminal victimization survey in a very similar way to the reliance on such surveys found in positivist victimology or it has looked for other forms of 'universal' standards either in the form of human rights or other kinds of ratified legal frameworks. This focus of attention is equally problematic for those who might claim a radical space in victimology informed by feminist concerns, as frequently the policy implications here result in campaigns around the law, that as Hudson (2006) has so usefully summarized in the term 'white, man's law'. Moreover, as Walklate (2007) has argued, while all of these avenues offer different and useful foci for policy from Amnesty International to the European Community, to the United Nations, at a fundamental level much of this kind of work results in a political and policy agenda not that dissimilar in its presumptions from that of a more conservative political persuasion as far as the victim of crime is concerned (again with the possible exception of the propositions already discussed). However, efforts have been made to break free of the conservative conundrum through what has been called 'critical victimology'.

Critical victimology

The term 'critical' has been used by a number of different writers to delineate an alternative way of thinking about the nature of victimization. Miers (1990), for example, uses it to draw attention to the process of acquiring both the label and status of victim. Fattah (1992) uses it to call for a better integration of criminological and victimological knowledge. The way in which this term has been used by Walklate (1990) and Mawby and Walklate (1994), however, denotes a substantially different theoretical and empirical starting place than either positive or radical victimology and subsequently leads to a different conceptualization of the relationship between the citizen and the state. We shall consider each of these issues in turn.

Critical victimology as articulated in the work of Walklate (1990, 2007) and Mawby and Walklate (1994) takes as its starting point the need to understand what constitutes the 'real'. Influenced by the work of Bhaskar (1978) and Giddens (1984), this form of victimology centres the need for an empirically informed policy agenda, but one which is as concerned with what 'goes on behind our backs' as it is with what we can see. Drawing explicitly on the theoretical work of Giddens, this concern implies the need to take account of a number of processes that contribute to the construction of everyday life:

> [P]eople's conscious activity, their 'unconscious' activity (that is, routine activities people engage in which serve to sustain and sometimes change the conditions in which they act), the generative mechanisms (unobservable and unobserved) which underpin daily life, and finally, both the intended and the unintended consequences of action which feed back into people's knowledge.
>
> (Mawby and Walklate 1994: 19)

A theoretical starting point such as this carries with it a number of implications for not only what kind of empirical investigation is most likely to reveal the processes just outlined (comparative and longitudinal) but also what might constitute the central concerns of such an area of analysis.

In the context of criminal victimization, Mawby and Walklate (1994) have argued that the kind of theoretical starting point just outlined not only generates a challenge to the domain assumptions of victimology as a discipline, but also generates a concern with three key policy-oriented concepts: rights, citizenship and the state. It has been seen that these concepts are also intimately connected with other versions of victimology, so we shall consider the nature of their interrelationship in this context too. What matters, of course, is to understand how they might be differently interpreted and harnessed in the political process. In other words, what gives this version of victimology its critical policy edge?

Critical victimology presumes that the state is not necessarily neutral or benign in its activities. Such a view stems from the work of Offe (1984). Appreciating the ways in which the state operates sometimes in the interests of its citizens, but always in the interests of self-maintenance, is central to understanding the underlying (generative) mechanisms which contribute towards the kinds of victimization that we 'see' as compared to those that we do not 'see'. The way in which the term 'victim' has been used symbolically in the political arena has already been commented on in this chapter and elsewhere. Perhaps what has not been sufficiently outlined is the way in which the notion of the victim as delineating 'all of us' also serves ideological purposes especially at times when the state is economically less well secure.

Offe and Ronge (1975) argue that as the contradictions within welfare state capitalism have become increasingly acute, the stability of the state could only be maintained by 'creating the conditions under which legal and economic subjects' could function as commodities. Arguably, the processes that have occurred within the UK since the mid–1970s have constituted an effort to 'commodify' citizenship. Embodying the citizen as a consumer of services, of course, serves not only to 'justify' the levels of expenditure available for those services, but also to maintain at an ideological level a notion of both the citizen and the state as being neutral entities. And, of course, as MacKinnon (1989: 162) has cogently argued, the state under discussion here is a patriarchal state: 'The liberal state coercively and authoritatively constitutes the social order in the interests of men as a gender – through its legitimating norms, forms, relation to society, and substantive policies.' But the state is not only gendered, but also embedded in notions of class and race that permeate its activities. This is neither more nor less the case than in the area of the law (see Naffine 1990). This does not mean that the state cannot be challenged. What it does imply, however, is that any challenge to the state and its activities of self-maintenance may not always have the 'progressive' outcome intended. Matthews (1994), for example, comments on the way in which the adoption of feminist-informed rape crisis programmes has in some circumstances resulted in their co-option by the state. Smart (1989) raises a similar dilemma for feminists who look to changing the law as a way of enhancing women's rights before the law. Such an outcome is not always or necessarily guaranteed.

For this version of critical victimology, then, the state is not an objective, neutral arbiter of the 'facts', but a self-interested and self-motivated mechanism in which its interests at different historical moments may be more or less paramount, dependent on economic circumstances (echoing some of the themes addressed in Chapter 2); and as Jessop (2002) argues looks for mechanisms that appeal to an imagined political community. An imagining that has increasingly come to mean the 'all of us' of criminal victimization (see also Walklate 2006). This does not mean that the state always remains impervious to questions of gender, race or class. However, it does mean that in order to understand the ways in which those questions may or may not be articulated in policy terms is connected with the underlying activities of the state itself. These processes set the scene in which some aspects of citizenship become visible and others remain invisible.

One that has remained invisible, and was commented on earlier, is the way in which, as Alison Young observes, victimization has become elided with citizenship: 'If everyone is a victim, then everyone has a part to play in the struggle against crime. More strongly, everyone has a *duty*: it is part of the offices of the citizen to minimize the risk of becoming a victim' (Young 1996: 56).

This elision between victimization and citizenship captures the commonality between left- and right-wing criminology/victimology on this issue, despite the surface manifestation of political differences. Of course, a continued commitment to a discourse on the question of citizenship rooted in notions of individualism simultaneously serves to blame, if not hide, those collectivities whose economic and material conditions have been worsening (relatively) since 1979. A critically informed victimology is one which is concerned to understand the mechanisms whereby such collectivities are hidden and what might constitute the real policy opportunities, economic circumstances notwithstanding, to equip those collectivities with 'rights'.

This is not the place to offer a picture of what such a policy agenda might concern itself with (for a detailed discussion of this, see Mawby and Walklate 1994: Chapter 9; Walklate 2007). Needless to say, such a policy agenda is one which does not privilege the notion of victims' rights but considers those policy possibilities which might ensure a more equitable experience of the criminal justice process for all groups of people who might come into contact with it. A key concern of critical victimology, then, is to challenge the use of the term 'victim' and the circumstances in which such a term may be applicable. In so doing, it constitutes a fundamental challenge to the domain assumptions of victimology as a discipline. An appreciation of that challenge will facilitate a deeper understanding of both the theoretical and policy agenda of a critical victimology.

A challenging victimology?

As was stated earlier, the work of Mendelsohn (1974) and von Hentig (1948) is frequently taken as the starting point for victimological concerns. While neither of these writers intended to suggest that there was such a being as the 'born victim', they were nevertheless searching for ways of differentiating the potential victim from the non-victim that could be applied in all victimizing situations. This concern with differentiation is clearly consonant with the work of the early criminologists.

Later versions of this kind of work are much more sophisticated than those of von Hentig and Mendelsohn, but they nevertheless share in the early criminological worldview that if criminals could be identified in some way then so could victims. Not only that – more often than not victims would be identifiable by some personal characteristic that marked them as being different from the norm. What constituted that norm was differently interpreted for different writers, but what they shared in common was an underlying presumption that it was characterized by the white, heterosexual male (see Walklate 2004: Chapter 2).

In this way victimology, unsurprisingly, shared in those fundamental tenets of early criminology – determinism, differentiation and pathology. These concerns are reflected in the work of the early victimologists whose typologies focused on either the personal characteristics of the victim (whether they were female, old, mentally defective and so on, for von Hentig) or the contribution that their behaviour made to the commission of a crime (from being totally innocent to the criminal who became the victim, for Mendelsohn). They are also reflected in the subsequent development of the discipline and its focus on the concepts of victim precipitation and lifestyle.

These two concepts, victim precipitation and lifestyle, constitute the core of much victimological thinking, as has been alluded to in this chapter. As concepts they have generated a significant amount of empirical work and consequently have contributed to the development of the victimological agenda. As concepts they also both implicitly and explicitly focus our attention on the behaviour of individual victims.

This concern to differentiate the victim from others, whether in terms of personal or behavioural characteristics, has constituted a key assumption of much victimological work. A critical victimology, as outlined earlier, clearly challenges the presumption that victims can be differentiated in this way. Critical victimology articulates the view that it is within the routine practices of everyday life that the processes of 'victimization' are produced and reproduced. There is, however, another theme implicit in this discussion. What has also been very powerful in the policy domain is the idea of the victim as being structurally neutral; yet as repeated evidence from criminal victimization survey data illustrates, the victim of crime is not a neutral entity but one that is clearly socially structured (see Walklate 2007) in which the harm done by crime is not shared equally among all society's citizens (see also Dixon et al. 2006).Yet, this neutral image is one that has become increasingly popular in policy terms and is self-evident in the contemporary policy agenda addressing the victim of crime under New Labour. So in the rest of this chapter we shall explore the current policy initiatives designed to ensure that the victim is no longer the 'forgotten party of the criminal justice system' alongside some of the interventions that have been introduced to address the claims of a more structurally informed concept of the victim of crime.

Rebalancing the criminal justice system

Contemporary criminal justice policy concerns in England and Wales are preoccupied with 'rebalancing' the criminal justice system to better meet the presumed needs of the victim of crime. In some respects, this rebalancing reached a peak in the passing of the Domestic Violence, Crime and Victims Act in 2004. This piece of legislation introduced surcharges on fines and fixed penalties for motoring offences that will contribute to the funding of a new Victims' Fund, it allows the Criminal Injuries Compensation Authority to recover payments made to victims from their offenders, it widens the opportunities for victims to be given and to provide information in cases where their offender receives a prison sentence, it provides for a Commissioner for Victims and Witnesses and sets out a Code of Practice for Victims. The breadth of this legislation in relation to victims of crime is consequently without precedent in England and Wales and arguably marks a further twist in the politicization of the victim of crime that for some encroaches on the rights of the defendant (see for example, Garland 2001; Williams 2005). Echoing work I have done elsewhere (Walklate 2007), I shall discuss these concerns with 'rebalancing' under three headings; tinkering with the criminal justice system, giving the victim a voice; and restorative justice, all of which have assumed a structurally neutral image of the victim of crime.

Tinkering with the criminal justice system

The adversarial criminal justice system offers no real status to the victim of crime over and above that of perhaps being a witness to a crime and thereby called to give evidence in court. In recognition of this lack of formal status, Mawby and Gill (1987: 229) argued that there were four areas in which victims' rights could be improved: the right to play an active part in the criminal justice system; the right to knowledge; the right to financial help; and the right to advice and support. These were claims that acknowledged, as Dignan (2005: 65) has argued, the ways in which the criminal justice system had historically failed the victim of crime. As he says, it had failed to recognize the harm done by crime; it had treated the victim instrumentally; and had failed to offer financial redress. All of which led researchers to talk about 'secondary victimization', the victimization that occurs as a result of involvement in the criminal justice system. It is the policy responses designed to address this secondary victimization that I have chosen to call 'tinkering with the criminal justice system' since it is the adversarial system of criminal justice itself that is frequently the barrier to the ultimate success or failure of the kinds of policy initiative to be discussed here. Arguably, two main strategies have been used to try to render the criminal justice system more responsive to the victim of crime: reorienting the work of the criminal justice professionals and developing policies in relation to the offender.

While all branches of the criminal justice professionals have been increasingly encouraged to place the victim of crime more to the centre of their routine daily work in recent years, that imperative has probably had its greatest impact on the probation service. It is a moot point as to the extent that either the public or the courts were ever convinced by probation as a mean of offender control, however, contemporarily the probation service no longer has as its central mission the goal of assisting, advising and befriending (deserving) offenders. This reorientation of probation work towards the victim of crime was put on a statutory footing by the Criminal Justice and Court Services Act 2000, although this change of focus was first introduced in the 1990 Victims' Charter. That charter obliged the probation service in England and Wales to contact the victims and/or families of life sentence prisoners prior to any consideration of their release. This task was widened in the 1996 Charter to include victims of serious violent or sexual offences. Under the Domestic

Violence, Crime and Victims Act 2004, local probation boards have obligations to the victim of an offender who receives a sentence of imprisonment of 12 months or longer after conviction of a sexual or violent offence and the victim of an offender convicted of a sexual or violent offence and receives a restricted (or other similar) hospital order. Consequently, the probation service is now required to take reasonable steps to establish any victim representations about licence conditions or supervision requirements subject to their offender's release from prison or hospital and to ensure that those responsible for making such decisions are informed of the victim's wishes. They must also provide the victims with any information about their offender's release and any conditions that may be attached to it.

The second strand of policies that tinker with adversarialism has looked to further the demands made on the offender with respect to the victim. There has been a long tradition within criminal justice policy of disposing the offender to pay compensation to the victim and while there is some evidence to suggest that victims are in favour of this kind of disposition, historically they have been very difficult to implement. There are a number of reasons for this but a prime one is the reluctance of the court to prioritize the victim in cases where compensation is appropriate. However, the invocation of ensuring that the offender 'pays' for their offence, whether that be in formal terms through a compensation order imposed by the court or through more rhetorical devices like being seen to be involved in community work, raises the problematic issue of the extent to which paying attention to the victim results in the further penalization of the offender. However, these moves notwithstanding, the adversarial system of justice, structurally, offers no voice to the victim. Recognition of this has led some to campaign for giving the victim such a voice and it is these policy interventions that we shall consider next.

Giving the victim a voice

Edwards (2004) suggests that there are four different ways in which the victim might participate within criminal justice decision making; in an expressive fashion through the offering of either information or feelings; by being required to provide information; through consultation and as a result having an informal influence on decisions; and, finally, by having control over the decision-making process. As we shall see, current policy in the UK falls short of offering the victim a say in the sentencing of an offender (although a number of criminal justice systems do so internationally); the UK scheme that is discussed in more detail later, however, was given an added edge with the introduction of a pilot scheme of victims' advocates in April 2006, for cases in which a conviction of murder or manslaughter has been secured. It is intended that the advocate will speak on behalf of the family so that the court can be told how the death and the events that have followed have affected them. Given that a conviction must be secured for an advocate to speak, it must be assumed that their representations are intended to influence sentencing.

The Victim Personal Statement Scheme, the scheme that operates on a more widespread basis at present, went nationwide in 2001. The Home Secretary Jack Straw was reported as saying that this scheme would: 'give victims a voice in a way that they have not had before. It will be a real opportunity to make their views known more formally to the police, crown prosecution service and the courts and to know they will be taken into account in the case. I want victims to feel they are at the heart of the criminal justice system' (*The Guardian*, 27 May: 6).

So does this scheme put victims at the heart of the criminal justice system?

The purpose of a victim personal statement is twofold; to offer the optional opportunity to the victim of crime to relate to all the agencies how a crime has affected them and to provide the criminal justices agencies with more information about the impact of a crime. This is an entirely voluntary scheme for the victim and is not intended to be used by the criminal justice agencies to affect sentencing outcomes. It is a two-stage process. The first stage involves taking a personal statement from the victim at the same time as a witness statement is taken. The second stage affords the opportunity for the victim to describe the impact of any longer term effects of the crime. Both statements form part of the case papers for any trial and both are seen to be the responsibility of the police to collect. While these statements provide an opportunity for the victim to raise any concerns that they may have about aspects of the crime and the offender not dealt with elsewhere by the criminal justice process (like bail proceedings, for example) and provide all agencies within the criminal justice process with more information, this will only be the case in those cases where the victim chooses to make such statements and in which the police pursue such statements leaving the space open for the deserving/undeserving distinction to appear. Indeed, Tapley (2005: 32) reports that 'Victim Personal Statements were not being offered to victims on a consistent and regular basis' echoing the finding of an earlier Probation Inspectorate (2003) that also found such statements were not being made generally available. Tapley (2005: 29) suggests that 'the redefinition of victims as consumers has resulted in the victims being denied the status of "active citizens" with rights and instead rendered them "passive consumers" of criminal justice services.' Lending further support to the view expressed by Padfield and Crowley 2003 quoted by Williams and Canton (2005: 4) that:

> The reality of the service offered to defendants, victims and witnesses is not improved by simply passing yet more legislation. Indeed the gap between the theoretical protections offered by statute and the reality to be seen in practice seems in danger of growing ever wider.

The qualitative evaluation of this scheme by Graham et al. (2004) points to similar issues in victims' understanding of the scheme and the kind of information they had been given about it but overall is suggestive that those who participated felt that it had been a positive process: 'It was seen as "fair" that the extent, severity, and dominance of those impacts could be considered in sentencing an offender.' (ibid.: 49).

It is important to note that victim (impact) statements used to inform sentencing raise serious alarm bells for those committed to the principle of the adversarial system. It is argued that this is a tactic that can introduce a level of arbitrariness to the sentencing process above and beyond that which already exists. Since, in essence, sentencing becomes reliant on the persuasive powers of the victims' statement and the efficiency and accuracy with which it has been recorded. In other words, in principle it is a process that becomes subject to the potential influence of factors outside those pertinent to the crime committed and that are before the court. If used in this way, the victim impact statement may erode the rights of the offender to a 'fair' trial, might result in the imposition of heavier penalties than might otherwise have been the case and, as a consequence, result in an increase in sentencing disparity. The statement schemes introduced into England and Wales are not intended to influence sentencing (it is as yet not clear how the victim advocates recently proposed might operate in this respect), although this does not mean that the greater awareness of the impact of a crime put before a court would not result in some of these effects. Indeed, it would be very surprising if this were not the case. Moreover, as Ashworth (2000) also observes, if such statements are put before the court with any evidential status that presumably the defendant must have a right of cross-examination. Though, as Wemmers (2005) reports, in jurisdictions where this is permitted, it would appear that cross-examination rarely occurs as the prosecution tends to edit out those aspects of such a statement that might prove to be controversial, which from a point of view rather defeats the object of them in the first place. In addition, it must also be remembered, of course, that victim impact statements are not the only source of arbitrariness in sentencing outcome.

Sanders (2002: 220) argues that 'VIS and its variants are probably more popular with people who have never used them that with those who have. They are good for idealised victims, rather than real victims' and goes on to suggest that these kinds of developments are characteristic of the exclusionary tendencies of contemporary criminal justice policy, that fail to recognize that quite often the individuals on either side of the witness box can be both victims and offenders at one and the same time. Some commentators argue that this problem is overcome by embracing the final strategy of victim participation in the criminal justice system to be discussed here: restorative justice.

Restorative justice

It is now nearly 30 years since the first appearance of the essay by Christie in the *British Journal of Criminology* entitled 'Conflicts as property' (Christie

1977). In that essay, Christie was keen to make the case that the law, and the emergence of the professions associated with the practice of law, in taking disputes out of people's own hands, had not only denied them the right to manage their own disputes but had also, as a consequence, denied the development of more constructive and imaginative responses to such disputes. One of the themes in this work places emphasis on 'reintegration'; on finding ways in which the offender is made aware of the consequences and impact of their offending behaviour yet simultaneously is reintegrated into (rather than ostracized from) the community, given wider popularity and dissemination in the work of Braithwaite (1989, inter alia).

The Crime and Disorder Act 1998 makes possible, at a number of different junctures, the introduction of restorative justice under this general rubric. For example, young offenders who receive warnings are referred to a youth offending team, which may, as a part of monitoring that offender, require some sessions on victim awareness. Furthermore those who come before the court may find themselves in receipt of a referral order, which may include the prevention of re-offending through a youth offender contract. Such a contract may include direct and/or indirect reparation to the victim and/or the wider community. If a young offender is convicted of an offence they may find themselves in receipt of a 'community order'. Under the action plan that should flow from this order, the offender may be required to make reparation to the wider community or to the victim of the offence or anyone else affected by it should they so wish it. The report by Miers et al. (2001) is clearly suggestive of the problems facing researchers in trying to evaluate the effectiveness of these initiatives. They found that, for example, interpretations of what constituted reparation was somewhat elastic across the different schemes they were concerned with. Such problems notwithstanding (and these problems are important in the contemporary political atmosphere), there are some issues of principle that are worth raising about the legislative move in this direction.

This policy commitment reflects a view that these strategies are not only workable but will also have the desired effect, that is, reducing offending behaviour. It also reflects a presumption that such strategies constitute the preferred model of reparation, and make sense, for both the individuals involved in the process and the communities of which they are a part, in both instances this means also to be understood by the victims. Some of the issues that are generated by these presumptions draw attention to the tension between what might be expected from policy, what actually has been and can be delivered from such policy and understanding what might already exist informally as ways of making amends between members of a community (see also Newburn and McEvoy 2003) and as Goodey (2005) has observed, restorative justice (RJ) is more often than not represented as victim-centred justice. Some proponents of this way of doing business would also point to United Nations resolutions and those passed by the Council of Europe as indications of a paradigm shift towards this way of conducting criminal justice work and while there has been a huge amount of activity and interest in restorative justice internationally, my comments here will inevitably reflect how that activity has played itself out in the England and Wales.

As Miers (2004) observes, in the UK the importance of the victim of crime to the criminal justice system has been variously described as a supplier of information, a beneficiary of compensation, a partner in crime prevention and a consumer of services. In his words: 'Restorative justice purports to take this relationship and these changes a step further – to one of victim participation in the system' (2004: 24) and 'has at its core the bringing together of victims and offenders' (Hudson 2003: 178). In the light of these efforts to shift criminal justice policy in the direction of such participation, much time and effort has been spent in the UK establishing whether or not this works and who it works for, without, and this is the nub of Miers' analysis, there being any consensus on what the question of what works actually means. What is clear is that, other achievements of RJ notwithstanding, it is possible to suggest that the victim of RJ has become the (young) offender.

Pitts (2001) has argued that the 'new correctionalism' of New Labour is drawing more and less problematic young people into the criminal justice system, leading Muncie (2002) to talk about the 'repenalisation' of youth offending. As Burnett and Appleton (2004: 48) observe, with respect to the claims made by the Youth Justice Board 2000–2001 Annual Review 'Building on success' (2002):

> It was reported that predicted reconviction rates for youth crime had been cut by nearly 15%. In making such claims it has been highly selective in utilising the findings of independent evaluations that the Youth Justice Board itself commissioned, thus conveniently drawing a veil over less encouraging findings.

So the question of which young people are being targeted and what aspects of their behaviour may be being changed by recent policy interventions, especially RJ interventions, appears to be very much a matter of conjecture and debate. (Echoing some of the observations also made by Miers 2004.) According to Muncie (1999), in giving a prominent position to RJ, New Labour has established not only a 'new correctionalism' but also an 'institutionalized intolerance' of the young, that has been exacerbated by the antisocial behaviour legislation in which if an individual breaches an antisocial behaviour order they can find themselves incarcerated for what was not a substantive criminal offence! Moreover, as Williams (2003) states:

> Although reparation orders were designed to be restorative, in many cases the pressure of work and practitioner cynicism have combined to create a production-line of mechanistic and unreflecting drudge-work which is of no benefit to victims and of little significance to offenders.

So, as both Muncie and Pitts have argued, drawing on the work by

Cohen (1985), we have a situation presently in which the net is being widened and the mesh being thinned, all at the same time. From a point of view it can be argued that restorative justice has become the policy means through which 'being tough on crime' and 'being tough on the causes of crime' has been articulated.

Awareness of these policy processes draws our attention to what Young (2001) has called the 'dynamic of essentialism': the repeated recreation of 'The Other', those problematic outsiders who are not 'us'. In this 'culture of control' (Garland 2001), of course, our collective response to 'The Other' is not about tolerance but intolerance not the least of which has been the targeting of young offenders in recent legislation. It is in this latter context that RJ initiatives have proved to be increasingly popular within contemporary criminal justice policy. From this point of view, as mentioned earlier; the victim is the offender; inexorably pushed upwards on the criminal justice ladder for offences that may have not previously received a formal sanction.

In many ways the previous discussion implies that while RJ initiatives have as their intent to desire to repair the harm done to the victim of crime through either face-to-face contact with their offender or through the offender making amends to their community in some way, RJ as a movement has reflected little on how it has imagined who the victim is. This does not mean that some RJ initiatives do not work well at a local level, that some victims who participate in such initiatives do not feel better about their participation or that some proponents of RJ are not aware of the problematic status that results for the victim consequent to a commitment to RJ. However, in a sociocultural process characterized by global doubt and uncertainty and a domestic preoccupation with control, the potential for sensitivity that the previous questions of RJ demand, is lost. Elsewhere I have called this the rhetoric of victimhood as a source of oppression (Walklate 2005) in which both RJ and victimology are implicated in being vehicles for contemporary state policy.

However, the responses to the victim of crime that have taken place in recent years have not confined themselves to the victim as a neutral entity. Some would say that there have been important developments within the criminal justice system in relation to questions of gender and ethnicity, both categories of 'victim' in which the evidence suggests that the harm done as a result of their victimization is disproportionate to their resources of dealing with it, and it is to a consideration of those policy possibilities that we shall now turn.

Feminism, policy and violence

As Chesney-Lind (2006) has observed much of the intellectual and policy activity that has taken place over the last 25 years, that has as its focus tackling the issue of violence against women, needs to be understood by reference to what is referred to as second-wave feminism. That movement, largely located at its inception within the Anglo-American-European axis, took for granted the gains that women had made in relation to civil rights but recognized that there were many areas of women's lives in which they still suffered as a result of their unequal relationship with men. That focus of concern drew attention to women's experiences of, among other things, violence at the hands of men in general but domestic violence and sexual violence in particular. It is possible to suggest that much has changed since those early campaigning days of the 1960s and 1970s in respect of these experiences, but arguably, much has also remained the same particularly when one considers the situation with regard to proceedings within the criminal courts. Here I shall discuss what the parameters of those changes might look like, in the context of domestic violence and sexual violence and the issues that remain unresolved within this contemporary picture.

Raising the profile of women's experience of violence at the hands of men that they know, usually their partner, has been a key feature of feminist campaigning from the formation of the first women's refuge in Chiswick in 1977 through to the Zero Tolerance campaigns supported by many local authorities in the 1990s. While the difficulties that women face in recognizing and reporting the criminal nature of their experiences are now more widely acknowledged, it is worthwhile remembering that such an acknowledgement is a relatively recent one and, moreover, as we shall observe, much remains to be achieved in this respect. One arena in which much effort has been made to appreciate the nature of domestic violence and to develop more appropriate response to such incidents has been the criminal justice system.

The cumulative effect of feminist campaigning, the drive for value for money and effectiveness to which the police had become subjected during the 1980s, alongside the increasing recognition of victims as consumers of criminal justice services (Mawby and Walklate 1994; Williams 1999) combined to produce Home Office circulars in 1986 and 1990 that gave the clear signal that domestic violence was to be treated as seriously as violence between strangers. Reiterated in 2000, these circulars have resulted in a marked change of direction for not only policing but also for the criminal justice system as a whole. In particular, these circulars formed the backcloth against which a 'presumption to arrest' the offender in domestic violence incidents has emerged. Despite ambivalent supportive evidence for arresting the offender (Sherman et al. 1991), this practice follows the North American model of mandatory arrest. In addition, it is important to note that evaluation of such strategies rarely compares women who have sought legal help with those who have not, rendering understanding the effectiveness of intervention problematic (Sherman and Smith 1992). Moreover, as Chesney-Lind (2006) documents, the implementation of the mandatory arrest stance in the USA has frequently resulted in unintended consequences, including the increasing arrest of women for their use of violence in fighting back against their male partner. This has, in her view, contributed to the rising statistics on female violence and the raised visibility of male victims of such violence some of which is now reflected in official statistics.

Alongside a presumption to arrest stance, police forces have also been active in developing specialist units to deal with domestic violence whose key task is to support the victim. It would appear that, although women who are supported through the work of such units have at their disposal a better service than existed prior to their implementation, problems clearly remain as to the extent to which the needs of women from ethnic minorities are understood and met (Patel 1992), whether or not such service delivery meets with notions of victim empowerment (Hoyle and Sanders 2000) and the extent to which many women still feel patronized and stereotyped by the police (Women's National Commission 2003). Problems such these are compounded by the findings of a Joint Inspectorate of Constabulary and Crown Prosecution Service report published in February 2004 that pointed to the fact that these agencies still did not share in a common definition of what counted as 'domestic' violence. In addition, this report evidenced that of 463 incidents to which the police were called, 118 were recorded as a crime, 90 people were charged with an offence of which 45 were convicted at court. The attrition rate in such cases is therefore still very much a problem despite all the positive interventions outlined earlier.

Nevertheless the commitment to responding to and dealing with domestic violence has continued with more recent policy interventions focusing on the courts. In 2003 the Crown Prosecution Service established five specialist, fast-track, domestic violence courts. The evaluation report on the work of these courts suggests that they enhanced the effectiveness of court and support services for victims, made advocacy and information sharing easier and improved victim satisfaction with and confidence in the criminal justice system (Cook et al. 2004: 6). It was announced in October 2005 that, on the basis of this success, this scheme was to be extended to 25 other court areas throughout England and Wales. Further to this the Domestic Violence, Crime and Victims Act (2004) extended the reach of the criminal justice system in tackling domestic violence by making a common assault an arrestable offence for the first time. Of course, it is too soon to say to what extent this continued criminalization of domestic violence is likely to result in long-term effects.

Similarly, responses to sexual violence (that, of course, might also be domestic) began life within the feminist movement. Rape crisis centres emerged during the 1970s in England and Wales in parallel with the development of the women's refuge movement. In a similar vein to the refuge movement, rape crisis centres were established with the central purpose of supporting women without any presumption that this required their involvement with the criminal justice system. Indeed, many individuals working within the rape crisis movement had, to say the least, rather prickly relationships with criminal justice systems. However, it was not until the early 1980s, largely through the impact of a 'fly on the wall'-style television programme covering the work of the Thames Valley Police with a woman complainant of rape, that criminal justice responses began to change. This wider exposure of police practices resulted in a reorientation of policing policy responses at that time in the form of the development of the 'rape suite'. These 'rape suites' were intended to offer a much more supportive environment for female complainants in an atmosphere that did not compromise the need to gather evidence. However, as Kelly (2001) reports, issues relating to sexual violence were largely sidelined after this initial flurry of activity, until the late 1990s, and did not really reappear until the problem of attrition in cases of rape reappeared. In reviewing responses to rape in a European context, Regan and Kelly (2003) show that with the exception of the Czech Republic, Germany and Latvia, conviction rates for rape have declined within all other European jurisdictions since 1977 with the greatest rate of decline being in Hungary at 27% closely followed by England and Wales at 22%. (The current conviction rate for cases of rape stands at 5.2% in England and Wales (Kelly et al. 2005)). This despite the fact that 11 countries during that same time period have either made rape a gender-neutral offence or included men within it, have removed the exemption of rape in marriage and have extended the definition to include other forms of penetration (Regan and Kelly 2003: 16). This leads Regan and Kelly (2003: 13) to suggest that: 'Legal reforms and changes in the investigation and prosecution of rape have had little, if any, impact on convictions.' Yet, as in the case of domestic violence, campaigns have continued to be focused on the law as constituting a mechanism for change. The Sexual Offences Act that came into force in 2004 did a number of things. It confirmed the gender-neutral nature of the act of rape and extended the definition to include the mouth and anus as other orifices of penetration by the penis. So in many ways this legislation can be seen as a landmark in achieving and addressing many of the historical complaints that radical feminism in particular had of the legal framework of rape in England and Wales.

Therefore, over the last two decades much time, effort and resources have been put in place to respond to all kinds of violence against women, much of it focused on the law and the work of criminal justice professionals. Yet a key problem still remains: the attrition rate. In the context of rape/sexual violence, the issue seems to be one associated with the changing nature of reporting behaviour (many more incidents between acquaintances being reported contemporarily than 25 years ago) but with success in conviction still only most likely to occur in those cases where the victim, and the associated evidence, are 'ideal' (Christie 1986). But what of other structurally informed responses to victimization?

Ethnicity and hate crimes

Criminal victimization data also point to the fact that the chances of criminal victimization are not only structured along gender lines they are also structured along ethnic lines. Increasing awareness of the level of routine harassment and its impact on the quality of life experienced by those from ethnic minorities has clearly influenced the policy agenda in England and Wales. However, there has been a growing elision between what is known about the experiences of people from ethnic minorities in relation to criminal victimization and what has come to be called 'hate' crime and it will be useful to reflect on the relationship between the two.

Lawrence (1999) suggests that there are two defining characteristics of hate crime: that the victim is interchangeable and merely needs to share in a common characteristic, and that there is little prior relationship between the victim and the offender, although the studies conducted by Ray and Smith (2001) and Mason (2005), for example, point out that the presumption of a lack of relationship between victim and offender is highly problematic. Nevertheless this presumption can be found in legal frameworks that have endeavoured to take this kind of criminal victimization seriously. In the UK, there is no legislative status that delineates hate crime from other kinds of crime, although the Association of Chief Police Officers does have an operational definition of such crime which states that it is 'a crime where the perpetrator's prejudice against an identifiable group of people is a factor in determining who is victimised'. However, while there are been several amendments to the law in England and Wales over recent years that permit for the 'aggravated' nature of any particular offence, relating in the legislation particularly to race (Crime and Disorder Act 1998) and religion (Anti-terrorism and Security Act 2001) at present, hate crime per se is not a meaningful legal category. It is nevertheless a label that inspires media headlines.

For example at the end of July 2005 the BBC reported that 'hate crime soars after bombings' and goes on to assert that there were '269 religious hate crimes in London in the three weeks after July 7th in comparison with 40 during the same time period in 2004' (BBC News, 2 November 2005). Indeed, the Home Office figures reported earlier for a different time period are suggestive of an overall increase in this kind of victimization. As Mason (2005: 2–3) states: 'In terms of incidents against members of the Asian and black communities, qualitative research, victimisation studies, and police statistics collectively paint a picture of verbal abuse, graffiti, property damage, threats and physical violence that is widespread and consistent.'

'Hate crime' is not only perpetrated against ethnic minority or religious minority groups as some of the statistics reported earlier indicate. Gay and lesbian people are also the target of 'hate crime', although assessing the nature and extent of this in England and Wales is not easy as Spalek (2006) observes. Mason (2005) reports that the Metropolitan Police recorded 754 homophobic incidents in the first six months of 2001 and Moran and Skeggs (2004) report on similar kinds of low-level harassment and more serious attacks experienced by the gay and lesbian community as those experienced by ethnic minority groups. GALOP (a gay, lesbian and transgender community safety charity operating in London) conducted a survey of gays' and lesbians' experiences in 2001 and reported that one in 10 people surveyed had experienced homophobic physical abuse with 4 per cent having experienced homophobic sexual abuse. Differences in reporting and recording practices and differences in experiences of lifestyle, as with the experiences of women and members of ethnic minorities, will all feed into what is seen to be the size of this kind of problem. There are, however, a number of problems associated with the emergence of 'hate' crime on the victimological, criminological and legal agendas some of which are worth reiterating here.

The first problem lies in the presumption that it is the stranger who is a danger to the potential victim of hate crime. As has already been observed in the work of Ray and Smith (2001) and Mason (2005) this is empirically problematic. Associated with this problem is also the tendency to elide all criminal victimization experiences of those belonging to minority groups as if they are all constituted and motivated in a similar way. It is important to remember that crime, and the experience of crime, is not only most likely to be committed by someone familiar to us, it is also an experience that is intra-class, intra-ethnic and intra-sexual. In other words, it is likely to be committed on us by someone very like us. This was one of the important interventions that were made by left realist victimology to the wider debate on criminal victimization in the late 1980s and there is little to suggest that this pattern has changed very much at one level. This does not mean to say that other forms of crime do not affect minority groups but it is offered as a careful reminder as to how the experience of criminal victimization is likely to be structured. The second problem, linked with this first, lies with the actual behaviour that is labelled as 'hate' crime. It is evident that the actual behaviour perpetrated as a hate crime may be just the same as other kind of crime, that is, vandalizing property or violence against the person. This leads Tomsen (2001: 1) to suggest that ' "hate crime" is a problematic label that may narrowly represent criminal motive and simplify the interpretation of victimisation and offending' that for him masks the perennial problem of how to deal with disaffected young males returning us to the question of gender discussed in Chapter 5.

Interestingly, despite the variation in academic and activist victim voices there appears to be a common arena in which both want to be heard: the law and criminal justice policy. As this chapter has demonstrated whether the victim of crime is envisaged as a structurally neutral entity or whether they are envisaged as structurally constituted, the law and criminal justice policy have become the common ground for trying to engineer change. The struggles that ensue as a result of this focus of activity derive not only from the way in which the law is constituted (Hudson

2006) but also the presumptions of the liberal state from which much of its practice is derived along with the search for universality. Whether or not such a search is in any way meaningful in the contemporary world is a moot point and need not concern us here but it does usefully remind us of the embedded relationship between criminology (and victimology) and the modern state.

Conclusion: criminal victimization and social responsibility

In a climate in which crime is seen as part of everyday life that we are all encouraged to be responsible for, in a very real sense we are all victims now. This is one of the main messages of crime (read victim) prevention policy. The symbolic representation of the victim in the political arena continues as a way of justifying both punitiveness and as a way of devising ever more imaginative ways of reintegrating the victim into the criminal justice process. The jury has still to give its verdict on how effective these imaginations might prove to be. Yet, it must be the case that some victims of crime will feel better and will be better taken care of as a result of initiatives like the ones under discussion here. How this might come about and for whom is likely to be the result of happenstance because of the kinds of policies being implemented. This end product is largely because of the ever present legacy of distinctions between the deserving and the undeserving, alongside the shallowness of soundbite politics in the criminal justice arena. As Crawford (2000: 303) states: 'Given the anxieties and emotions that crime evokes and its capacity to bifurcate through deep-seated fears of "otherness", crime may be an inappropriate vehicle around which to construct open and tolerant communities.' Insert 'victims' for 'crime' in this quote and therein lies the crux of the victim policy problem: what do we mean by 'victims' and 'criminal victimization'? If the greater involvement of the victim of crime within the criminal justice process is considered to be one of the mechanisms for encouraging greater awareness of the impact of crime and discouraging further offending behaviour, we must ask whose vision of justice is this most likely to work for and under what circumstances. Is it likely to work in communities in which intimidation and the fear of being labelled a 'grass' are the norm or is it more likely to work in communities not so structured with alternative forms of social control? Is it likely to work in communities riven with ethnic, religious or racial divides? If so, what would meaningful victim involvement look like and what resources would be needed to put such involvement in place? If we do want open and tolerant communities, as the earlier quote from Crawford implies, then we need to address the reality of crime and criminal victimization in communities as people actually live and experience those communities, not as we wish they were.

As the previous chapter has argued, the distribution of the rewards and punishments in any society is predicated on some notion of what is considered to be 'socially just'. The previous chapter also articulated some views on the ways in which conceptions of the welfare state have changed in emphasis since the late 1940s and how those changes could be connected to the processes of criminalization. This chapter has been concerned to address a different though connected thread in those processes. Here we have been concerned to document explicitly the different strands of thought found in the disciplinary concerns of victimology and the ways in which those strands of thought connect in different ways with the world of politics. What remains is to make explicit the ways in which these concerns are also connected to images of a socially just society.

The changing balance between the state and the individual has been described in different ways, from the removal of the 'nanny state' and the 'dependency culture' to the rise of possessive individualism. However this process is described and whatever moral connotations such descriptions invoke, its impact in terms of criminal victimization has been not only symbolic (the invocation of victimization as 'belonging') but also material. In other words, there is a real sense in which the drive to enhance social responsibility in this individualized form of 'active citizenship' and/or consumerism takes its toll on those sections of society least able to afford it not only in economic terms but also in terms of personal coping strategies (see also Dixon et al. 2006). This 'fact' is recognized by conservative and liberal criminologists both in the UK and the USA. Where they differ, of course, is in their explanation of its underlying cause and what is likely to improve it. But few would disagree that the changing relationship between citizen and state has done little to alleviate the lot of the 'dangerous classes' frequently leaving such 'dangerous classes' to construct their own ways of managing (see, for example, Walklate and Evans 1999).

It is notable that in this chapter we have focused primarily on the relevance and impact of mainstream victimological work. This is not intended to imply that attention has not been paid in policy and practical terms to more structurally informed aspects of criminal victimization. For example, it is possible to highlight the huge progress that has been made in policing responses to 'domestic' violence since the mid–1980s. Moreover, some would argue that the recognition and acceptance of 'institutional racism' brought about subsequent to the report of the Lawrence Inquiry has led to some progress and understanding around racial victimization. However, what these developments actually represent in terms of progressing a more structurally informed image of the victim of crime is a moot point. Lack of space inhibits further discussion of these issues here. For now it is perhaps sufficient to observe that if there is any mileage left in criminology's commitment to the modernist project, that mileage may lie in a fuller embrace of the implications of a more careful understanding of the interconnections between criminal justice and social justice.

Further reading

Various attempts have been made to document the nature of victimology: see, for example, Walklate (1989) and Mawby and Walklate (1994). For a different orientation on victimization, Elias (1993) provides a provocative account of the interconnections between levels of victimization and the associated political choices. The book of readings edited by Maguire and Pointing (1988) still provides a sound feel for the different concerns of those who populate the victims' movement. For a different take on the notion of victimhood, see Spalek (2006) and for up-to-date coverage of victimology and victim policy-related issues, see Dignan (2005), Goodey (2005) and Walklate (2007).

chapter eight

Conclusions: new directions for criminology?

Positivism, modernism and gender
A word on cultural criminology
Gender, race and class
Criminology and risk
Criminology and trust
Criminology, the citizen and the state
Criminology, political economy and social capital
Conclusion

> The crisis in criminology is a crisis of modernity. The twin pillars of the modernist project of reason and progress, the use of law in the control and adjudication of human affairs and the intervention of government to engineer a just social order totter under the weight of their own inconsistencies and ineffectiveness.
>
> (Young 1998: 262)

So what does this crisis look like?

Positivism, modernism and gender

The influence of positivism on the criminological agenda has been profound. The desire to produce and work with the objectively measurable facts of crime, as has been shown, is intimately connected with the emergence of criminology as a 'modern' social science. It is also intimately connected with the subject matter of the discipline itself and the diversity of interests that people the discipline.

Lawbreaking behaviour can, to a greater or lesser extent, be measured.

Some lawbreaking behaviours are more hidden than others. Some behaviour can be newly defined as lawbreaking. Moreover, there may well be a complex definitional process that contributes to the behaviour that is only partially evident. At any rate, lawbreaking behaviour is in some respects more easily measurable than 'social relationships' or the 'structure of society'. Criminal behaviour is real and it is real in its consequences. That is not to say the social relationships and/or social structures are not real, but merely to emphasize the powerful impact that the observable nature of criminal behaviour has had on the nature of the discipline itself.

In some respects the material reality of crime, however accurately it is measured, has served to fuel the hold that positivism has had on the criminological agenda. Counting crime, and the work of the criminal justice agencies, is in some respects the bedrock of criminological investigation. The presence of this bedrock has been felt in a number of different ways, from the mind imaging of neuroscience to the geographically focused criminal victimization survey of the left realist. Each in its own way has endeavoured to contribute to the objective measurement of the phenomenon of crime and each in its own way has contributed to the further perpetuation of the power of positivism. However, what underpins the continued influence of positivism is perhaps more fundamental than this discussion has so far implied.

The continued, almost implicit, acceptance of the ideas of positivism in criminology also reflects the discipline's intimate connection with the ideas of modernism. Born out of the ideas of the Enlightenment, the modern society was conceived as being that society in which decisions were made rooted in rational knowledge rather than superstition or belief. The later emergence of positivism, the gathering of information about that which could be observed, as opposed to data that could be felt or believed, constituted the main strategy through which rational knowledge could be constructed and gave life to the criminological project in the form of the nineteenth-century work and ideas of Lombroso. From this kind of knowledge, policies could be formulated that might contribute to the better management of social change. In this latter respect, the fundamental concerns of mainstream criminological work have changed little since the days of Lombroso. Of course, what is embedded in these ideas is a set of presumptions around what counts as rational knowledge and who can possess such knowledge, as much as how that knowledge is to be gathered. The political meshing of these ideas and the way in which they frame much contemporary criminological research as funded by the Home Office in the UK is reflected in another oft-quoted adage from Tony Blair: 'What counts is that which can be counted.'

Implicit in the modern, positive view of social reality is a presumption that human experience and male experience are one and the same. Seidler (1994) has argued that the implicit acceptance of this view has had a profound effect on social theory and it is easy to see that same profound effect on criminological theory (see Chapter 5). Seidler states:

> It is for men to be the guardians of 'reason' and 'objectivity' and so to refuse to be drawn into the unbounded and the chaotic, that, like the feminine, can so easily overwhelm. Social theory and philosophy have to stay within the limits of reason, learning to stay within the province of what can be clearly said.
>
> (Seidler 1994: 202)

The significance of recognizing the gendered base to knowledge, however, runs much deeper than a desire to think more carefully about how research agendas are constructed or sampling procedures put in place, as the critique of left realism in Chapter 4 demonstrates.

Recognition of the gendered base to knowledge demands a critical assessment and recognition of the ways in which the concepts used and deployed within criminology and victimology may not fully resonate with human experience. In other words, it requires a critical examination of the ways in which these concepts may articulate a male view of the world, not conspiratorially, but in a taken-for-granted way which (potentially) sets the agenda for the discipline in a particular (and limiting) manner. Given this interplay between positivism, modernism and gender, it is no wonder that some have looked to the development of theoretical and conceptual concerns for criminology which emanate from agendas outside criminology rather than continuing to struggle with the powerful influence of its internal agenda.

To summarize: the emergence of the modern form of criminology, and the context in which that occurred, ties the discipline to traditional conceptions of knowledge and traditional conceptions of what counts as rational knowledge. Once it is recognized that these interconnections have a gendered base, then it is possible to appreciate why feminism, along with the more recent work on masculinities, represents such a profound challenge for the discipline of criminology. At a minimum, this challenge suggests that there is a different way of working with the relationship between what might be considered scientific and what might be considered rational. The implications of such alternatives challenge criminology in a number of different ways.

The challenge to the conventional link between science, rationality and the policy agenda, which has been a recurring theme in this book, has come from not only those exploring gender issues but also those working with postmodernist ideas. Both standpoints, when applied to understanding knowledge and the knowledge production process, challenge the traditional universalism associated with traditional conceptions of science. The critique of left realism (and right realism) from those working within postmodernism evidences this. Challenging universalism implies (at a minimum) that knowledge is relative.

The resistance towards accepting knowledge as relative is present in both criminology and victimology. This is the result not only of an underlying search for the causes of crime and the tension between those who wish to centre the individual and those who wish to centre the social as the locus in which the causes of crime can be found, but also of the drive to produce policies – and, moreover, policies that work.

This is not to suggest that the search for causes and for effective policies is fruitless if the relativity of knowledge is accepted. However, it does suggest that such a search and such policies might be much more specifically and locally nuanced than has hitherto been the case. Arguably, however, it is necessary for both criminology and victimology to engage in a much more self-reflexive critique with respect to the conceptual apparatus within which they operate, before this position can be reached.

Thus the challenge of both feminism and postmodernism to the traditional implicit relationship between science, modernism and gender found in both criminology and victimology constitutes more than a polemical call for an appreciation of the relative nature of knowledge and the knowledge production process. It also requires a critical consideration of what is or is not made visible or invisible in the conceptual and research agendas constructed within these disciplines. This is necessary in relation to questions not only of gender, but also of class, race, age, community and so on. Whose knowledge counts, how and why?

One way to begin to map an understanding of these processes is to render more explicit other taken-for-granted aspects of the way in which criminology and victimology have constructed their frameworks for understanding crime. The analysis offered here will endeavour to achieve this by exploring the pertinence of taking a look at the emergence of what has been called cultural criminology and offering a review and further understanding of the relationship between gender, ethnicity and class, risk, trust, the relationship between the citizen and the state, the concept of social capital and the notion of political economy for the future development of both criminology and victimology.

A word on cultural criminology

Hayward and Young (2004: 259) define cultural criminology in the following way:

> Above all else, it is the placing of crime and the agencies of control as cultural products – as creative constructs. As such, they must be read in terms of the meanings they carry. Furthermore, cultural criminology seeks to highlight the interaction between these two elements: the relationship between constructions upwards and constructions downwards. Its focus is always upon the continuous generation of meaning around interaction; rules created, rules broken, a constant interplay of moral entrepreneurship, moral innovation and transgression.

How might this be translated into a specific criminological agenda?

First, this way of thinking about crime and the problem of crime is situated squarely within the way in which the media (film, TV, newspapers etc.) interplay with people's experiences, on the one hand, or provide a vehicle for experiences, on the other, referred to in Chapter 1. Some would argue that in contemporary society, all experience is mediated in this way. Moreover, the media now frequently provide us all with 'instantaneous' experience, minute-by-minute reporting, of real events such as wars or, as in the USA, live reportage of criminal trials. The line between this kind of experience and real experience is for many people increasingly fuzzy. There is a similar fuzziness to the difference between belonging to a 'real' community and what might be called a 'virtual' community and, as a consequence, whom people are using as their reference point moral or otherwise. A good example here is internet chat rooms and the potential they offer for criminal activity for paedophiles where the move from the virtual to the real may not be necessary at all in terms of what such people might be seeking but is nevertheless meaningful to them. It is the way in which crime is constantly constructed and reconstructed against this kind of backcloth that is of interest to the cultural criminologist. So their focus of attention becomes: the motive for crime as being about thrill, pleasure seeking and risk taking; the context of crime being the spaces left available to people in which they can be creative; the recognition of crime as about doing something different, of actually feeling alive; a methodology that embraces the view that such behaviour can only be studied by being immersed in them and being reflective on that immersion; with the result criminology cannot be a science in the positivistic sense (and, some would say, in any sense). So in cultural criminology there are no rigid definitions between the expert and the criminal or between crime and normality.

The consequence of this focus is that cultural criminology itself is likely to produce quite challenging and alternative forms of knowledge, which according to Hayward and Young (2004) makes it dangerous. In particular, cultural criminology would challenge much of the material discussed in this book. It would challenge even the possibility of doing comparative work and would certainly challenge the possibility of there being a universal definition of crime. More importantly, it works with quite a different sense of motivation for the criminal, not as being rational but as being a risk taking, thrill seeking and even desiring of sensation. In this sense, cultural criminology endeavours to capture the way in which the postmodern world (as opposed to the modern world in which criminology has its origins) results in individuals seeking out their own ways of making sense of the world in which the emphasis on difference and diversity are put to the fore in the contemporary global world. The (re-)emergence of this kind of criminology has been subjected to a thoroughgoing critique by O'Brien (2005). Summarizing his key concerns he asks:

> Under what circumstances and within what cultural criminological construction does graffiti writing or riding a motorcycle recklessly

> help to explain why Mark Thatcher is a free man while so many untried and unconvicted inmates of the world's prisons are not?
>
> (ibid.: 610–11)

This is a good question and one that returns us to the other lacunae of criminological and victimological explanation.

Gender, race and class

Chapter 5 discussed the problem of the primacy given to gender as the explanatory variable in the context of crime. The question that such a universalizing tendency poses is worthy of further comment. Recall from Chapter 5 Hagan and McCarthy's comments in response to criticism of their work:

> [We] also assumed gender would play a more important role than it did. Together these findings suggest that we need to give more thought to the ways that gender's relationship with crime is conditioned and mediated by background and foreground variables.
>
> (Hagan and McCarthy 2000: 235)

Recall, also, that Messerschmidt makes the same point:

> Gender, race and class are not absolutes and are not equally significant in every social setting where crime is realised. That is, depending on the social setting, accountability to certain categories is more salient than accountability to other categories.
>
> (Messerschmidt 1997: 113)

The work reported on by Walklate and Evans (1999) would make the same point about the role of community relationships. The complex ways in which different variables may interact with each other in determining both structural conditions for action and biographical responses of action demands critical reflection and examination. As was stated earlier, it means exploring femininities as well as masculinities. It means exploring whiteness as well as 'blackness'. It means exploring class. It means exploring different sexualities and challenging normative heterosexuality (Collier 1998). It means exploring the real world as opposed to just the discursive one. Such a process may call into question all kinds of knowledge claims, including those made by feminists, and will certainly call into question any policy process that assumes that what works in one setting may work in another. These questions also lead us into another contentious issue: that of sameness or difference.

The question of sameness or difference is the question of the relationship between understanding the experience of men and women as standing for the experience of all men and all women. The same might be said about other universalizing tendencies, for example, to do with blackness or Islam. The tension between these also reflects the tensions between universality and relativity, generalizability and specificity, modernism and postmodernism. It may be, of course, that what is at issue here is not the tension between sameness and difference itself but the actual posing of them as dichotomous. As Giddens (1984) has argued, such dualisms might be better conceptualized as dualities – in other words, as processes which interact with one another so that at one and the same time we are both the same and different, we operate with both claims to universal and local (relative) knowledge and so on. Thus, of course, recalling Messerschmidt's (1993) discussion of gender as an accomplishment, at one and the same time we are also accomplishing social class, negotiating age, dealing with race and racism, living in 'high-risk' or 'low-risk' communities. This leads us to a consideration of other domain assumptions reflected within criminology as a discipline.

Criminology and risk

A deep-rooted social expectation apparently associated with the exponential growth of scientific knowledge is that (modern) life should no longer be risky. Such cultural values pervade the issues of health, the food we eat, the leisure activities we engage in and what we expect the 'professionals' in each of these domains to be able to provide for us. The concepts of risk and risk assessment increasingly inform such public perceptions and have certainly informed the criminological agenda. The notions of risk and risk assessment are clearly connected to the idea of a (masculinist) science embedded within criminology and victimology, discussed earlier. As a consequence, these characteristics have resulted in the implicit acceptance of the idea of risk as a forensic concept. In other words, there has been an acceptance that in the possibility of understanding risk and utilizing risk analysis lies risk management. The control of outcomes: the control of probabilities that determine the likely consequences of particular courses of action. This is, as Douglas (1992) argues, what is culturally expected from the scientific enterprise. There are a number of both general and specific difficulties in criminology's continued acceptance of the concept of risk formulated in this way.

Bernstein (1996: 334) says: 'The past seldom obliges by revealing to us when wildness will break out in the future.' This quote clarifies the basis on which risk assessments are made. Probability theory, rooted as it is in historical data, can only ever be just that: theory. Events can always happen otherwise, despite cultural values and beliefs to the contrary. Of course, in a sense this is precisely the purpose of risk management: to minimize the impact of events happening otherwise. It cannot, however, eliminate their possible occurrence. This is as effectively the case for crime as it is for any other social problem in which risk assessment is considered salient.

While the notion of 'wildness' might draw attention to the ultimate ineffectiveness of trying to predict and/or control outcomes, it does not necessarily facilitate an understanding of the risks we see as opposed to the risks we do not see. Of course, as both Beck (1992) and Wildavsky (1988) argue, the latter process is also culturally constructed – as much to hide the extent to which the scientific enterprise has contributed to rising levels of risk as to find ways to control such levels of risk. This argument is well documented by Adams (1995). In the context of criminology, awareness of these general processes (potentially) returns us to the role of the state in hiding the crimes that are defined as risky and those that are not as well as hiding the implication of the state in such processes.

This discussion so far has addressed some of the general problems inherent in an uncritical acceptance of a conventional understanding of risk and risk analysis. A more specific analysis, which carries with it quite focused implications for the criminological exploration of risk, is raised by Douglas:

> In spite of evidence to the contrary, avoiding loss is written into the psychology textbooks as the normal, rational, human motive. But all this means is that the commercial, risk-averse culture has locally vanquished the risk-seeking culture, and writes off the latter as pathological or abnormal. To ignore such a large segment of the human psychology tells us more about the assumptions upholding the modern industrial way of life than about human nature's risk-taking propensities.
>
> (Douglas 1992: 30)

In one sense, it could be argued that both criminology and victimology have implicitly accepted this modern version of the risk-averse culture that Douglas talks about. This emphasis on risk avoidance is deeply embedded in the discourses around crime prevention that emanate from theories of all political hues. It also reflects a version of (masculine) knowledge that prefers to assert control via reasonable and rational argument rather than by brute force through the management of risk (risk assessment).

In other words, what is to be found in the criminological and victimological literature is a version of knowledge that values reason, in which risk avoidance is presumed to be reasonable and risk-seeking behaviour is presumed to be unreasonable. As a consequence, risk-seeking behaviour is downgraded, obscured, hidden from the debate but not necessarily from social reality or individual experience. That these values concur with those that support a conventional view of science and what counts as scientific knowledge is, therefore, of no great surprise.

It is the pervasiveness of this search for 'zero risk' that facilitates an understanding of the way in which the criminological and victimological agendas have been set, especially in relation to crime prevention. The search for the causes of crime has never been that separate from the search for the control of crime: crime prevention. An emphasis on risk avoidance fits so much more neatly in a discipline implicated in the policymaking process in this way. However, the effects of adopting an implicit zero-risk position are far reaching. This is especially the case in relation to constructing an adequate understanding of both the cause and the effect of criminal behaviour and the nature and extent of criminal victimization.

To summarize: criminology's (and victimology's) implicit acceptance of a conventional scientific agenda and its associated modernist and masculinist stance has resulted in that discipline's failure to work more critically with the concept of risk. In addition, this failure has resulted in, for the most part, a masculinist interpretation of and debate around what counts as risky behaviour, endorsing some behaviours for men as acceptably risky and some behaviours for women as unacceptably risky – both sides of this coin downgrading the potential value of exploring the pleasures of crime (as alluded to in Chapter 5) and emphasizing the apparent victimhood of women (also alluded to in Chapter 5). For example, in the context of the 'fear of crime' debate, this failure has impacted the way in which much criminological work hides men's fears (and their thrills) and simultaneously consigns women to possessing 'legitimate fears'.

To summarize: the criminological and victimological analysis of risk reflects the extent to which both these areas of study are tied implicitly to particular conceptions of the knowledge production process and the role of the scientific endeavour in that process. In particular, the failure to explore risk as both a gendered concept and a gendered experience has limited both of these disciplinary agendas in different but pervasive ways.

This does not mean, of course, that criminologists have failed to appreciate the nature of contemporary society as a risk society: a society preoccupied with control. There have been many commentaries that reflect this concern. The point here is to recognize how that concern has been constructed. Attempts have been made to challenge these assumptions, some of which have been referred to in Chapter 4 and some of which are related more directly to the fear of crime debate in which these issues appear to have their most visible salience (see Sparks 1992; Walklate 1997). However, more recent events, most notably the terrorist attacks in New York, Madrid, London and Mumbai, arguably call for criminology to think again both how it defines what counts as criminal and how as a discipline it has become embedded in a particular way of thinking about what constitutes risk in this risk society. (This is not the place to address this debate in detail but see, for example, Mythen and Walklate 2006.) All these efforts demonstrate that it is possible to work with alternative conceptualizations of risk that have the potential for enhancing criminological work. However, risk is only one side of a two-sided relationship. The other side of this relationship is trust.

Criminology and trust

> As a general rule, trust arises when a community shares a set of moral values in such a way as to create expectations of regular honest behaviour.
>
> (Fukuyama 1996: 153)

The concept of trust has been relatively under-explored in the social sciences. In discussing the question of 'ontological security', Giddens (1991) has argued that trust is most clearly evidenced in traditional societies through kinship relations, local communities or religious commitment. However, the absence of these mechanisms in late modern societies renders trust no more than a matter for individual contractual negotiation. Gellner (1989), too, argues that urban life is incompatible with trust and social cohesion, suggesting that such processes are rooted in rural, tribal traditions. Yet, as Fukuyama (1996) implies (see section opening), trust is also an essential part of modern life. Without it economic relations cannot be completely controlled and flourish. Trust is therefore essential.

The kinds of trust that exist, however, may not always be necessarily about creating 'regular honest behaviour' as Fukuyama states. It is just as likely to be about creating regular dishonest behaviour. It is the regularity or otherwise of behaviour that sustains or threatens social relationships. It is within this notion of regular social expectations that the question of trust becomes pertinent to criminology and victimology. This requires further exploration.

It may be argued that work emanating from the feminist movement, especially radical feminism, has been implicitly and explicitly concerned to problematize the question of trust in relation to women's experiences of criminal victimization. That work has clearly rendered problematic the notion of the safe haven of the home. Put another way, it has challenged the view that women need not fear men whom they know: work colleagues, boyfriends, relatives. These were 'trustworthy' men. The view that 'All men are potential rapists' offers a definite challenge to such a presumption. The recognition that the familiar and the familial are not necessarily any more trustworthy than the stranger puts a very different picture on the screen of who is and who is not trustworthy, a picture which feminist research has demonstrated routinely informs women's sense of 'ontological security'. Such work implies that just as the concept of risk is gendered so might be the concept of trust.

Giddens (1991) and Beck (1992) both argue that the increasing awareness of the importance of trust is the concomitant effect of greater awareness of the possible future damage of risk-taking activity alongside the challenge to universalism posed by postmodernism. As Misztal states:

> By destroying the grounds for believing in a universal truth, postmodernity does not make our lives more easy but only less constrained

> by rules and more contingent. It demands new solutions based on the tolerant co-existence of a diversity of cultures. Yet although post-modernism encourages us to live without an enemy, it stops short of offering constructive bases for mutual understanding and trust.
>
> (Misztal 1996: 239)

In a sense, this quote endorses the view of Fukuyama expressed earlier. It certainly centres the need for understanding the changing nature of trust, especially in the context of social relationships that are increasingly characterized by diversity and the celebration of difference. To 'live without an enemy' requires trust. But how does trust manifest itself?

The relevance of this question has been explored in the criminological context by Nelken (1994) in relation to the value of comparative research in exploring issues in relation to corporate crime. Walklate and Evans (1999) have discussed the way in which questions of trust underpin people's sense of ontological security in two high-crime areas, suggesting that they may be understood through the notion of a 'square of trust' (see Figure 8.1). In this square of trust, whom you can trust, how you trust and how much you can trust (Nelken 1994) at an individual level depends on where an individual is located with respect to its constituent mechanisms. For example, based on our fieldwork in one community (which we named Oldtown) it would appear that people trust as much as the local neighbourhood dogma permits, while simultaneously endeavouring to avoid 'public shaming' (being labelled a 'grass'). This takes the form, primarily, of trusting other local people because they are local (mechanisms of sociability). This does not mean, however, that other individuals are not trusted. But those others are trusted in a highly individualistic and fragile manner and that trust is dependent on what those individuals do with the trust invested in them. This may, for example, include trusting individual police officers and individual officials from other agencies, but it certainly does not mean offering generalized trust to those official agencies (the state). The risks of 'public shaming' are too high a price to pay for whatever benefits might accrue from such a cooperative venture. These processes do not mean, however, that the anarchistic politics of the criminal gangs (organized crime) has won the hearts and minds of this community. But it does mean that we may have to rethink some of the mechanisms whereby

Figure 8.1 The square of trust

Source: Walklate and Evans (1999: 135)

social solidarity is produced and maintained (the organized nature of the community).

Trusting relationships look somewhat different, however, in the other community (Bankhill) that was part of our investigation. The responses here appeared to suggest that older people were still willing to offer a generalized trust to the 'official agencies' (the state) and that there are friendship and community groups that strive to offer some kind of militation against a totally atomized existence (mechanisms of sociability). However, the belief that 'this area is going downhill rapidly' (the level of disorganization in the community) and the expressed fears of young people (the disorganized nature of local crime) undermined the sense of belongingness on which the potential for trusting relationships inherent in the call for help from the 'officials' might be developed. Thus there was an absence of social solidarity and a withdrawal from the processes on which such solidarity might be predicated.

For younger people in this community the picture was somewhat different. They know they cannot be seen to be talking to 'officials' (the state), which for them might include older people. They also know that to stay out of trouble of different kinds they have to manage the tightrope of being known (their mechanisms of sociability), but not being a 'grass' or participating in criminal activity (the disorganized nature of crime). For them, living in their locality was no worse than living anywhere else and trust existed between those who know each other but not much beyond. (For a more detailed discussion of these examples, see Evans et al. 1996; Walklate 1998; Walklate and Evans 1999.)

The different ways in which the questions of whom you trust, when you trust and how much you trust manifested in this discussion may be rooted in the different histories of the two areas that were under investigation. However, while that trust may be rooted in history, it is not historical. It is a real mechanism whereby individuals create a way of managing their routine daily lives, which differently situates them in relation to the state, crime, community, social relationships and protection. The people in Oldtown, for example, would not readily call on the police for protection but would more routinely draw on their own community resources in the form of organized criminality to provide such protection. In Bankhill, by way of contrast, there was an absence of being able to rely on the police or organized local structures to provide protection, resulting in an increasing tendency to withdraw from public involvement in either.

As we have gone on to argue, these two research areas were not unusual places. The research reported here echoes the work of Sampson et al. (1997) on collective efficacy and developed by Dekeseredy et al. (2003) in relation to violence against women. These kinds of locations are often those that have suffered disproportionately as the gap between rich and poor has grown – as we have increasingly become a 30/40/40 society (Hutton 1995). But how useful is such an analysis in other locations that have not suffered as the gap between rich and poor has grown? What do the issues relating to trust and community safety look like here? (See Walklate 2002.) But above and beyond these empirical questions, what do such findings imply for the policy process? As Chapter 4 implies, policy cannot be taken 'off the shelf' and assumed to work in the same way in widely different localities. Furthermore, policy may need to be very differently informed. At a maximum, this means taking local variation into account and, at a minimum, considering the 'locally powerful': who is influential and how you get things to work (see Walklate 2001a, 2001b).

Such tensions return us to the issue raised earlier concerning whose knowledge counts as legitimate and under what circumstances. They also highlight the importance of understanding the nature of the diversity surrounding the crime question and the impact that may have on the policy process. As Cook (2006: 174) states: 'The vexed issue of trust cannot be addressed merely by politicians and their acolytes "getting the message over" in more effective ways or through other "technical" means. In other words we cannot expect trust to just reappear by doing things better, technically, than we did before.' This discussion returns us to the third issue relevant to a further development of the criminological and victimological agendas: the relationship between the citizen and the state.

Criminology, the citizen and the state

Arguably, how people manage their routine daily lives informed by the concepts of risk and trust constitutes the surface manifestation of this deeper structural relationship: the relationship between the citizen and the state. Understanding the nature of this structural relationship reveals much about the mechanisms of social inclusion and exclusion and how they work. Placing this relationship at the centre of criminological concern does not presume that the state, the institutions of the state or any individual necessarily operates in a conspiratorial manner. However, it does presume that the risks we are encouraged to see, as opposed to those that we are not, serve the interests of the state. Hence the undoubted value of comparative research of both a theoretical and an empirical nature in order to better explore and expose such processes. Neither does this view necessarily imply that individual citizens are cultural dopes; but it does assert that to understand how they are constructed in terms of legitimacy does frame the options present in their everyday lives.

So while the relationship between the citizen and the state has changed in emphasis in the UK since 1945, there are also strong historical continuities in that relationship. These historical continuities are informed by a distinction between the deserving and undeserving, the principle of less eligibility and the notion of the dangerous classes. These dangerous classes, of course, provide the criminal justice system with much of its work, so for that reason alone it is important to gain a clear understanding of the surface manifestation of these deeply rooted processes. Some are clearly evident in the different community-based responses to crime problems identified here. So, if the lived experiences of those people living in high-crime areas are taken into account, there is clearly another layer of questions to be considered concerning what works, for whom, how, why, where and when. However, in order for such accounting to occur it is important that academics, politicians, policymakers and the locally powerful pay constant vigilant attention to the questions of whose policy and whose community it is. As Giddens states:

> In order to work, partnerships between government agencies, the criminal justice system, local associations and community organisations have to be inclusive – all economic and ethnic groups must be involved. . . . To be successful, such schemes demand a long-term commitment to social objectives.
>
> (Giddens 1998: 88)

As he goes on to point out, such an approach does not necessarily mean that any link between unemployment, poverty and crime is denied; but it does mean that policies need to be coordinated with common goals and objectives.

However, a genuine desire for policy to work for change needs to be cognisant of the importance of the local context in which that policy is set. In some settings, this might mean taking gender into account, in others, it might mean that other structural variables are more important. But above all, policy needs to work with rather than against the historical and socioeconomic circumstances that structure any local context. It also requires a desire for policy to work to be both authentic and genuine for the communities themselves. Such a desire may also require a closer critical examination of what we understand by crime, community, prevention and protection, who is responsible for the delivery of these and how that might be implemented. So, while Putnam (2000) may be correct in drawing our attention to the decline in civic participation, the corollary that this also entails a decline in community is not proven, neither is the assumption that communities have become increasingly brittle and fragile. Some may have, others certainly have not. In both research and policy terms this means that we need a much more careful understanding of how communities work for people themselves: what their networks look like, how 'social capital' works in their area and for whom. Some of the answers to such an exploration may well be less than pleasant politically, but ignoring them is not helpful either. So what might the key concerns of a future criminology look like?

Criminology, political economy and social capital

As has been argued elsewhere in this book, much of what has happened in relation to responding to crime as a social problem has become increasingly characterized by what Garland (2001) has called a 'culture of control'. Ironically, in some respects this has facilitated the coexistence of a criminology of everyday life alongside a criminology of the 'other': the demonizing of the deviant. And while Garland offers us an elegant analysis of this 'new punitiveness' and the increasing complexity of the criminal justice process and the range of actors involved in this, he places less emphasis on the underlying market forces that have arguably generated such changes. This is not the case in the more recent work of Taylor (1999).

Arguably following the version of left realism articulated in the work of Currie (see Chapter 4), Taylor centres the importance of understanding the changing nature of market society as underpinning what he sees to be nine crises of contemporary society. These 'crises' – among them the gender order, young people, parenting and the job market – have all been touched on at different points in this book. What is important about the analysis offered by Taylor is his desire to revisit questions of political economy. The questions go beyond debates about privatization and focus our attention on the political economy of market society and simultaneously on the hidden economy of local society. For example, they encourage us to consider the market culture that both promotes insider dealing and at the same time produces residual territories of social exclusion from which the state has largely withdrawn. However, as has already been argued, it should not be assumed that these processes have denied human agency; quite the contrary. It is at this juncture that criminology may benefit from revisiting not only questions of political economy and the processes they engender but also questions to do with social capital.

Hagan and McCarthy (1997) offer a sound review of the different kinds of capital individuals might possess. Yet even as their study demonstrates the diminished social capital possessed by the young homeless in their investigation, and the downward spiral of life that that propelled them into, did not mean that these young people were not equipped with networks that enabled them to survive. It is worth reconsidering the discussions in Chapters 6 and 7 in the light of this. Would policies intended to address antisocial behaviour work better if they recognized individuals' coping skills? Would policy responses designed to deal with hate crime, or domestic violence, have a better chance of 'success' if they incorporated such an understanding too? But, of course, social capital is not just possessed by individuals. It can also be possessed collectively (see the discussion of the work by Walklate and Evans 1999, referred to earlier). And while debates about social capital have existed among some sociologists and political theorists for some time, criminology might do well to pay greater heed to them. We need to look for ways of understanding how social capital works, or not, at individual, interpersonal, organizational, collective and societal levels if criminology wishes to retain its commitment to the modernist project. Questions such as these inevitably raise fundamental questions about the state, its local legitimacy, social justice and democracy and return us to the relationship between criminal justice and social justice with which this book began.

Conclusion

In summing up, then, a number of themes suggest themselves. It is clear that criminology has much yet to learn from both feminism and postmodernism in their endeavours to problematize both the nature of knowledge and the knowledge construction process and how this may or may not relate to the policy arena. Both areas of debate render problematic the notions of 'crime' and 'policy'. The questions raised by these areas of concern, however, do not necessarily lead to a retreat into relativism but may demand a more careful working with what is known, how, where and when and what might work under what circumstances. It is clear that centring a more refined understanding of the concepts of risk, trust, political economy and social capital and the underlying relationship that these concepts rest on, might lead to far more fruitful theoretical and empirical agendas for both criminology and victimology. The concerns of this book centre a concern with social justice for criminology and victimology and while this might echo idealism, it concurs with Cook's (2006) agenda and the need to focus 'upstream': that is, to look for policies that 'seek to address root causes and to prevent inequalities, rather than downstream policies which seek to understand and ameliorate them' (ibid.: 188).

Glossary

Administrative criminology A term coined by Jock Young to describe the criminological research conducted by the UK Home Office during the 1980s with a focus on managing the problem of crime.

Categorical theory A concern with the ways in which the social construction of the terms 'man' and 'woman' impact on the lives of individuals.

Citizenship A term encompassing those who are included and excluded from the rewards of the social system.

Classical criminology Criminological work that considers the individual as having free will and engaging in crime as a process of rational decision making.

Crime Lawbreaking behaviour.

Criminal victimization survey A sample survey of the general population designed to measure experiences and perceptions of crime. They were developed to offer a picture of the 'dark' figure of crime, that is, crime not reported or recorded in official statistics.

Critical criminology A term used in a variety of ways but in general referring to the kind of criminology that is concerned to unravel the ways in which talk about crime both defines and controls crime as a problem. It pays particular attention to the ways in which the variables of race, class and gender are played out in the criminal justice system.

Critical victimology A term used in a variety of ways, but referring here to the potential use and value of applying the structuration theory of Giddens to the victimization experience.

Cultural criminology A way of thinking about crime that situates our understandings within the processes in which criminal behaviour is creatively produced, interacted with and assigned meaning in a cultural context.

Differential opportunity A term associated with the work of Cloward and Ohlin referring to the different structures of opportunities for achieving both legitimate and illegitimate goals within any particular community.

Functionalism A view of society as interdependent parts whose consensual coexistence is necessary for the adequate functioning of the whole.

Hegemonic masculinity The version of masculinity that has consensual legitimacy, resulting in its perpetuation as a dominant though not determining form.

Labelling theory A theory that focuses on the processes by which people come to be defined as criminal and the subsequent impact that has on their criminal career.

Left realism A way of thinking about crime largely emanating from the United Kingdom in the mid-1980s and concerned to take crime seriously and to reclaim the law and order debate from right-wing politics.

Liberal feminism A movement concerned to redress the sex balance by ensuring women are included in the intellectual and empirical process.

Marxist criminology An attempt to use Marxist theorizing to develop a political economy of crime with particular emphasis on how the law itself serves the interests of the powerful.

Modern Taken to characterize societies in which the power of reason has superseded the power of belief.

Multi-agency A term coined in the early 1980s to describe policy initiatives designed to ensure cooperation between the various agencies within the criminal justice system.

Multiple and/or repeat victimization A patterning of victimization resulting in a small proportion of the total number of victims experiencing most of the victimization.

New Labour The Labour Party since the 1990s.

Positivism A way of thinking about knowledge and the knowledge production process that centres on that which can be objectively observed and/or measured.

Positivist criminology A process of gathering the facts concerning the causes of crime.

Positivist victimology A process of gathering the facts concerning the causes of victimization.

Postmodern feminism Feminist work that celebrates the differences between women and challenges any claim to universal knowledge.

Radical criminology A brand of criminology largely associated with the work of Taylor, Walton and Young that attempted to marry Marxism with labelling theory.

Radical feminism Work that is concerned to address men's oppression of women.

Radical victimology Work within victimology, influenced by Marxism, concerned to address the role of the law and the state in creating victimization.

Rational choice theory A modern version of classical criminology focusing on the offender as a rational decision maker.

Realism A view of the knowledge construction process concerned to identify the underlying mechanisms that contribute to the surface manifestation of particular kinds of practices and behaviour.

Relative deprivation A concept developed within left realism to focus attention on the extent to which people's perceptions of their own position in comparison with that of others might lead to their involvement in crime.

Restorative justice A concern to look for ways of better managing both the offender and experiences of the criminal justice process by making good the harm done by crime. This generally involves looking for ways of including the victim of crime more effectively.

Right realism Largely emanating from the United States, this label refers to a collection of theoretical and policy concerns about crime that centre the cause of crime within the individual.

Risk society A society preoccupied with safety.

Routine activity theory A view of the crime problem as being rooted in the product of three factors: a motivated offender, a potential victim and the absence of a capable guardian.

Sex role theory Takes as a given the biological origins of the differences between men and women.

Social capital The social networks and embedded relationships that enable people to achieve, or not achieve, their potential.

Social control theory Associated with the work of Hirschi, this approach focuses attention on the ways in which people are encouraged to conform to the rules of society and the effectiveness of those mechanisms of conformity.

Social disorganization Associated with the work of the Chicago School of the 1920s and 1930s, rooted in the ideas of social ecology concerned to understand the growth and development of the city and the social adaptations made to those processes. This work drew particular attention to the 'zone of transition' (q.v.).

Social exclusion This refers to those individuals and/or communities largely outside mainstream society. Those who are economically deprived and may also suffer other deprivations in health, education, employment opportunities and so on.

Social justice The way in which any society organizes itself to distribute the rewards and punishments in that society.

Socialist feminism Feminist work appreciating the ways in which age, sex, gender and class weave a complex web in women's lives.

Square of crime Developed by left realists to describe the key elements of the crime problem: the offender, the victim, the reaction of the formal agencies and the reaction of the public.

Strain theory Associated with the work of Robert Merton, this theory draws attention to the tensions between the legitimate and illegitimate means of achieving the norms and values of a particular society.

Underclass A term often used in the 1990s to refer to those sections of society that live outside its mechanisms of rewards.

Victim personal statement A voluntary policy initiative designed to record and present to the court the impact that a crime has had on the victim. It is not intended to affect sentencing but to better inform the court of the nature and impact of crime.

Zone of transition That part of the city characterized by high fluidity in population movement and with a high proportion of rented accommodation. In social disorganization theory, this part of the city experienced most social problems in the process of adapting to city growth. In contemporary terms, this would be referred to as the inner city.

References

Adams, J. (1995) *Risk*. London: UCL Press.

Ashworth, A. (2000) Victims' rights, defendants' rights, and criminal procedure. In A. Crawford and J. Goodey (eds) *Integrating a Victim Perspective within Criminal Justice: International Debates*. Aldershot: Ashgate.

Audit Commission (1996) *Misspent Youth*. London: Audit Commission.

Banks, M. (2005) Spaces of (in)security: media and fear of crime in local context. *Crime, Media Culture: An International Journal* 1(2): 169–89.

Beck, U. (1992) *The Risk Society*. London: Sage.

Becker, H. (1963) *The Outsiders*. New York: Free Press.

Bell, D. (1976) *The Cultural Contradictions of Capitalism*. London: Heinemann.

Bernstein, P.L. (1996) *Against the Gods: The Remarkable Story of Risk*. New York: John Wiley & Sons.

Bhaskar, R. (1978) *A Realist Theory of Science*. Brighton: Harvester.

Bonger, W.A. (1916) *Criminality and Economic Conditions*. Vancouver, BC: Political Economy Group.

Bottoms, A.E. (1983) Neglected features of the contemporary penal system. In D. Garland and P. Young (eds) *The Power to Punish*. London: Heinemann.

Bowlby, J. (1965) *Child Care and the Growth of Love*. Harmondsworth: Penguin.

Box, S. (1983) *Crime, Power and Mystification*. London: Macmillan.

Braithwaite, J. (1989) *Crime, Shame and Reintegration*. Cambridge: Cambridge University Press.

Brittain, A. (1989) *Masculinity and Power*. Oxford: Basil Blackwell.

Brogden, M., Jefferson, T. and Walklate, S. (1988) *Introducing Policework*. London: Unwin Hyman.

Brown, B. (1986) Women and crime: the dark figures of criminology. *Economy and Society* 15(3): 33–56.

Brown, D. and Hogg, R. (1992) Law and order politics – left realism and radical criminology: a view from down under. In R. Matthews and J. Young (eds) *Issues in Realist Criminology*. London: Sage.

Brown, S. (1998) *Understanding Young People and Crime*. Buckingham: Open University Press.

Burnett, R. and Appleton, C. (2004) Joined-up services to tackle youth crime: a case study in England. *British Journal of Criminology* 44(1): 34–54.

Burney, E. (2002) Talking tough, acting coy: what happened to the anti-social behaviour order? *The Howard Journal* 41(5): 469–84.

Cain, M. (1986) Realism, feminism, methodology and law. *International Journal of the Sociology of Law* 14: 255–67.

Cain, M. (1990) Towards transgression: new directions in feminist criminology. *International Journal of the Sociology of Law* 18: 1–18.

Cameron, D. and Fraser, E. (1987) *The Lust to Kill*. Oxford: Polity Press.

Carlen, P. (1983) *Women's Imprisonment*. London: Routledge & Kegan Paul.

Carlen, P. (1988) *Women, Crime and Poverty*. Milton Keynes: Open University Press.

Carlen, P. (1992) Criminal women and criminal justice: the limits to and potential of feminist and left realist perspectives. In R. Matthews and J. Young (eds) *Issues in Realist Criminology*. London: Sage.

Carlen, P. (1996) *Jigsaw: The Politics of Youth Homelessness*. Buckingham: Open University Press.

Cavender, G. (2004) Media and crime policy: a reconsideration of David Garland's culture of control. *Punishment and Society* 6(3): 335–48.

Chadee, D. and Ditton, J. (2005) Fear of crime and the media: assessing the lack of relationship. *Crime, Media, Culture: An International Journal* 1(3): 322–32.

Chambers, G. and Millar, A. (1983) *Investigating Sexual Assault*. Edinburgh: Scottish Office.

Chambliss, W.J. (1975) Towards a political economy of crime. *Theory and Society* 2: 149–70.

Chesney-Lind, M. (2006) Patriarchy, crime and justice: feminist criminology in an era of backlash. *Feminist Criminology* 1(1): 6–26.

Christie, N. (1977) Conflicts as property. *British Journal of Criminology* 17: 11–15.

Christie, N. (1986) The ideal victim. In E.A Fattah (ed.) *From Crime Policy to Victim Policy*. London: Macmillan.

Clarke, R. (1980) Situational crime prevention: theory and practice. *British Journal of Criminology* 20(2): 136–47.

Cloward, R. and Ohlin, L. (1960) *Delinquency and Opportunity: A Theory of Delinquent Gangs*. New York: Free Press.

Cohen, A.K. (1955) *Delinquent Boys*. London: Free Press.

Cohen, L.E. and Felson, M. (1979) Social change and crime rate trends: a routine activity approach. *American Sociological Review* 44(4): 588–608.

Cohen, S. (1985) *Visions of Social Control*. Oxford: Polity Press.

Coleman, C. and Moynihan, J. (1996) *Understanding Crime Data*. Buckingham: Open University Press.

Collier, R. (1998) *Masculinities, Crime and Criminology*. London: Sage.

Connell, R.W. (1987) *Gender and Power*. Oxford: Polity Press.

Connell, R.W. (1997) Gender politics for men. *International Journal of Sociology and Social Policy* 17 (1/2): 62–77.

Cook, D. (2006) *Criminal and Social Justice*. London: Sage.

Cook, D., Burton, M., Robinson, A. and Vallely, C. (2004) *Evaluation of Specialist Domestic Violence Courts/Fast Track Systems*. London: Crown Prosecution Service/Department of Constitutional Affairs.

Cooke, P. (1990) *Back to the Future*. London: Unwin Hyman.

Cornish, D. and Clarke, R.V. (1986) *The Reasoning Criminal: Rational Choice Perspectives on Offending*. New York: Springer.

Cottle, S. (2005) Mediatised public crisis and civil society renewal: the racist murder of Stephen Lawrence. *Crime, Media, Culture: An International Journal* 1(1): 49–71.

Cowie, J., Cowie, V. and Slater, E. (1968) *Delinquency and Girls*. London: Heinemann.

Crawford, A. (2000) Salient themes and the limitations of restorative justice. In A. Crawford and J. Goodey (eds) *Integrating a Victim Perspective within Criminal Justice*. Aldershot: Ashgate.

Crawford, A., Jones, T., Woodhouse, T. and Young, J. (1990) *The Second Islington Crime Survey*. Barnet: Centre for Criminology, Middlesex Polytechnic.

Currie, E. (1985) *Confronting Crime*. New York: Pantheon.

Currie, E. (1995) The end of work: public and private livelihood in post-employment capitalism. In S. Edgell, S. Walklate and G. Williams (eds) *Debating the Future of the Public Sphere*. Aldershot: Avebury.

Daly, K. (1997) Different ways of conceptualising sex/gender in feminist theory and their implications for criminology. *Theoretical Criminology* 1(1): 25–52.

Datesmann, S. and Scarpitti, F. (eds) (1980) *Women, Crime and Justice*. New York: Oxford University Press.

DeFleur, L.B. (1975) Biasing influences and drug arrest records. *American Sociological Review* 40: 88–103.

Dekeseredy, W.S., Schwartz, M., Alvi, S. and Tomeaszewski, A. (2003) Perceived collective efficacy and women's victimization in public housing. *Criminal Justice* 3(1): 5–27.

De Maillard, J. and Roche, S. (2005) Crime and justice in France: time trends, policies and political debates. *European Journal of Criminology* 1(1): 111–52.

Dennis, N. and Erdos, G. (1992) *Families without Fatherhood*. London: Institute of Economic Affairs.

Dignan, J. (2005) *Understanding Victims and Restorative Justice*. Maidenhead: Open University Press.

Dixon, M., Reed, H., Rogers, B. and Stone, L. (2006) *CrimeShare: The Unequal Impact of Crime*. London: IPPR.

Dobash, R.P., Dobash, R.E. and Gutteridge, S. (1986) *The Imprisonment of Women*. Oxford: Basil Blackwell.

Douglas, M. (1992) *Risk and Blame: Essays in Cultural Theory*. London: Routledge.

Downes, D.M. and Rock, P. (1988) *Understanding Deviance*. Oxford: Oxford University Press.

Eagle Russett, C. (1989) *Sexual Science: The Victorian Construction of Motherhood*. Cambridge, MA: Harvard University Press.

Eaton, M. (1986) *Justice for Women?* Milton Keynes: Open University Press.

Edgar, D. (1991) Are you being served? *Marxism Today* May.

Edwards, I. (2004) An ambiguous participant: the crime victim and criminal justice decision-making. *British Journal of Criminology* 44(6): 946–6.

Edwards, S. (1989) *Policing 'Domestic' Violence*. London: Sage.

Elias, R. (1985) Transcending our social reality of victimization: towards a new victimology of human rights. *Victimology* 10: 6–25.

Elias, R. (1986) *The Politics of Victimization*. Oxford: Oxford University Press.

Elias, R. (1993) *Victims Still*. London: Sage.

Etzioni, A. (1996) *The New Golden Rule*. London: Profile Books.

Evans, K., Fraser, P. and Walklate, S. (1996) Whom can you trust? The politics of grassing on an inner city housing estate. *Sociological Review* 44(3): 361–80.

Eysenck, H. and Gudjonnson, G.H. (1990) *The Causes and Cures of Crime*. New York: Plenum.

Farrington, D.P. and Morris, A.M. (1983) Sex, sentencing and reconviction. *British Journal of Criminology* 23(3): 229–48.

Fattah, E.A. (ed.) (1992) *Critical Victimology*. London: Macmillan.

Felson, M. (2002) *Crime and Everyday Life*, 3rd edn. London: Sage.

Felson, M. (2006) *Crime and Nature*. London: Sage.

Foucault, M. (1977) *Discipline and Punish*. Harmondsworth: Penguin.

Fukuyama, F. (1996) *Trust*. London: Penguin.

Furedi, F. (1997, 2002) *The Culture of Fear*. London: Cassell.

Gadd, D. (2000) Masculinities, violence and defended psychosocial subject. *Theoretical Criminology* 4(4): 429–50.

Galtung, J. (1967) *Theory and Method of Social Research*. London: Allen & Unwin.

Garland, D. (1985) *Punishment and Welfare*. Aldershot: Gower.

Garland, D. (1988) British criminology before 1935. *British Journal of Criminology* 28(2): 1–17.

Garland, D. (1999) The commonplace and the catastrophic: interpretations of crime in late modernity. *Theoretical Criminology* 3(3): 353–64.

Garland, D. (2001) *The Culture of Control*. Oxford: Oxford University Press.

Garland, D. (2002) Of crimes and criminals: the development of criminology in Britain. In M. Maguire, R. Morgan and R. Reiner (eds) *The Oxford Handbook of Criminology*. Oxford: Oxford University Press.

Garofalo, J. (1986) Lifestyle and victimization: an update. In E.A. Fattah (ed.) *From Crime Policy to Victim Policy*. London: Macmillan.

Geis, G. (1973) Victimisation patterns in white collar crime. In L. Drapkin and E. Viano (eds) *Victimology: A New Focus*, vol. 5. Lexington, MA: D.C. Heath and Co.

Gellner, E. (1989) Trust, cohesion and the social order. In D. Gambetta (ed.) *Trust: Making and Breaking Co-operative Relations*. London: Basil Blackwell.

Gelsthorpe, L. (1989) *Sexism and the Female Offender*. Aldershot: Gower.

Gelsthorpe, L. (2002) Feminism and criminology. In M. Maguire, R. Morgan and R. Reiner (eds) *The Oxford Handbook of Criminology*. Oxford: Oxford University Press.

Gelsthorpe, L. and Morris, A. (eds) (1990) *Feminist Perspectives in Criminology*. Buckingham: Open University Press.

Gibbons, D.C. (1994) *Talking about Crime and Criminals*. Englewood Cliffs, NJ: Prentice-Hall.

Giddens, A. (1984) *The Constitution of Society*. Cambridge: Polity Press.

Giddens, A. (1991) *Modernity and Self Identity*. Oxford: Basil Blackwell.

Giddens, A. (1998) *The Third Way*. Oxford: Polity Press.

Glueck, S. and Glueck, E. (1950) *Unraveling Juvenile Delinquency*. New York: Commonwealth Fund.

Goldson, B. and Muncie, J. (eds) (2006) *Youth, Crime and Justice: Critical Issues*. London: Sage.

Goodey, J. (2000) Biographical lessons for criminology. *Theoretical Criminology* 4(4): 473–98.

Goodey, J. (2005) *Victims and Victimology*. London: Longmans.

Goring, C. (1913) *The English Convict*. London: HMSO.

Gottfredson, M. and Hirschi, T. (1990) *A General Theory of Crime*. Stanford: Stanford University Press.

Graham, J., Woodfield, K., Tibble, M. and Kitchen, S. (2004) *Testaments of Harm: A Qualitative Evaluation of the Victim Personal Statement Scheme*. National Centre for Social Research, May.

Hagan, J. and McCarthy, B. (1997) *Mean Streets: Youth, Crime and Homelessness*. Cambridge: Cambridge University Press.

Hagan, J. and McCarthy, B. (2000) The meaning of criminology. *Theoretical Criminology* 4(2): 232–42.

Hall, S., Cricher, C. and Jefferson, T. (1978) *Policing the Crisis*. London: Macmillan.

Harding, S. (1991) *Whose Science? Whose Knowledge?* Buckingham: Open University Press.

Hayward, K. and Young, J. (2004) Cultural criminology: some notes on the script. *Theoretical Criminology* 8(3): 259–74.

Hedderman, C. and Gelsthorpe, L. (1998) *Understanding the Sentencing of Women*. London: Home Office.

Heidensohn, F. (1985) *Women and Crime*. London: Macmillan.

Heidensohn, F. (1996) *Women and Crime*, 2nd edn. London: Macmillan.

Heidensohn, F. (2002) Gender and crime. In M. Maguire, R. Morgan and R. Reiner (eds) *The Oxford Handbook of Criminology*. Oxford: Oxford University Press.

Hindelang, M.J. (1979) Sex differences in criminal activity. *Social Problems* 27: 143–56.

Hindelang, M.J., Gottfredson, M.R. and Garofalo, J. (1978) *Victims of Personal Crime: An Empirical Foundation for a Theory of Personal Victimization*. Cambridge, MA: Ballinger.

Hirschi, T. (1969) *Causes of Delinquency*. Berkeley: University of California Press.

Hollway, W. and Jefferson, T. (1997) The risk society in an age of anxiety: situating the fear of crime. *British Journal of Sociology* 48(2): 255–65.

Hollway, W. and Jefferson, T. (2000) The role of anxiety in the fear of crime. In T. Hope and R. Sparks (eds) *Crime, Risk and Insecurity*. London: Routledge.

Home Office (2001) *Statistics on Women and the Criminal Justice System*. A Home Office publication under Section 95 of the Criminal Justice Act 1991. London: Home Office.

Home Office (2003) *Respect and Responsibility – Taking a Stand Against Anti-Social Behaviour*. London: Home Office.

Home Office (2005) *Rebuilding Lives*. London: Home Office.

Hood-Williams, J. (2001) Gender, masculinities and crime. *Theoretical Criminology* 5(1): 37–60.

Hooks, B. (1999) *Ain't I a Woman Too?* Cambridge, MA: South End Press.

Hopkins Burke, R. (2001, 2005) *An Introduction to Criminological Theory*. Cullompton: Willan.

Hoyle, C. and Sanders, A. (2000) From victim choice to victim empowerment. *British Journal of Criminology* 40(1): 14–36.

Hudson, B. (2003) *Justice in the Risk Society*. London: Sage.

Hudson, B. (2006) Beyond white man's justice: race, gender and justice in late modernity. *Theoretical Criminology* 10(1): 301–18.

Hutton, W. (1995) *The State We're In*. London: Random House.

Jamieson, J. (2006) New Labour, youth justice and the question of 'respect'. *Youth Justice* 5(3): 180–93.

Jefferson, T. (1993) Theorising masculine subjectivity. Plenary address, Masculinities and Crime Conference, Brunel University, September.

Jefferson, T. (1994) Theorising masculine subjectivity. In T. Newburn and E. Stanko (eds) *Just Boys Doing Business*. London: Routledge.

Jefferson, T. (1997) The Tyson rape trial: the law, feminism and emotional truth. *Social and Legal Studies* 6(2): 281–301.

Jefferson, T. (1998) 'Muscle', 'hard men' and 'Iron' Mike Tyson: reflections on desire, anxiety and the embodiment of masculinity. *Body and Society* 4(1):77–98.

Jefferson, T. (2006) Hegemonic masculinity. In E. McClaughlin and J. Muncie (eds) *The Sage Dictionary of Criminology*, 2nd edn. London: Sage.

Jefferson, T., Sim, J. and Walklate, S. (1992) Europe, the left and criminology in the 1990s: accountability, control and the social construction of the consumer. In D. Farrington and S. Walklate (eds) *Victims and Offenders: Theory and Policy*. London: British Society of Criminology and Institute for the Study and Treatment of Delinquency.

Jessop, B. (2002) *The Future of the Capitalist State*. Cambridge: Polity Press.

Jordan, B. (2005) New Labour: choice and values. *Critical Social Policy* 25(4): 427–46.

Karmen, A. (1990) *Crime Victims: An Introduction to Victimology*. Pacific Grove, CA: Brooks Cole.

Kasperon, R. and Kasperon, J. (1996) The social amplification and attenuation of risk. In *Annals of the American Academy of Political and Social Science* 545: 116–25.

Katz, J. (1988) *The Seductions of Crime*. New York: Basic Books.

Kauzlarich, D., Matthews, R.A. and Miller, W.J. (2001) Towards a victimology of state crime. *Critical Criminology* 10: 173–94.

Kelly, L. (2001) *Routes to Injustice: A Research Review on the Reporting, Investigation and Prosecution of Rape Cases*. London: Crown Prosecution Inspectorate Service.

Kelly, L., Lovett, J. and Regan, L. (2005) A gap or a chasm? Attrition in reported rape cases. Home Office Research Study 293. London: Home Office.

Kinsey, R., Lea, J. and Young, J. (1986) *Losing the Fight against Crime*. Oxford: Basil Blackwell.

Kretschmer, E. (1926) *Physique and Character*. New York: Harcourt Brace.

Lawrence, F.M. (1999) *Punishing Hate: Bias Crimes under American Law*. Cambridge, MA: Harvard University Press.

Lea, J. (2002) *Modernity and Crime*. London: Sage.

Leonard, E.B. (1982) *A Critique of Criminology Theory: Women, Crime and Society*. London: Longman.

Lilly, J.R., Cullen, F. and Ball, R. (1995) *Criminological Theory: Context and Consequences*. Thousand Oaks, CA: Sage.

Lister, R. (1990) *The Exclusive Society: Citizenship and the Poor*. London: Child Poverty Action Group.

MacInnes, J. (1998) *The End of Masculinity*. Buckingham: Open University Press.

MacInnes, J. (2004) The sociology of identity: social science or social comment? *British Journal of Sociology* 55(4): 531–43.

MacIntyre, A. (1988) *Whose Justice? Which Rationality?* London: Duckworth.

MacKinnon, C. (1989) *Towards a Feminist Theory of the State*. Cambridge, MA: Harvard University Press.

MacLean, B. (1992) A programme of local crime survey research for Canada. In T. Lowman and B. MacLean (eds) *Realist Criminology, Crime Control and Policing in the 1990s*. Toronto: Toronto University Press.

Maguire, M. (2002) Crime statistics, patterns and trends, in M. Maguire, R. Morgan and R. Reiner (eds) *The Oxford Handbook of Criminology*, 3rd edn. Oxford: Oxford University Press.

Maguire, M. and Pointing, J. (eds) (1988) *Victims of Crime: A New Deal?* Milton Keynes: Open University Press.

Marshall, T.H. (1981) *The Right to Welfare and Other Essays*. London: Heinemann.

Mason, G. (2005) Hate crime and the image of the stranger. *British Journal of Criminology* 45(6): 837–60.

Matthews, N. (1994) *Confronting Rape*. London: Routledge.

Matthews, R. and Young, J. (eds) (1992) *Issues in Realist Criminology*. London: Sage.

Matza, D. (1964) *Delinquency and Drift*. New York: John Wiley & Sons.

Mawby, R. and Gill, M. (1987) *Crime Victims: Needs, Services and the Voluntary Sector*. London: Tavistock.

Mawby, R. and Walklate, S. (1994) *Critical Victimology: The Victim in International Perspective*. London: Sage.

Mayhew, P. and Hough, M. (1988) The British Crime Survey: origins and impact. In M. Maguire and J. Pointing (eds) *Victims of Crime: A New Deal?* Milton Keynes: Open University Press.

Mendelsohn, B. (1974) The origins of the doctrine of victimology. In I. Drapkin and E. Viano (eds) *Victimology*. Lexington, MA: Lexington Books.

Merton, R.K. (1938) Social structure and anomie. *American Sociological Review* 3: 672–82.

Merton, R.K. (1968) *Social Theory and Social Structure*. New York: Free Press.

Messerschmidt, J. (1986) *Capitalism, Patriarchy and Crime: Towards a Socialist Feminist Criminology*. Totowa, NJ: Rowman and Littlefield.

Messerschmidt, J. (1993) *Masculinities and Crime*. Lanham, MD: Rowman and Littlefield.

Messerschmidt, J. (1997) *Crime as Structured Action*. London: Sage.

Miers, D. (1978) *Responses to Victimisation*. Abingdon: Professional Books.

Miers, D. (1989) Positivist victimology: a critique. *International Review of Victimology* 1(1): 3–22.

Miers, D. (1990) Positivist victimology: a critique, part 2. *International Review of Victimology* 1(3): 219–30.

Miers, D. (2004) Situating and researching restorative justice in Great Britain. *Punishment and Society* 6(1): 23–46.

Miers, D., Maguire, M., Goldie, S., Sharpe, K., Hale, C., Netten, A., Uglow, S., Doolin, K., Hallam, A., Enterkin, J. and Newburn, T. (2001) An exploratory evaluation of restorative justice schemes. Crime Reduction Research Series Paper 9. London: Home Office.

Misztal, B. (1996) *Trust in Modern Societies*. Oxford: Polity Press.

Mooney, J. (1993) The North London domestic violence survey. Paper presented to British Criminology Conference, Cardiff.

Mooney, J. (2003) It's the family stupid: continuities and reinterpretations of the dysfunctional family as the cause of crime in three political periods. In R. Matthews and J. Young (eds) *The New Politics of Crime and Punishment.* Cullompton: Willan.

Moran, L. and Skeggs, B. with Tyrer, P. and Corteen, K. (2004) *Sexuality and the Politics of Violence and Safety.* London: Routledge.

Morash, M. (2005) *Understanding Gender, Crime and Justice.* London: Sage.

Morris, A. (1987) *Women, Crime and Criminal Justice.* Oxford: Basil Blackwell.

Morris, L. (1994) *Dangerous Classes: The Underclass and Social Citizenship,* London: Routledge.

Mugford, G. and O'Malley, P. (1990) Heroin policy and the deficit model. The limits of left realism. Unpublished paper.

Muncie, J. (1999) *Youth and Crime.* London: Sage.

Muncie, J. (2002) Policy transfers and 'what works': some reflections on comparative youth justice. *Criminal Justice* 1(3): 27–35.

Muncie, J., McLaughlin, E. and Langan, M. (eds) (1996) *Criminological Perspectives: A Reader.* London: Sage.

Murray, C. (1990) *The Emerging British Underclass.* London: Institute of Economic Affairs.

Mythen, G. and Walklate, S. (2006) Criminology and terrorism: which thesis? Risk society or governmentality? *British Journal of Criminology* 46(3): 379–98.

Naffine, N. (1987) *Female Crime.* Sydney: Allen & Unwin.

Naffine, N. (1990) *Law and the Sexes.* London: Allen & Unwin.

Nelken, D. (1994) Whom can you trust? The future of comparative criminology. In D. Nelken (ed.) *The Future of Criminology.* London: Sage.

Newburn, T. (1996) Back to the future: youth crime, youth justice, and the rediscovery of 'authoritarian populism'. In J. Pilcher and S. Wagg (eds) *Thatcher's Children? Politics, Childhood and Society in the 1980s and 1990s.* London: Routledge.

Newburn, T. and McEvoy, K. (2003) (eds) *Criminology, Conflict Resolution and Restorative Justice.* London: Macmillan.

Oberwittler, D. and Hofer, S. (2005) Crime and justice in Germany: an analysis of recent trends and research. *European Journal of Criminology* 2(4): 465–508.

O'Brien, M. (2005) What's cultural about cultural criminology? *British Journal of Criminology* 45(5): 599–613.

Offe, C. (1984) *Contradictions of the Welfare State.* London: Heinemann.

Offe, C. and Ronge, V. (1975) Theses on the theory of the state. *New German Critique* 6 (Fall): 139–47.

Outhwaite, W. (1987) *New Philosophies of Social Science: Realism, Hermeneutics and Critical Theory.* London: Macmillan.

Padfield, M. and Crowley, R. (2003) Procedural and evidential protection in the English courts. In M. Tonry (ed.) *Confronting Crime: Crime Control Policy under New Labour.* Cullompton: Willan.

Pain, R., Francis, P., Fuller, I., O'Brien, K. and Williams, S. (2002) 'Hard to reach'. Young people and community safety: a model for participatory research and consultation. Briefing note, Policing and Reducing Crime Unit. London: Home Office.

Painter, K. (1991) *Marriage, Wife Rape and the Law.* Manchester: University of Manchester, Department of Social Policy.

Parsons, T. (1937) *The Structure of Social Action.* New York: McGraw-Hill.

Parton, N. (1985) *The Politics of Child Abuse*. London: Macmillan.
Patel, P. (1992) Plenary address, Violence Against Women Conference, Manchester Metropolitan University, May.
Peelo, M. (2006) Framing homicide narratives in newspapers: mediated witness and the construction of virtual victimhood. *Crime, Media, Culture: An International Journal* 2(2): 159–75.
Peelo, M. and Soothill, K. (2000) The place of public narratives in reproducing social order. *Theoretical Criminology* 4(2): 131–48.
Philo, G. (1999) *Message Received: Glasgow Media Group Research 1993–1998*. New York: Addison-Wesley-Longman.
Phipps, A. (1988) Ideologies, political parties, and victims of crime. In M. Maguire and J. Pointing (eds) *Victims of Crime: A New Deal?* Milton Keynes: Open University Press.
Piipsa, M. (2003) Violence against women as conveyed by surveys: the Finnish case. *Journal of Scandinavian Studies in Criminology and Crime Prevention* 3: 173–93.
Pitts, J. (2001) The new correctionalism: young people, youth justice and New Labour. In R. Matthews and J. Pitts (eds) *Crime, Disorder and Community Safety*. London: Routledge.
Pollak, O. (1950) *The Criminality of Women*. New York: A.S. Barnes/Perpetua.
Prideaux, S. (2005) *Not So New Labour*. Bristol: Policy Press.
Putnam, R.D. (2000) *Bowling Alone: The Collapse and Revival of American Community*. New York: Simon & Schuster.
Quinney, R. (1972) Who is the victim? *Criminology* November: 309–29.
Quinney, R. (1977) *Class, State and Crime: On the Theory and Practice of Criminal Justice*. New York: McKay.
Ray, L. and Smith, D. (2001) Racist offenders and the politics of 'hate crime'. *Law and Critique* 12: 203–21.
Regan, L. and Kelly, L. (2003) *Rape: Still a Forgotten Issue*. London: Metropolitan University, Child and Woman Abuse Studies Unit.
Rock, P. (1986) *A View From the Shadows*. Oxford: Clarendon.
Rock, P. (1990) *Helping Victims of Crime: The Home Office and the Rise of Victim Support in England and Wales*. Oxford: Clarendon.
Roshier, B. (1989) *Controlling Crime*. Milton Keynes: Open University Press.
Russell, D. (1990) *Rape in Marriage*. New York: Collier.
Sampson, R., Raudenbush, W. and Felton, E. (1997) Neighbourhoods and violent crime: a multilevel study of collective efficacy. *Science* 77, 15 August.
Sanders, A. (2002) Victim participation in an exclusionary criminal justice system. In C. Hoyle and R. Young (eds) *New Visions of Crime Victims* Portland, OR: Hart Publishing.
Schlesinger, P., Humber, H. and Murdock, G. (1991) The media, politics of crime and criminal justice. *British Journal of Sociology* 42(3): 397–40.
Scott, J. (1994) *Wealth and Poverty*. London: Macmillan.
Scraton, P. (1990) Scientific knowledge or masculine discourses? Challenging patriarchy in criminology. In L. Gelsthorpe and A. Morris (eds) *Feminist Perspectives in Criminology*. Buckingham: Open University Press.
Scraton, P. and Chadwick, K. (1991) The theoretical and political priorities of critical criminology. In K. Stenson and D. Cowell (eds) *The Politics of Crime Control*. London: Sage.
Scully, D. (1990) *Understanding Sexual Violence*. London: Unwin Hyman.

Seidler, V. (1994) *Unreasonable Men: Masculinity and Social Theory*. London: Routledge.

Sherman, L. and Smith, D. (1992) Crime, punishment and stake in conformity: legal and informal control of domestic violence. *American Sociological Review* 57: 670–90.

Sherman, L., Schmidt, J., Hartin, P. and Cohn, E. (1991) From initial deterrence to long term escalation: short custody arrest for ghetto poverty violence. *Criminology* 29(4): 821–49.

Sim, J., Scraton, P. and Gordon, P. (1987) Introduction: crime, the state, and critical analysis. In P. Scraton (ed.) *Law, Order and the Authoritarian State*. Milton Keynes: Open University Press.

Smart, C. (1977) *Women, Crime and Criminology*. London: Routledge & Kegan Paul.

Smart, C. (1989) *Feminism and the Power of Law*. London: Routledge.

Smart, C. (1990) Feminist approaches to criminology: or postmodern woman meets atavistic man. In L. Gelsthorpe and A. Morris (eds) *Feminist Perspectives in Criminology*. Buckingham: Open University Press.

Smolej, M. and Kiviuori, J. (2005) The association between crime, media and fear of violence. In R. Siren and P. Honkatukia (eds) *Victimisation to Violence in Finland: Results from 1980–2003 National Surveys*. Publication No. 216. Helsinki: National Research Institute of Legal Policy.

Social Exclusion Unit (1998) *Bringing Britain Together*, Cm. 4045. London: The Stationery Office.

Social Exclusion Unit (2001) *Preventing Social Exclusion*. London: Social Exclusion Unit.

Spalek, B. (2006) *Crime Victims: Theory, Policy and Practice*. London: Palgrave.

Sparks, R. (1992) Reason and unreason in left realism: some problems in the constitution of the fear of crime. In R. Matthews and J. Young (eds) *Issues in Realist Criminology*. London: Sage.

Squires, P. (2006) New Labour and the politics of anti-social behaviour. *Critical Social Policy* 25(1): 144–68.

Stanley, L. and Wise, S. (1987) *Georgie, Porgie: Sexual Harassment in Everyday Life*. London: Pandora.

Stanko, E.A. (1985) *Intimate Intrusions: Women's Experience of Male Violence*. London: Virago.

Stenson, K. and Brearly, N. (1989) Left realism in criminology and the return to consensus theory. In R. Reiner and M. Cross (eds) *Beyond Law and Order*. London: Macmillan.

Stenson, K. and Sullivan, R.R. (eds) (2001) *Crime, Risk and Justice. The Politics of Crime Control in Liberal Democracies*. Cullompton: Willan.

Stone, L. (1995) *Uncertain Unions and Broken Lives*. Oxford: Oxford University Press.

Sutherland, E.H. (1947) *Principles of Criminology*. Philadelphia: Lippincott.

Tapley, J. (2005) Public confidence costs – criminal justice from a victim's perspective. *British Journal of Community Justice* 3(2): 39–50.

Taylor, I. (1999) *Crime in Context*. Oxford: Polity Press.

Taylor, I., Walton, P. and Young, J. (1973) *The New Criminology*. London: Routledge & Kegan Paul.

Thatcher, M. (1977) *Let Our Children Grow Tall*. London: Centre for Policy Studies.

Tolson, A. (1977) *The Limits of Masculinity*. London: Tavistock.

Tomsen, S. (2001) Hate crimes and masculinity: new crimes, new responses, some familiar patterns. Paper presented to the 4th National Outlook Symposium on Crime in Australia, Canberra: Australian Institute of Criminology.

Utting, D. (1993) Family factors and the rise of crime. In A. Coote (ed.) *Families, Children and Crime*. London: Institute for Public Policy Research.

Valier, C. (2004) *Crime and Punishment in Contemporary Culture*. London: Routledge.

von Hentig, H. (1948) *The Criminal and his Victim*. New Haven, CT: Yale University Press.

Walby, S. and Myhill, A. (2001) New survey methodologies in researching violence against women. *British Journal of Criminology* 41(3): 502–22.

Walklate, S. (1989) *Victimology: The Victim and the Criminal Justice System*. London: Unwin Hyman.

Walklate, S. (1990) Researching victims of crime: critical victimology, *Social Justice* 17(3): 25–42.

Walklate, S. (1995) *Gender and Crime*. Hemel Hempstead: Harvester Wheatsheaf.

Walklate, S. (1996) Can there be a feminist victimology? In P. Davies, P. Francis and V. Jupp (eds) *Understanding Victimization: Themes and Perspectives*. Newcastle: University of Northumbria Press.

Walklate, S. (1997) Risk and criminal victimization: a modernist dilemma? *British Journal of Criminology* 37(1): 35–45.

Walklate, S. (1998) No more excuses! Young people, victims and making amends. *Policy Studies* 19(3/4): 213–22.

Walklate, S. (2001a) Victim impact statements: a voice to be heard in the criminal justice system? In B. Williams (ed.) *Reparation and Victim Focused Social Work*. London: Jessica Kingsley.

Walklate, S. (2001b) So who's bowling alone? Crime community and politics. Paper presented to the Crime Prevention, Safety, Security and Democracy Conference, Goteburg, December.

Walklate, S. (2002) It's all a question of trust. In A. Crawford (ed.) *Crime and Insecurity in Europe*. Cullompton: Willan.

Walklate, S. (2003) I can't name any names but what's his face up the road will sort it out: community and conflict resolution. In K. McEvoy and T. Newburn (eds) *Criminology and Conflict Resolution*. London: Macmillan.

Walklate, S. (2004) *Gender, Crime and Criminal Justice*, 2nd edn. Cullompton: Willan.

Walklate, S. (2005) Imagining the victim of crime: the rhetoric of victimhood as a source of oppression. *Social Justice: Emerging Imaginaries of Repression and Control*. Special Issue edited by R. Lippens and T. Kearon 32(1): 89–99.

Walklate, S. (2007) *Imagining the Victim of Crime*. Maidenhead: McGraw-Hill/Open University Press.

Walklate, S. and Evans, K. (1999) *Zero Tolerance or Community Tolerance: Managing Crime in High Crime Areas*. Aldershot: Ashgate.

Walton, P. and Young, J. (1998) *The New Criminology Revisited*. London: Routledge.

Wemmers, J. (2005) Victim policy transfer: learning from each other. *European Journal of Criminal Policy and Research* 11(1): 121–33.

Wertham, F. (1949) *The Show of Violence*. New York: Doubleday.

Wildavsky, A. (1988) *Searching for Safety*. Oxford: Transition.

Williams, B. (1999) *Working with Victims of Crime: Policies, Politics and Practice.* London: Jessica Kingsley.

Williams, B. (2003) Community justice, victims and social justice. Professorial inaugural lecture, de Montfort University.

Williams, B. (2005) *Victims of Crime and Community Justice.* London: Jessica Kingsley.

Williams, B. and Canton, R. (2005) Editorial: victims of crime, offenders and communities. *British Journal of Community Justice* 3(2): 1–8.

Williams, F.P. and McShane M.D. (1994) *Criminological Theory*, 2nd edn. Englewood Cliffs, NJ: Prentice-Hall.

Wilson, E. (1983) *What is to be done about Violence against Women?* Harmondsworth: Penguin.

Wilson, J.Q. (1975) *Thinking about Crime.* New York: Vintage.

Wilson, J.Q. and Herrnstein, R. (1985) *Crime and Human Nature.* New York: Simon & Schuster.

Wilson, J.Q. and Kelling, R. (1982) Broken windows. *Atlantic Monthly* March: 29–38.

Women's National Commission (2003) *Seen but not Heard: Women's Experiences of the Police.* London: Women's National Commission.

Wootton, B. (1959) *Social Science and Social Pathology.* London: George, Allen & Unwin.

Young, A. (1992) Feminism and the body of criminology. In D.P. Farrington and S. Walklate (eds) *Offenders and Victims: Theory and Policy.* London: British Society of Criminology and Institute for the Study and Treatment of Delinquency.

Young, A. (1996) *Imagining Crime.* London: Sage.

Young, J. (1986) The failure of criminology: the need for a radical realism. In R. Matthews and J. Young (eds) *Confronting Crime.* London: Sage.

Young, J. (1988) Risk of crime and the fear of crime: a realist critique of survey based assumptions. In M. Maguire and J. Pointing (eds) *Victims of Crime: A New Deal?* Milton Keynes: Open University Press.

Young, J. (1992) Ten points of realism. In J. Young and R. Matthews (eds) *Rethinking Criminology: The Realist Debate.* London: Sage.

Young, J. (1994) Incessant chatter: recent paradigms in criminology. In M. Maguire, R. Morgan and R. Reiner (eds) *The Oxford Handbook of Criminology.* Oxford: Oxford University Press.

Young, J. (1998) Breaking windows: situating the new criminology. In P. Walton and J. Young (eds) *The New Criminology Revisited.* Basingstoke: Macmillan.

Young, J. (1999) *The Exclusive Society.* London: Sage.

Young, J. (2001) Identity, community and social exclusion. In R. Matthews and J. Pitts (eds) *Crime, Disorder and Community Safety.* London: Routledge.

Young, J. and Matthews, R. (1992) *Rethinking Criminology: The Realist Debate.* London: Sage.

Young, J. and Matthews, R. (2003) New Labour, crime control and social exclusion. In R. Matthews and J. Young (eds) *The New Politics of Crime and Punishment.* Cullompton: Willan.

Index

30/30/40 society, 111, 156

absent fathers, 49, 51, 52, 53
active citizenship, 109, 132, 143
Adams, J., 152
administrative criminology, Home Office, 45–7, 60, 161
adversarialism, 130, 131, 133
age fallacy, 6
Amnesty International, 123, 125
antisocial behaviour, 55, 93, 114, 115–17, 135, 159
Appleton, C., 135
Ashworth, A., 133
atavism, 20
Audit Commission, 113

Bankhill, 156
Banks, M., 6
Beccaria, Cesare, 18–19
Beck, U., 152, 154
Becker, Howard, 27–8
behaviour
  criminal *see* criminal behaviour
  criminality of behaviour, 22–8
  lawbreaking *see* lawbreaking behaviour
behaviourism, 40
Bell, D., 56
Bentham, Jeremy, 18, 19
Bernstein, P.L., 151
Beveridge reforms, 106, 107, 109
Bhaskar, R., 49, 66–7, 81
biogenetics, 20
biography, psychoanalysis, 99–100
biological factors
  criminal behaviour, 21
  lawbreaking behaviour, 9, 20
  sex role theory, 92
  socio-biological explanations, 39–42
biosocial theory, 21
black crime, 33
Blair, Tony, 79, 146
Bonger, W.A., 29
born criminal, 21
Bottoms, A.E., 122
Bowlby, John, 50, 51
Box, S., 124
Braithwaite, J., 8, 9, 26, 83, 114, 134
Brearly, N., 72
British Crime Survey, 46–7, 113
Brittain, A., 96
Brogden, M., 71
Brown, B., 84
Brown, D., 74, 77
Brown, S., 113, 118
Bulger, James, 53, 113
Burnett, R., 135
Burney, E., 115

Cain, M., 73–4, 88, 89, 101

Cameron, D., 86
Canton, R., 132
capitalism, 18, 30, 31, 60, 110, 126–7
Carlen, P., 77, 85, 87–8, 89, 101, 111–12, 118
categorical theory
  gendering the criminal, 95–6
  meaning, 161
causes of crime
  biological factors, 9, 20, 21, 39, 41
  criminogenic situations, 44, 63, 88, 107
  left realism, 60
  Marxist criminology, 30
  positivist criminology, 20
  radical criminology, 32
  rational choice theory, 42, 43
  relative deprivation, 12, 61–2, 77, 81, 162
  right realism, 38, 39, 41, 42, 43, 49, 54, 55
  slogans, 12, 79, 108, 113
  social conditions, 46
Cavender, G., 7
Centre for Contemporary Cultural Studies, 33
Chadee, D., 6
Chadwick, K., 34, 35
Chambers, G., 165
Chambliss, W.J., 29–30
Chesney-Lind, M., 136, 137
Chicago School, 22, 25, 27, 163
children, criminal behaviour, 19
Christie, N., 133–4, 139
cities
  delinquent subcultures, 24
  relative deprivation, 12
  social ecology, 22–3
  zone of transition, 23
citizenship
  active citizenship, 109, 132, 143
  citizen and state, 13, 15, 57, 107–9, 111–13, 157–8
  commodification, 127
  consumers, 47, 106
  meaning, 161
  public services, 47
  social policy, 106
Clarke, R., 42–3, 46, 58
class
  dangerous classes, 55, 107, 108, 110, 111, 112, 143, 157
  delinquency, 93
  explanatory variable, 73
  gender, race and class, 150–1
  lawbreaking behaviour, 8
  young males, 24–5, 28
  see also underclass
classical criminology, 18–20, 57, 161
Cloward, R., 24, 25, 27, 161
Code of Practice for Victims, 129
Cohen, Albert K., 24, 93–4
Cohen, L.E., 44, 45
Cohen, S., 27, 136
Coleman, C., 8
Collier, R., 101, 103, 104, 150
Commissioner for Victims and Witnesses, 129
common sense
  Braithwaite's facts compared, 8–10
  crime talk, 4, 5–6, 9
  criminal justice policy, 71
  populism, 70
communitarianism, 13, 110, 121
communities
  community based initiatives, 79–80
  criminal justice policy, 13
  social capital, 80, 158
compensation, 10, 107, 129, 131, 135
Comte, Auguste, 71
Connell, R.W., 94, 95, 96, 98
conscientious activity, 31
conservative criminology, 44, 47, 48, 59
Conservative Party
  criminal justice policy, 12–13
  individual responsibility, 38
conservative victimology, 120
constitutional factors, 39, 40, 41
conventional victimology, 120
Cook, D., 105, 107, 110, 111, 116, 118, 138, 157, 160
Cooke, P., 3
Cornish, D., 42–3, 58
Cottle, S., 7
Cowie, J., 85
Crawford, A., 68, 70, 142
crime
  factual knowledge, 7–10

fear, 7
information sources, 7–10
meaning, 161
patterning, 9
universal explanation, 4, 11, 21, 101
see also criminal behaviour; lawbreaking behaviour
Crime and Disorder Act 1998, 51, 79, 113–15, 134, 140
Crime and human nature, 39
crime prevention policies
costs, 43
left realism, 63–5, 70–2
local communities, 79–80
modernization, 18
rational choice theory, 42, 43
situational crime prevention, 42, 43, 47
crime problem
gender, 84, 86, 91, 95, 103
left realism, 59, 60, 61, 64, 66, 74–6, 79, 82, 163
lived experiences, 158
management, 46, 66
political debate, 43, 79, 120
public perception, 7
right realism, 38, 43, 46, 56, 57, 82
risk society, 12
routine activity, 163
unit of analysis, 4
United States, 74–6
welfare ethic, 38
crime rates, trends, 8, 38, 41, 48
crime surveys
British Crime Survey, 46–7, 113
democratic basis, 68, 70
International Victimization Survey, 121
Merseyside and Islington, 59
victimization, 10, 46–7, 61, 64, 67–9, 72–3, 121, 161
crime talk
common sense, 4, 5–6, 9
fallacies, 6
influences, 6–7
religion, 18
criminal activity
abusive families, 50
class, 30
hidden nature, 9
Internet, 149
left realism, 61
masculinity, 102
patriarchy, 87
predisposition, 5
states, 124
young people, 156
criminal behaviour
behaviour of criminals, 17–22
children, 19
criminality of behaviour, 22–8
decriminalization, 5
definitions, 4, 5–6
Marxist criminology, 31
measurement, 4
patterning, 23
positivism, 22
risk-taking, 54
routine activity, 44
techniques of neutralization, 25–6
underclass, 52–5
see also lawbreaking behaviour
Criminal Injuries Compensation Board/Authority, 10, 107, 129
criminal justice policy
conservative criminology, 44, 47, 48, 59
formation, 11–12
Labour Party, 12–13, 78
left realism, 76
neo-conservatism, 80
political parties, 12–13, 14
rebalancing system, 129–36
social justice, 13, 105–6
tinkering with system, 130–1
young people, 113–17
criminal justice process
adversarialism, 130, 131, 133
equity, 128
innocence presumption, 19
labelling theory, 28
new punitiveness, 159
right realism, 57
social justice, 117
victims, 132, 142
criminal justice professionals, 6, 130, 139
criminal law, criminal behaviour, 5
criminal victimization
common sense, 5

ethnicity and hate crimes, 140–2
factual knowledge, 10–11
images, 6
information sources, 10
politics and welfare, 119–44
risk, 45
secondary, 130
social responsibility, 142–3
surveys, 10, 46–7, 61, 64, 67–9, 72–3, 121, 161
women, 11, 72
criminality of the state, 28–36
criminalization, processes, 33–4
criminals
behaviour of criminals, 17–22
characteristics, 5, 8
criminology
administrative criminology, 45–7, 60, 161
citizen and state, 157–8
classical criminology, 18–20, 57, 161
concerns, 5
conservative criminology, 44, 47, 48, 59
criminal justice policy, 11–13
critical criminology, 26, 29, 33–6, 161
cultural criminology, 148–50, 161
discipline, 2, 13, 18
doing gender, 96–9
domain assumptions, 2
feminism, 84–90
gender criminology, 39, 83–104
key features, 1–16
males, 90–1
malestream, 84, 86, 102, 103
Marxist criminology, 29–32, 33, 77, 162
masculinity, 100–1
modernism, 2–4
multidisciplinary character, 2
new directions, 145–60
objectivity, 4
other, 69, 159
perspectives, 17–37
policymaking, 11
political economy and political economy, 159–60
positivist criminology, 18, 20–2, 162
radical criminology, 32–4, 162
risk, 151–3
transgressive criminology, 88, 89
trust, 154–7
universal explanation of crime, 4, 11, 21, 101
critical criminology
criminality of the state, 34–6
Marxism, 26, 29, 34
meaning, 161
social problems, 33, 34
critical victimology, 125–8, 161
Crowley, R., 132
Crown Prosecution Service, 138
cultural criminology, 148–50, 161
culture of control, 55, 57, 122, 136, 159
culture of fear, 12
Currie, Elliott, 51, 54, 60, 74–7, 81

Daly, K., 103
dangerous classes, 55, 107, 108, 110, 111, 112, 143, 157
dark figure of crime, 46, 65, 161
Darwin, Charles, 20
Datesmann, S., 85
De Maillard, J., 7
DeFleur, L.B., 85
Dekeseredy, W.S., 156
delinquent subcultures, 24
demonization, 12, 49, 54, 69, 113, 116, 159
Dennis, N., 53, 54
dependency, 54, 55, 109–10, 143
deviancy
labelling theory, 27–8
social theory, 33
strain theory, 24, 26, 27
differential association, 92
differential opportunity, meaning, 161
discrimination, 34, 85, 86, 89
Ditton, J., 6
Dixon, M., 129
Dobash, R.P., 85
domestic violence
2004 Act, 129, 131, 138
common sense, 9
families, 51
feminism, 84, 86, 137
police, 73, 76, 137, 138, 143
United States, 137–8

Douglas, M., 151, 152
Downes, D.M., 72
dramatic fallacy, 6
Durkheim, Emile, 24

Eagle Russet, C., 102
Eaton, M., 85, 101
Edgar, D., 106
Edwards, I., 131
Edwards, S., 73, 85
Elias, R., 123, 144
Enlightenment, 2–3, 146
environment
  control, 3
  designing out crime, 23
  operant conditioning, 40
  rape suits, 139
  social ecology, 22
Erdos, G., 53, 54
essentialism, 77, 87, 88, 114, 136
Etzioni, A., 13, 115
Evans, K., 23, 102, 143, 150, 155, 156, 159
evolution, 20
exclusive societies, 12
Eysenck, Hans Jürgen, 21, 40

families
  absent fathers, 49, 51, 52, 53
  abusive families, 50
  broken families, 49, 50, 51
  divorce, 49, 53
  dysfunction, 52, 55
  feminism, 50, 51, 54–5
  importance, 50–2
  lawbreaking behaviour, 49–55
  persistent offending, 54
family structures
  dismembered families, 53
  feminism, 54–5
  social change, 9, 54, 117
  social order, 55, 76
family values, 51, 53
Farrington, D.P., 85
Fattah, E.A., 125
Felson, M., 6, 16, 44, 45, 58, 69
feminism
  criminology, 84–90
  critical victimology, 127
  domestic violence, 84, 86, 137
  families, 50, 51, 54–5
  left realism, 72–4
  liberal feminism, 85–6, 89, 162
  methodology/policy, 72–4
  policy and violence, 136–9
  postmodern feminism, 88–9, 90, 162
  power relations, 50–1
  radical feminism, 86–7, 89–90, 162
  second-wave, 137
  socialist feminism, 87–8, 90, 163
  victimology, 120–1
  women and crime, 84
Fraser, E., 86
free will, 18, 19, 20, 21, 30, 54, 161
French Revolution, 19
Fry, Margery, 107
Fukuyama, F., 154, 155
functionalism
  meaning, 161
  New Labour, 121
  sex role theory, 92
  social order, 24
Furedi, F., 12

Gadd, D., 99
Galtung, Johan, 68
Garland, D., 2, 11, 12, 13, 55, 58, 122, 130, 136, 159
Garofalo, J., 45
Geis, G., 124
Gelsthorpe, L., 84, 85, 86, 102
gender
  categorical theory, 95–6
  crime problem, 84, 86, 91, 95, 103
  criminology, 39, 83–104
  gender blindness, 83–4
  gender, race and class, 150–1
  inequalities, 13
  men *see* males; masculinity; young males
  positivism, modernism and gender, 145–8
  sex role theory, 91–5
  see also women
General Theory of Crime, 26
generative mechanisms, 67, 69
Gibbons, D.C., 4, 36, 42, 43
Giddens, A., 35, 67, 96, 98, 110, 126, 151, 154, 158, 161
Gill, M., 130

modern, meaning, 162
modern society, risk society, 12
modernism
  criminology, 2–4
  left realism, 77–8
  positivism, modernism and gender, 145–8
  reason, 3
Mooney, J., 54, 55, 73
Moran, L., 141
Morash, M., 104
Morris, A. M., 84, 87, 108
Morris, L., 110
Moynihan, J., 8
Mugford, G., 70
mugging, 33
multi-agency
  co-operation, 71
  intervention, 63–4
  meaning, 162
multiple/repeat victimization, meaning, 162
Muncie, J., 30, 33, 79, 113, 114, 118, 135
Murray, C., 52–3
Myhill, A., 121
Mythen, G., 153

Naffine, N., 84, 102, 127
nanny state, 108, 143
Neighbourhood Watch, 109
Nelken, D., 155
neo-classical compromise, 19
new correctionalism, 79, 114, 135
The New Criminology, 32, 33
New Labour
  communitarianism, 13, 110, 121
  law and order, 72, 113–15
  left realism, 78–80, 115
  meaning, 162
  new correctionalism, 135
  self-discipline, 55
  victimology, 129
  see also Labour Party
Newburn, T., 113, 134
nuclear family
  disintegration, 53
  family values, 51
  left realism, 76
  patriarchy, 55

Oberwittler, D., 7
O'Brien, M., 149
Observer Wife, 50
Offe, C., 126
Ohlin, L., 24, 25, 27, 161
O'Malley, P., 70
operant conditioning, 40
other
  categorical theory, 95
  criminology of the other, 69, 159
  deviancy, 105
  dynamics of essentialism, 114, 136
  postmodern feminism, 88
Outhwaite, W., 67, 68

Padfield, M., 132
Painter, K., 73
Parsons, Talcott, 24, 29, 92, 93
Parton, N., 113
Patel, P., 138
patriarchy
  criminal activity, 87
  nuclear family, 55
  social relationships, 72
Peelo, M., 7
Philo, G., 7
Phipps, A., 122, 123
Piipsa, M., 121
Pitts, J., 114, 135
police
  crime control, 63
  dispersal order, 115
  domestic violence, 73, 76, 137, 138, 143
  funding, 47
  left realism, 61, 62, 63
  lived realities, 62
  minimal policing, 73
  public-police relationship, 57, 109
  rape suits, 139
  Victim Personal Statement Scheme, 132
Policing the Crisis, 33
political economy, 32, 33, 34, 159–60
political parties, criminal justice policy, 12–13, 14
politicality of crime, 30, 31
politicality of law, 30–1
politics
  dramatization, 6

law and order debate, 10
slogans, 12, 79, 108, 113
Pollak, O., 85
positivism
knowledge, 2, 11, 66
meaning, 162
modernism and gender, 145–8
reason, 3
social democratic positivism, 46
social positivism, 69
positivist criminology, 18, 20–2, 162
positivist victimology, 120–2, 162
possessive individualism, 56
postmodern feminism
difference, 88
gendering the criminal, 88–9, 90
meaning, 162
universality, 90
postmodernism
binary relationship, 74
difference/diversity, 56
left realism, 74, 78, 81
power relations, feminism, 50–1
Prideaux, S., 121
prisons
classical criminology, 19
exclusionary punishment, 106
psychiatry, 2, 19, 32
psychoanalysis, 83, 99–100
psychology, 2, 4, 9, 11, 21, 32, 40, 42, 50, 152
public expenditure, 47, 48, 108
punishment
classical criminology, 18, 19
right realism, 48
Putnam, R.D., 114, 158

Quinney, R., 30, 31, 123

racism, 34, 88, 89, 143, 151
radical criminology, 32–4, 162
radical feminism, 86–7, 89–90, 162
radical victimology, 122–5
rape, 9, 50, 55, 65, 84, 86, 100, 127, 138, 139
rational choice theory
meaning, 162
right realism, 42–4, 46, 49
rationality
calculation, 18, 21
social conditions, 30
Ray, L., 140, 141
Reagan, Ronald, 74
realism
left *see* left realism
meaning, 162
right *see* right realism
social problems, 48–9
reason
lawbreaking behaviour, 18, 19
modernism, 3
recapitulation, 20–1
Regan, L., 139
relative deprivation
cities, 12
left realism, 61–2, 77, 81
meaning, 162
specificity, 62
religion, 3, 18, 20, 140
residence, lawbreaking behaviour, 8
respect agenda, 116
Respect Task Force, 38
restorative justice, 113, 116, 130, 133–6, 162
right realism
administrative criminology, 45–7
critique, 47–9
meaning, 162–3
rational choice theory, 42–4, 46, 49
routine activity theory, 44–5
social order, 56
social problems, 38, 47, 49, 53, 56
understandings, 38–58
United States, 38
risk
assessment, 151–2
criminology, 151–3
management, 13
risk society, 12, 153, 163
risk-taking, 54
Roche, S., 7
Rock, P., 72, 108
Ronge, V., 126
Roshier, B., 11
routine activity theory
meaning, 163
right realism, 44–5
Russell, D., 73, 86

Sampson, R., 156

Sanders, A., 133, 138
Scarpitti, F., 85
Schlesinger, P., 7
science
  knowledge, 3–4
  power of reason, 3
Scott, J., 111
Scraton, P., 34, 35, 102
Scully, D., 103
security, 12
Seidler, V., 3, 147
self-control, 26
sex role theory
  gendering the criminal, 91–5
  meaning, 163
sexism, 34, 85, 86, 88
sexual harassment, 72
sexual violence, 89, 95, 103, 137, 138, 139
shaming, 114, 155
Sherman, L., 137
Sim, J., 71, 72
Skinner, B.F., 40
Smart, C., 84, 86, 127
Smith, D., 137, 140, 141
Smolej, M., 7
social analysts, 70, 71
social bonds, 26
social capital
  communities, 80, 158
  cultural criminology, 148
  meaning, 163
  political economy, 159–60
  rewards/punishments, 13
  young people, 114–15, 116
social conditions, 20, 23, 30, 46, 54, 86
social control theory
  crime control, 18
  criminality of behaviour, 26–7
  meaning, 163
social democracy
  left realism, 66, 71
  positivism, 46
social disorganization
  criminality of behaviour, 22–6
  meaning, 163
social dynamics, 32
social ecology, 22–3, 44, 163
social exclusion
  imprisonment, 106
  inequality, 111
  management of society, 80
  meaning, 163
  social justice, 105
  Third Way, 110
  universal rights, 109
  young people, 106
Social Exclusion Unit, 23, 79
social factors, lawbreaking behaviour, 8–9
social justice
  appreciation, 105
  criminal justice policy, 13, 105–6
  meaning, 110–11, 162
social order
  consensus, 12
  family structures, 55, 76
  functionalism, 24
  government, 110, 145
  inclusive society, 69, 78
  liberal state, 127
  poverty, 107
  right realism, 56
  rule of law, 122
  socio-biological explanations, 41
social problems
  control, 3, 159
  critical criminology, 33, 34
  left realism, 67, 74, 77
  radical criminology, 33
  right realism, 38, 47, 49, 53, 56
  risk assessment, 151–2
  zone of transition, 23, 163
social processes, lawbreaking behaviour, 5, 32
social psychology, 61, 91
social reaction, 32, 33
social reality, 2, 7, 31, 33, 66–8, 72, 78, 94, 95, 146, 152, 166
social sciences, social problems controlled, 3
social scum, 52, 110
socialist feminism, 87–8, 90, 163
socialization, 26, 31, 52, 91–4, 101
socio-biological explanations, 39–42
Soothill, K., 7
Spalek, B., 140, 144
Sparks, R., 153
square of crime, 61, 63, 81, 163
square of trust, 155

Squires, P., 115, 116
Stanko, E.A., 86
Stanley, L., 73
states
  citizen and state, 13, 15, 57, 107–9, 111–13, 157–8
  contract with state, 18–19, 107
  criminal activity, 124
  criminality of the state, 28–36
  liberal state, 127
  nanny state, 108, 143
  see also welfare state
Stenson, K., 16, 72
Stone, L., 49
strain theory, 24–6, 27, 163
Straw, Jack, 113, 132
structuration theory, 161
Sullivan, R.R., 16
surveys
  crime *see* crime surveys
  social surveys, 64, 67–9, 71, 72–3
Sutherland, E.H., 91, 92, 93
symbolic interactionism, 22, 27

Tapley, J., 132
Taylor, I., 4, 11, 32–3, 35, 37, 66, 77, 85, 159, 162
technology, social effects, 3
terrorism, 7, 31, 101, 122, 140, 153
Thatcher, Margaret, 47, 74, 108
Thatcher, Mark, 150
Thinking about crime, 39
Third Way, 110, 112
Tolson, A., 91
Tomsen, S., 141
transgressive criminology, 88, 89
trust, 154–7
Tyson, Mike, 99

underclass
  crime, 52
  criminal behaviour, 52–5
  criminogenic poverty, 107
  illegitimacy, 52, 53
  labour market behaviour, 52–3
  Lumpenproletariat, 52
  meaning, 52, 163
  social justice, 15
  social scum, 52, 110

United States
  Constitution, 19
  domestic violence, 137–8
  left realism, 74–7
  right realism, 38
universal explanation of crime, 4, 11, 21, 101
universalism, 88, 95, 96, 142, 147, 150, 151, 154
Utting, D., 54

Valier, C., 7
vandalism, 113, 141
victim personal statement, 131–3, 163
Victim Support, 10, 109
victimization prevention
  criminological research, 13
  public policy, 10
victimology
  challenging victimology, 128–9
  conservative, 120
  conventional, 120
  critical, 125–8, 161
  feminism, 120–1
  meaning, 119–28
  positivist, 120–2, 162
  radical, 122–5
  state crime, 124
victims
  2000 Act, 130
  politicization, 10
  voices, 131–3
  see also criminal victimization
Victims' Charter, 130
voluntary sector, 10
von Hentig, H., 119–20, 128

Walby, S., 121
Walklate, Sandra, 23, 45, 102–4, 107, 114, 120–1, 123, 125–30, 136–7, 143–4, 150, 153, 155–7, 159
Walton, P., 37, 57, 162
welfare dependence, 54, 55
welfare ethic, 38
welfare state
  capitalism, 126–7
  deserving/undeserving poor, 107
  inclusive society, 69, 110
  insurance-based benefits, 107

neo-liberalism, 54
understanding, 106–11
Wemmers, J., 133
Wertham, F., 119
white-collar crime, 8, 31, 97, 98
wickedness, 5, 31, 48
Wildavsky, A., 152
Williams, B., 130, 132, 135, 137
Williams, F.P., 36
Wilson, E., 50
Wilson, James Q., 21, 39–42, 46, 48, 56, 58, 115
Wise, S., 73
Wollstonecraft, Mary, 85
women
criminal victimization, 11, 72
dependency, 109–10
oppression, 86, 95, 135, 162
rape, 9, 50, 55, 65, 84, 86, 100, 127, 138, 139
sexual harassment, 72
sexual violence, 89, 95, 103, 137, 138, 139
single parent households, 53
social surveys, 72–3
violence, 76
women and crime, 84
see also gender
Wootton, B., 85, 108

Young, Alison, 88, 89, 122, 124, 127
Young, Jock, 12, 16, 36, 41, 42, 46, 56–7, 59–65, 69–73, 75, 77, 80–2, 114, 145, 148, 149, 161, 162
young males
class, 24–5, 28
gender criminology, 39
lawbreaking behaviour, 8, 11
socio-biological explanations, 39–40
victims, 10–11
work attitudes, 53
young people
antisocial behaviour, 115–17
balanced intervention, 79
criminal justice policy, 113–17
criminal victimization, 11
lawbreaking behaviour, 8
Youth Justice Board, 114, 135

Zero Tolerance, 137
zone of transition, 23, 163